BRIDGING
THE
GLOBAL GAP

BRIDGING
THE
GLOBAL GAP
A HANDBOOK TO LINKING CITIZENS
OF THE FIRST AND THIRD WORLDS

MEDEA BENJAMIN & ANDREA FREEDMAN
A project of GLOBAL EXCHANGE

SEVEN LOCKS PRESS
Cabin John, MD/Washington, DC

Library of Congress Cataloging-in-Publication Data

Benjamin, Medea, 1952-
    Bridging the global gap: a handbook to linking citizens of the
First and Third World / Medea Benjamin & Andrea Freedman.
        p. cm.
    Includes index.
    ISBN 0-932020-73-9: $11.95
    1. International cooperation. I. Freedman, Andrea. II. Title.
JC363.B44   1989
303.48′2—dc20   89-10508
                                                            CIP

Typesetting by Compositors, Inc., Cedar Rapids, Iowa
Cover design by Pat Morrison
Printed by McNaughton and Gunn, Inc., Saline, Michigan

Printed on acid-free paper.

For information contact:

SEVEN LOCKS PRESS
P.O. Box 27
Cabin John, MD 20818
(301) 320-2130

This book is dedicated to the memory of Samora Machel, a nurse by training, leader in southern Africa's liberation struggle, and first President of Mozambique. His fervent belief in internationalism as a key to building a more just world continues to inspire us all.

> "International solidarity is not an act of charity.
> It is an act of unity between allies fighting on
> different terrains toward the same objectives.
> The foremost of these objectives is to aid the
> development of humanity to the highest level
> possible."
> —*Samora Moises Machel (1933-1986)*

Acknowledgments

We have many people to thank for their contributions, but our first "acknowledgment" must be that this book is just a beginning. We hope that we have sparked a debate within the internationalist community on the effectiveness and vision of its work, and any misrepresentations or oversights in this airing of the issues are ours alone.

So many colleagues shared their perspectives, networks, and editorial comments with us. Many thanks go to Myra Alperson, Barbara Atkinson, Becky Buell, Roger Burbach, Jim Cason, Ann Clark, Nancy Cole, Kevin Danaher, Tom Fenton, Paul Freundlich, Tom Hampson, Mary Heffron, Steve Hellinger, Jeff Hollander, Larry Hollar, Kathie Klarreich, Steve Lydenberg, Jack Malinowski, Frances Moore Lappe, Diane Narasaki, Jim Paul, Tom Peterson, Todd Putnam, Rachel Schurman, Mike Shuman, Tim Smith, Vivian Stromberg, Dorie Wilsnack, Alan Wright, and Haleh Wunder. Special thanks to our editor and copy editor, Jane Creighton and Sara Miles, for unscrambling any jumbled thoughts and for conveying their enthusiasm for this project.

We are indebted to a corps of interns and volunteers who contributed thousands of hours of research help. They are: Michele Allen, Candace Brightman, Kathi Gin, Paige Eaves, Deborah Freedman, Kirsten Jones, Nancy McKee, Fulvia Musti-Ciarla, Alexis Olian, Eleonora Quijada, Amy Schultz, Amy Swartz, Caroline Todd, and Laurel White. This book began as a research project while the authors worked at the Institue for Food and Development Policy/Food First. We are grateful for the financial support from the members of Food First, and especially for grants from the Max and Anna Levinson Foundation and the Evangelical Lutheran Church of America.

In the process of writing this book, we felt the need to create an organization to help tie together the various threads of this internationalist movement. The organization, founded in 1989 as Global Exchange, was built on the hard work and support of the following people: Nick Allen, Fafa Auxila, Alvin Benjamin, Marilyn Borchardt, Becky Buell, Jon Christensen, Lorraine Coleman, Kevin Danaher, Ross Hammond, Kim Harris, Steve Hecker, Judy Hurley, Kirsten Irgens-Moller, Christopher Kashap, Kathie Klarreich, Audee Kochiyama-Holman, Nina Korican, Suzanne Ludlum, Tim Maher, Sara Miles, Kit Miller, Maya Miller, Warren Mills, Crosby Milne, Annie Mize, Prexy Nesbitt, Deaneen Newell, Stuart Ozer, Ana Perla, Mark Rand, Judy Revord, Kyle Richmond, Laura Rodriguez, Akinyele Sadiq, Liana Shamlian, Michael Shimkin, Denise Stanley, Rick Tejada-Flores, and Walter Turner.

On a personal note, we'd like to thank our families—Arlen, Rose, and Alvin Benjamin, Sheila and Cy Freedman—and especially our husbands, Kevin Danaher and Jeff Walker, for the patience and support they extended to us throughout the work on this book.

Finally, this book would have been impossible without the cooperation of the hundreds of community activists we interviewed. Your adventures, insights, and commitment inspired us on a daily basis. *Bridging the Global Gap* is as much a product of your hard work and introspection—not to mention fun—as it is ours! Enjoy it, and keep in touch.

Medea Benjamin and Andrea Freedman
Global Exchange, San Francisco
August, 1989

Table of Contents

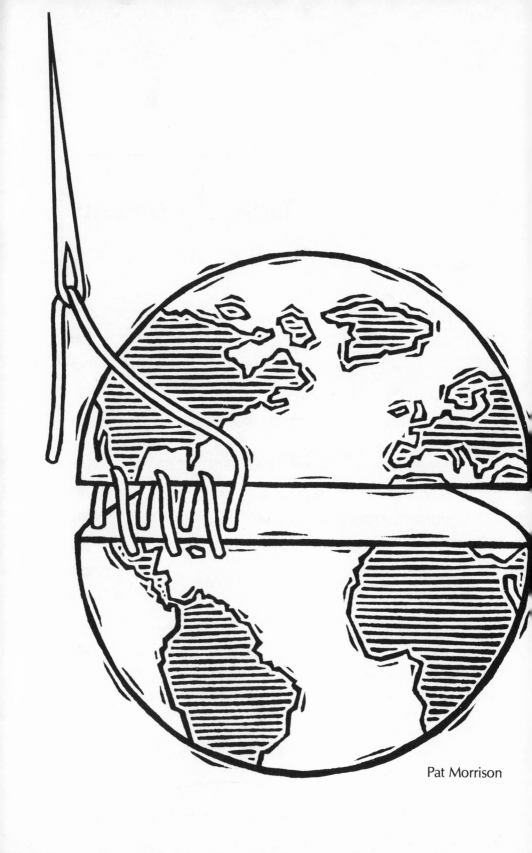

Pat Morrison

Introduction:
A New Spirit
of Internationalism

"During the Spanish Civil War, I remember my parents, both excellent teachers, telling us, their children, how they kept reading the papers every morning, looking anxiously for assistance coming from the governments of the Western democracies. It was a betrayal of the Western world's commitment to democracy, disappointment after disappointment, morning after morning.

"And then something remarkable happened! The Western governments did not want to help, but (and what an important but!) workers, peasants, farmers, professionals, intellectuals, students, and others came from these same countries (and other countries) to help. They frequently came illegally, even against the wishes of those 'democratic' governments. Many were average North Americans representing the best tradition of commitment to liberty and justice that sectors of popular forces have always had."

—Vicente Navarro,
Professor of Public Health
Johns Hopkins University
member of the Spanish anti-fascist
underground in the 1950s and 1960s.

Vicente Navarro is referring to the spirit of internationalism, a spirit that moves ordinary citizens to take a stand on international issues. The 1980s have witnessed an extraordinary surge in internationalism in the United States.

1

Spurred by the mutual fear of nuclear annihilation, for example, many U.S. citizens have initiated people-to-people ties with their Soviet counterparts.[1] Many more, appalled by hunger in a world of plenty and frustrated by government policies that fail to address the roots of hunger, have forged direct ties with the poor in the Third World.

For the past few years we have been talking with friends all over the globe who are the protagonists of this movement to link North Americans and Third World communities. They have formed sister cities, sister schools, and sister churches. They have created alternative trade organizations to experiment with new models of mutually beneficial trade. They have accompanied human rights activists whose lives are in danger. They have used their technical skills to support grassroots organizations. They have challenged transnational corporations to become more socially and environmentally responsible. They have pressured U.S. policymakers to reshape U.S. policies to reflect the interests of the Third World majority.

Many of the participants in this movement are motivated by a deep moral commitment to side with the poor in their struggle for justice. Some are environmentalists drawn to internationalism through a recognition that concerns such as the destruction of the rain forests, the greenhouse effect, and the debt crisis transcend national boundaries. Others have lived abroad— perhaps as Peace Corps volunteers or as exchange students— and have formed strong personal bonds with Third World people. Still others are immigrants, workers, and political activists who recognize the parallels between hunger and poverty at home and abroad.

The resulting movement is building a kind of internationalism this country has never before witnessed. In contrast to those who fought in the Spanish Civil War, today's internationalists are unlikely to take up arms and fight on another country's soil. Instead, representatives from unions, schools, churches, community groups, and city governments are searching for nonviolent ways to wage peace and end poverty. They are traveling across the globe to discover concrete ways of supporting their Third World counterparts. In the process, they are redefining the real "national interests" of the United States, and demanding that we revamp our foreign policy to reflect the interests of the world's majority.

The hundreds of internationalists we interview in this book range in profession from homemaker to hog farmer, from carpenter to engineer. They are teenagers and octogenarians. Their level of commitment varies from twenty minutes a month to sixteen hours a day, seven days a week. They may consider themselves capitalist or socialist, atheist or religious. But what they all have in common is the ability to see the world beyond their own borders—and to see it not as passive observers but as active participants in shaping its future.

But "taking foreign policy into our own hands" also conjures up images of the well-meaning American who goes to the Third World to "set things straight," and ends up doing more harm than good. What, then, is the proper role of internationalists?

Those of us who want to see an end to hunger and injustice—as well as an end to foreign policies based on fear and competition—can side with the poor in two ways. We can directly support grassroots organizations built by and for the Third World poor themselves. And we can work to remove the obstacles that our government places in the path of those who are working for change.

As we at Global Exchange address the issues of poverty and injustice on campuses and in community centers and churches across the country, over and over again we are asked, "But what can we do?" Never before have we had so many answers. While human rights work, alternative trade, sister cities, and the like may seem like disparate swipes at an unjust world order, in the process of writing this book we have come to see them as an integral whole. We are confident that if this internationalist movement continues to attract new adherents and broaden its scope, it will:

- break down contentious barriers and expand our nation's cultural and educational horizons, building sensitivity and understanding about Third World people;
- create new models for providing material assistance that combine environmentally and socially sound development with education and advocacy here at home;
- shift the direction of our foreign policy by cutting ties with

repressive regimes and ending the tradition of intervening against popular movements for change; and
- foster broader democratic participation here at home by fortifying the bedrock of democracy—an alert, educated, and participating citizenry.

The internationalism we describe in this book is based on a healthy combination of honest self-interest mixed with deep compassion. It recognizes that the interests of the Third World poor coincide with the interests of the majority of North Americans. Less poverty abroad would mean fewer companies abandoning the United States in search of cheaper labor; higher standards of living in Third World countries would mean more markets for our goods; greater democracy overseas would mean less U.S. tax dollars wasted on military aid to repressive regimes. As the late President of Mozambique, Samora Machel, stated, "International solidarity is not an act of charity. It is an act of unity between allies fighting on different terrains toward the same objectives. The foremost of these objectives is to aid the development of humanity to the highest level possible."

Internationalism does not mean abandoning our problems at home for more "glamorous" struggles abroad. On the contrary, it means showing the connections between local and international struggles. It demands that we integrate our efforts to change foreign policy with our efforts to eliminate hunger and homelessness in our own communities. It also demands that we struggle against racism and sexism at home and abroad, and that these efforts be an essential part of the "new internationalism."

This book strives to capture this new spirit of internationalism. We hope to give those already involved an extra push—especially in those inevitable moments of self-doubt. For those who are not involved, we hope to spark their desire to get on board. The voices in this book will prove that a spirited, committed group of individuals can indeed make a difference.

BRIDGING
THE
GLOBAL GAP

Loren Hedstrom (left), Jacqueline and Phillip Kane (right), and Katherine Stokes (bottom, middle), participants in a new kind of tourism, have all been transformed by their Third World experience.

Travel With a Purpose

Several years ago, when I turned sixty-five, I went on a trip to the Philippines sponsored by the development group, Oxfam. I went for very personal reasons—my husband and I were separated, my four children were on their own, and I just decided it was a good time to explore my interest in other cultures. I had no knowledge and no real interest in the Philippines. But I knew about the work of Oxfam America and wanted to learn more about how its projects work.

During the two weeks we were there, we met with all kinds of people—peasants, factory workers, priests, professionals. It was a year before the fall of Marcos, and many of the people we met with were involved in the struggle to overthrow him.

After the first five days of the trip, we split up into groups of two. Each pair teamed up with a Filipino companion and we broke up according to our interests. One group went to see some development projects Oxfam was supporting. Two others joined a group of factory workers. The religious members of our group went to stay with rural Christian communities. I went with a peasant organizer to the remote villages she was working in.

They were five extremely demanding days. We spent our time slogging through the thick jungle in the rain, or trudging along footpaths in the hot sun, moving from one remote village to a remoter village. I fell into rice paddies and got leeches on my legs. The homes we stayed in—that were so simple and yet shared so graciously—had no electricity, no running water, and no toilets. In one house there were twelve of us in one room, sleeping side by side on straw mats.

I became very close to the mother in one family, despite the fact that she didn't speak a word of English. Her thatched roof leaked during the torrential downpours, and in the middle of the night I woke to find her sheltering me with her only covering. She showed me how to wash clothes in a fast-flowing brook without losing them, how to make the most of a meager meal, how to go to the bathroom off the side of the house when it's raining too hard to venture out. We were like two peas in a pod. I also became close to our Filipino guide. Her mother had left years ago to be a domestic worker in Europe, and I temporarily became the mother she didn't have.

I was overwhelmed by the level of poverty I saw; I'd never thought of the Philippines as such a poor country. But what struck me even more was the people's dignity and hospitality. They were unbelievably bright and creative. They were beautiful people—their patched clothes were as clean as could be. And they struggled to better their lives under the most difficult circumstances imaginable.

I'd say the most striking thing I learned was that the Filipino people held the U.S. government and U.S. corporations directly responsible for the economic injustices of their country. Whether it was middle-class people in Manila or poor peasants way out in the countryside, they all said the same thing: "Stop your government from supporting Marcos and get your military bases out of our country." I had not realized the extent to which U.S. foreign policy was based on military might, or that the United States was so involved in preserving the status quo at the expense of the poor in the Philippines. It was a real shock to me.

It was especially difficult to be constantly asked what we were going to do when we got back. Their country was a dictatorship, they said, but they were risking their lives to change it. Our country was a democracy, so certainly now that we understood the truth we'd be able to fix things.

I live in a conservative, middle-class suburb in New England, and when I first came home I didn't even attempt to talk to other people about my experiences. It took me a good six weeks to calm down and organize my thoughts. I finally put together a slide show and got up the courage to talk at some churches, schools, women's groups. I tried to make people understand that the hardships I, a sixty-five-year-old woman, had endured for a week were the hardships others were enduring for a lifetime.

On one level, the knowledge I have gained makes me feel terrible. I feel terrible that such injustice exists, and that we Americans are responsible for a good piece of it. But on another level, I feel tremendously inspired by the people I met—their courage, their imagination, their endurance against unbelievable odds. I learned that even those who live under the most terribly oppressive conditions have options and can take responsibility for changing their lives.

My daughter says to me, "Relax, Mom. You've paid your dues. You're almost seventy years old and you have a right to enjoy the years you have left." But after I've seen a bit of how this world works, I feel a tremendous responsibility to do something.

I look at people in this country who are taking real risks—sanctuary workers, tax resisters—but I don't have the guts to do those things yet. It's hard to change overnight, especially at my age and living in such a conservative community. But I'm still thinking, still looking, still asking myself what risks I am willing to take and what risks are worth taking. One thing is certain—my experience in the Philippines changed my view of the world and from now on, there's no turning back.

—Katharine Stokes

My wife Jacqueline and I are both retired; we've been married for forty-seven years. She was a guidance counselor for many years. I am a double retiree— lieutenant colonel in the U.S. Army and a supervisor on the New York City Board of Education.

Now that we're retired and have a little savings, we thought we might do some traveling. We heard about a trip one of the church groups was organizing to southern Africa. We'd heard a lot about South Africa in the papers and on television, and we thought it would be nice to see for ourselves what was really going on.

I remember when we told our children and friends where we were going, they thought we were crazy. They said, "Here you are living in the South Bronx—one of the poorest areas in our country—and you have to go thousands of miles away on your vacation to see more poor people?"

It's true we could have stayed right here at home and used the money we spent on the trip to help people in our community. But my wife and I strongly believe that we must show our concern for all people who suffer indignities.

It was a real people-to-people trip. We were fifteen in all, and three of us were black Americans. We rode on miles of dusty, rocky roads to visit with people in the black townships and resettlement areas. We went into their homes. We ate our meals with them. We went to church and prayed with them. We witnessed firsthand the toll that apartheid exacts in family separations, forced relocation, and human rights abuses. And we forged such strong bonds with the people we met that we really became part of one family.

We not only learned about their country, but we also helped dispel the myths they held about our own. We were the first black Americans many of them had ever seen. Their view of black America came from watching Bill Cosby, "Different Strokes," and the Jeffersons on television. They were amazed when we told them that many American blacks were not well educated and wealthy, but suffered—like them—from unemployment, inadequate housing and poor health care.

And over and over again, we heard the same thing—that policies like sanctions and divestment were the only pressure that would move the South African government to change. "Please go home and tell your people to keep the pressure on," they implored.

We were all inspired to take the message home and talk to as many people as possible about what we had witnessed. One of the tour members wrote a book about the experience. Others collected money through their churches to buy an ambulance for one of the black townships we visited. Some of the members have been working to get a hundred full scholarships for South African and Namibian students to study in the United States. Others have started letter-writing campaigns to free political prisoners. And everyone has done presentations. My wife and I have done over forty—in churches, homes, libraries, hospitals, and colleges. We've talked to everyone from third graders to graduate students. We also wrote articles, like the one in the church publication *Maryknoll* that reaches 800,000 people.

As my wife says, we're "on fire." We want to talk to anyone we can, anywhere we can. We want to tie the issues of southern Africa to the issues of poverty, discrimination, and unemployment here in our own country. Because what became very clear to us on our trip was that whether we're talking about South Africa or the South Bronx, we are all affected by the same forces that keep people impoverished.

—Philip Kane

I'm a hog farmer from Scandia, Kansas. As a member of the district council for the American Lutheran Church, in 1982 I was invited to join a Lutheran delegation going to Mexico and Nicaragua. The church agreed to pay part of the trip, so I figured, "why not?"

In Mexico we met with church leaders who started talking to us about this "preferential option for the poor" that the Latin church had taken. They were living and working among the poor. That was all well and good but then they started talking about why people were poor, and they said the United States was part of the reason. Well, I was a very conservative Republican—I come from Reagan country, you know—and I got quite upset about the things I was hearing.

Then we went to Nicaragua and I heard more of the same. I didn't know anything about the history of Nicaragua, and they told us about the U.S. involvement over the years and how it helped keep this small elite in power.

But what really turned me around was listening to the people, listening to their dreams about their future. We talked to a lot of small farmers, just like me, who for the first time in their lives had a piece of land because the revolution was redistributing land to people who needed it. Now I'm all for respecting private property, but I do think there's a limit on how much land one person should be allowed to own. But you see, they had this small elite who owned most of the land and got very rich off the backs of the poor—and that's just not fair.

I listened to what these people were doing. They weren't forcibly taking over other people's land. No, they were setting up sensible criteria for how much land a person could have and how to fairly redistribute the rest. So when I saw what they were trying to do, I couldn't help supporting them.

This kind of experience is a very heavy thing—it shakes up everything you ever learned, everything you ever believed. It's really a life-changing experience. And of course, it's very hard to come back home to the same conservative community in Kansas and try to communicate what you have learned.

When I got back I prepared a talk, taped it, and took it to a friend of mine who's a Baptist pastor. He listened to it and then turned to me and said, "Loren, are you prepared to have your lifelong friends turn their backs on you? Because when they hear this talk, that's just what'll happen." And he was right. My wife thought I'd been brainwashed. My son-in-law thought I'd gone mad—he still does. And a lot of my friends stopped talking to me.

But you know in Nicaragua I'd been touched by people with a deep inner vision. We met with Ernesto Cardenal, the priest who's the Minister of Culture. We met with Miguel D'Escoto, the priest who's the Foreign Minister. And I think a bit of their inner vision rubbed off on me.

Back home, I got in my car and started traveling all over the Midwest, talking in churches and Lions Clubs. I always get a mixed reaction. With some people, you can see the sparks fly. Others come up to me afterward and put their arms around me.

I was lucky with my wife. I started giving her some books to read and I took her to all the talks I gave. And sure enough, she started joining right in. Sometimes at the talks she'd get so riled up I'd have to say to her, "Whoa, mama, take it easy."

As I said, this kind of travel experience is a very emotional one. It's not fun and games. Because if you really allow yourself to sit back and listen to people, you'll never be the same again.

I look at the United States in a whole different light now. I keep telling people I had to get out of the country to see my own country. Before I'd read about how a few people own most of this country's wealth, but I didn't pay attention. Now that just doesn't seem right anymore. So I became the district coordinator for the Lutheran hunger program and work on poverty and justice issues right here.

Sure, my life was a lot simpler before the trip. But at this point I'd have it no other way. I feel freer now than I've ever felt in my life. I reread the Scriptures now, and they have a whole new meaning. And while it's true I've lost some old friends, I now have new friends all over the country. I'm part of a growing network that supports and nurtures each other. You should see us when we get together—we're more than friends, we're family. And that's what keeps me going.

—Loren Hedstrom

Katharine Stokes, Philip and Jacqueline Kane, and Loren Hedstrom are all participants in a new brand of travel to the Third World. In contrast to commercial tours, which often view the Third World as an unending source of sun, sand, and sex, this kind of tourism—referred to as alternative tourism, socially responsible tourism, or social tourism—sees travel as a way to establish the basis for deepening our understanding and strengthening our ties with the Third World.

Although a handful of such tours existed in previous decades, alternative tourism in the United States is truly a phenomenon of the 1980s. By 1987, hundreds of alternative tour groups had sprung up throughout the United States. The range of possibilities is astounding: study tours to Cuba and Nicaragua, bicycle treks to China, peace tours to the Pacific Islands, reforestation brigades to Central America, socially conscious pilgrimages to the Holy Lands, locally run village resorts in West Africa, homestays with Rastafarians in Jamaica.

The impetus for an alternative to commercial tourism has come from an amalgam of sources. The major push did not come from well-meaning "first worlders," but from the Third World itself. "It was the church and community leaders in the Third World who began examining the effects of commercial tourism on their own societies," recalls Peter Davies of the Center for Responsible Tourism. "It really started with the church in Asia, which took a hard look at the issue of sex tourism and then branched out to look at the entire industry."

Beginning in the late 1970s, several regional church groups, predominantly from Asia and the Pacific, initiated a series of conferences to look at the effect of tourism in the Third World. Delegates at these conferences decried the growth of prostitution and the degradation of local cultures and values. They claimed that while tourism created jobs, the jobs were unskilled, low-paying, seasonal, and exaggerated colonial stereotypes of "master" and "servant". They also asserted that the real beneficiaries of tourism were not the poor Third World host countries, but the rich industrialized countries that control the entire industry—the hotels, the airlines, the tour operators and agencies.

Church leaders criticized Third World commercial tourism from a moral point of view as well. Travel by relatively rich people to the lands of predominantly poor people, with the sole motivation of pleasure, they maintained, has no possible justification in either biblical or theological terms. "The tourist who can live in such a compromising situation, where the cost of one night's accommodation in a hotel exceeds the monthly salary of the average citizen of the host country, has dulled his or her sensitivity to the suffering of the people," Australian priest Ron O'Grady insisted. "The inherent hedonism of such travel in countries where poverty is rampant makes a mockery of the poor and cannot be part of a Christian lifestyle."[1]

The regional conferences culminated in the 1980 International Workshop on Tourism, held in the Philippines. Hosted by the Christian Conference of Asia, it included representatives from Catholic and Protestant groups in Asia, Africa, the Caribbean, Europe, and the United States.

The Workshop concluded that tourism was "wreaking havoc" throughout the Third World and the delegates decided to continue their critique of tourism by forming the Ecumenical Coalition for Third World Tourism. Based in Bangkok, this coalition now has several regional branches throughout the world.[2] A major campaign of the Coalition has been to reduce the negative cultural effects of Third World tourism.

The German group, New Angle Films, for example, produced a series of films under church auspices illustrating some of the pernicious effects of tourism. One film about Sri Lanka follows a thirteen-year-old boy who dropped out of school to become a "beach walker," using his charm to get money and gifts from tourists. While he earns twice as much as his father, his father worries what will become of his son when he is no longer a "cute young boy" but an uneducated, unskilled man with Western tastes. Airlines such as Lufthansa have agreed to show these films on their charter flights to the Third World.

Another example of educational efforts to reform tourist behavior is the Code of Ethics elaborated by the Christian Conference of Asia.[3] After discussions between the Australian Council of Churches and the Indonesian airline, Garuda, the airline published a version of the code to place in the seat pocket of its flights to Indonesia.

Criticism of commercial tourism has also come from a very different quarter—the workers employed in the industry. Since 1978, the International Union of Food and Allied Workers (IUF), a federation of 1.4 million union members with headquarters in Geneva, has been evaluating the effects of the tourist industry. They have noted with concern tourism's devastating effect on the environment and its tendency to create low-paid, subservient jobs for Third World workers, while reserving the managerial positions for foreigners.

Furthermore, the unionists complain that Third World tourism as practiced by commercial tours makes no attempt to form bonds between First and Third World workers. They cite a study of a popular tourist resort in Sousse, Tunisia, which found that 90 percent of the tourists claimed they had come for "the sun, the beach, the sea and the palm trees," and only 10 percent professed any interest in Tunisian society and history. The tourists spent an average of twenty-two hours a day inside the hotel complex, and 65 percent did no sightseeing at all. The IUF claimed that this type of tourism "makes a mockery of the pious notion that tourism encourages human exchange and understanding among nations."[4]

The Call for a New Kind of Tourism

Knowing that tourism was around to stay, church groups and trade unions began to channel criticism of commercial tourism into a call for the creation of an alternative—tourism controlled by local people that would make use of locally available resources in the interests of strengthening local economies and cultures. "If tourism is to be salvaged," stated the resolution of the 1980 Christian Conference of Asia, "a thorough re-thinking and restructuring of the whole industry is called for, taking as its basic premise not profit-making and crass materialism, but the fundamental spiritual and human development of peoples everywhere."[5]

The IUF has called on workers in the industrialized countries to seek contact with workers in the country they're visiting, to learn about the local culture, and to exchange experiences and opinions. As IUF General Secretary Dan Gallin told us, "Vacation should not be thought of as a time to escape from reality, but as a time to raise our awareness about that reality. Of course vacations should be fun, but they can be both fun and educational. They can be an opportunity for workers to learn about different societies and to create ties with other workers."

To begin this process, the IUF is collaborating with alternative travel groups, such as Dev Tours in France, to create package tours for union members that combine leisure with union principles.

Alternative Tourism in Central America

In the United States, the push for alternative tourism has come from a totally different source: public unrest over the heavy U.S. role in the conflict in Central America. Starting in 1980, more and more U.S. citizens, confused by the views propounded by the White House and the media, decided to go to Central America and take a look for themselves.

The numbers are extraordinary: between 1980 and 1988 an estimated 80,000-100,000 North Americans visited Central America, mainly through study tours, delegations, and work brigades. United States senior citizens joined Elders Brigades to help harvest Nicaraguan coffee. Peace activists joined their Central American counterparts in peace walks through the region. Religious groups met with base Christian communities to learn about liberation theology in practice. And special tours were conducted for almost every imaginable grouping, including doctors, lawyers, and—literally—Indian chiefs.

Visitors are usually moved by a desire to see for themselves what the conflict is all about. Most alternative tour operators are eager to expose participants to the reality of Central America in the hopes of changing U.S. policy in the region. Although there is usually some time for fun and relaxation, visitors are more often busy meeting with local representatives—government officials, union and peasant groups, businesspeople, women's organizations, and church officials.

One of the largest groups leading tours to Central America is the Center for Global Education at Augsburg College in Minneapolis. In 1982 the Center began taking Lutheran students and church members to Mexico to study liberation theology and global development issues. "The crisis in Central America really changed our focus," director Joel Mugge explains. "People started asking us if we could take them to Central America so they could see for themselves what was happening there. So we took a few church groups down, but then we started getting requests from all directions—colleges, lawyers, teachers. We now take about seven hundred people to Central America every year, and we have offices in Washington D.C., Mexico, and Nicaragua."

Trip organizers want visitors to gain a deeper understanding of the Central American conflict, but some also initiate visitors into more active participation. One remarkable group in this category is Witness for Peace. Most Witness for Peace participants go to Nicaragua in groups of fifteen to twenty for two-week stints. After a two-day training workshop in Mexico City or the United States and two days of interviews in Managua with church, government, and opposition leaders, they travel to the countryside to accompany poor Nicaraguans in areas most affected by the war. Volunteer Peter Olson explains it this way: "Standing with the Nicaraguan people has included many things. It has meant helping to cultivate crops in dangerous areas, digging a bomb shelter at a daycare center, helping to bury children and adults, helping out with a vaccination drive. Above all, it has meant joining hands with our Nicaraguan sisters and brothers time and again in praying for peace and reconciliation."

Witness for Peace began sending delegations to Nicaragua in October 1983. By mid-1988 more than three thousand people, from every state and every major religious denomination, had participated. These are no ordinary tourists, but people who are willing to demonstrate their nonviolent resistance to U.S. intervention in Nicaragua. As the steering committee notes, "Our faith calls us to be peacemakers. We do not take this action lightly. We know there are risks in a war zone. But we believe that those who work for peace must be willing to take the same risks as those who fight in war." (There have been no casualties among Witness for Peace volunteers, although some team members were captured by the contras, detained, and later released unharmed.)

As a consequence of this massive flow of North Americans to Central America, many participants have become interested in finding out more about the rest of the world. Joel Mugge of the Center for Global Education told us, "We have a lot of people coming back from Central America who then say, 'Well, I think I understand what's happening in Central America now, but what's happening in the Philippines?'" This has spurred the Center to work in other areas. It now has tours to the Philippines, to the Caribbean, and has recently initiated study tours to Cuba.

"We'd like to branch out into still other parts of the world," Joel says. "We'd also like to get away from the simple crisis orientation of our work. For while Central America is a region that currently demands action on the part of North Americans, we'd really like to look at alternative political and theological approaches that societies have taken. This kind of travel is a way for Americans to not only see the Third World with new eyes, but to see our own society as reflected through Third World eyes. And this, of course, creates a whole new awareness of our responsibility to both the Third World and our own society."

Other Sectors Promoting Alternative Tourism

Groups that fund development projects in the Third World, such as Oxfam and the National Council of Negro Women, also provide tours to the Third World. Offered primarily as a service to their members, these tours provide a firsthand look at development issues and projects.

Newcomers to the alternative tourism scene are environmental activists, who now promote vacations that range from studying Ecuador's tropical rain forests to planting trees in the Nicaraguan countryside. Some of these tours combine outdoor adventure with environmental conservation. Journeys International, for example, channels a portion of the tour costs into special projects like seed distribution in Nepal or reforestation in Peru.

Alternative tourism to Africa blossomed for a period in the 1970s with the publication of Alex Haley's book, *Roots*. Tourist agencies throughout the United States began offering tours geared at black Americans eager to discover their ancestors' homeland. Some merely capitalized on the book itself, but others truly sought to build connections between black Americans and Africans. "I remember there were charter flights leaving from New York almost every week," says Willis Logan, head of the Africa Desk of the National Council of Churches. "But those kinds of tours have died down to a trickle."

The vast majority of tours to Africa are still safari tours that look at African wildlife but ignore the social conditions of the countries they visit. There are exceptions, however. A group called Into Africa Tours, for example, combines safaris in Kenya with a homestay on a family farm and visits to villages to meet with local people.

The women's movement has also engendered some alternative tours linking women in industrialized countries with women's struggles in the Third World. The New York-based group MADRE takes North Americans to meet with women in Central America. Woman to Woman gives female activists from the United States a chance to meet with Mexican women about issues such as land reform, union organizing, sexism, and forced sterilization.

A call for alternative tourism has also come from groups examining the revolutionary processes taking place not only in the Soviet Union, Eastern Europe, and China, but in other Third World countries as well. The Venceremos Brigade and the Center for Cuban Studies have been leading tours to Cuba for years, despite the restrictions that various U.S. administrations have placed on travel to the island. The travel agency Marazul has arranged dozens of tours to Cuba, Nicaragua, Grenada (until the

U.S. invasion in 1983), and in 1987 began its first friendship tours to Vietnam.

"We think it's important for Americans to see Third World countries with social systems different from our own," says Marazul's Bob Guild. "It helps challenge what they read in the press; it helps break down fear and hostility. We're not saying they should love these systems; we're just saying they should try to understand them."

Key Differences Between Alternative and Commercial Tourism

Not all alternative tours are built on exactly the same principles. Some put more emphasis on the environment than on meeting local people. Some emphasize homestays while others rely on hotels or hostels. Some try to ensure that visitors respect local customs and cultures while others are concerned with how visitors will use the cross-cultural experience once they return home.

But most alternative tours share a number of key principles that sharply distinguish them from commercial package tours. Among them are the following:

• *Alternative tourist groups try to keep as much of the tourist dollar as possible in the host country.*

Most commercial tours leave little of the tourist dollar in the host country. A U.S. tour party usually pays the tour operator in the United States, travels on a U.S. airline, stays in a U.S.-owned hotel, is guided around by U.S. guides, and often eats food imported from the United States. Studies show that tour operators claim at least 20 percent of total package prices. Airlines take another sizable chunk. So the share that remains in the tourist's own country can easily exceed 75 percent.

Alternative tours tend to emphasize staying in locally owned lodgings, eating at local restaurants, and employing local counterparts to help lead the group. A program in Africa called "Tourism for Discovery," for example, is designed to keep tourist dollars in local hands. The program was initiated in Casamance, Senegal, by villagers unhappy with multinational control over tourism in their country. They built simple huts within the village itself and invited visitors to share in the ordinary life of the people, and join in festivities and dances, thus providing ample opportunity for visitors to talk with the local people. Similar programs have since cropped up in Benin, Mali, and Niger and have become quite popular with European tourists.[6]

Alternative tourism stresses not only local spending but simple living. While commercial agencies lure tourists with promises of opulence (under the Duvalier dictatorship, Haiti's luxurious Habitation Leclerc hotel, for example, was promoted as the "most extraordinarily lascivious and decadent place on earth"), alternative tours call for moderation. The Connecticut group, Plowshares International, which leads immersion seminars to the Third World, requires participants to agree to a "covenant of lifestyle" that says they must "live 'simply but safely' at the level of our hosts, eating local food and using local transportation so as to experience the richness and diversity of the culture as 'visitors' and not as 'tourists.'" Plowshares participants are also requested not to bring more than $100 for purchasing gifts.

• *Most people who join alternative tours show a genuine interest in learning about the countries they're visiting.*

"I'm amazed when I talk to people who have been on a Club Med vacation to Haiti, let's say, and can't recall what country they were in," says Bob Guild of Marazul Tours. "Our philosophy is that travel is not just lying on the beach, but also learning about the country whose beach we're lying on."

Many alternative tour groups provide participants with reading packets months before the trip. Some make advanced reading and preparation a requirement for participation. "We send people a list of materials that are mandatory reading and then a list of other suggestions," says Alice Frazer Evans of Plowshares Institute. "Some of our participants read everything and more, and then turn around and send us recommendations. Some of the busy business executives get the materials and take them on the plane, hoping for a long flight. But we do insist that people prepare as much in advance as they can, so they can make the most out of the experience."

• *Alternative tourism is not just a profit-making venture.*

While commercial tour operators have one goal—profits—

alternative tour operators are primarily interested in fostering cross-cultural ties.

Alternative tours often go to countries spurned by commercial operators because they are areas in upheaval—Central America, southern Africa, the Philippines, the Middle East. "We go to many of the 'hot spots'," says Mary Hoffman of The Travelers Society, "not because they are profitable but because they happen to be where some of the most interesting experiments are taking place, or because they are countries that North Americans should know more about. We started tours to Grenada when the socialist government of Maurice Bishop came to power, which was precisely the time that commercial travel agencies took Grenada off their list. We sponsor a lot of tours to Jamaica, another country that has been blacklisted by many tourist agencies because of negative publicity around violence and political unrest."

Though cultural and economic exchanges remain their focus, alternative tour groups do not disdain making profits—it's just that the operating principles make them hard to come by. "We would love to make a profit on our trips," says Kathie Klarreich, who leads tours for Caribbean Exchange. "We could then afford to offer scholarships and develop a really effective follow-up program. But the reality is that these trips are expensive to run. If we want to compensate our hosts fairly and keep the tours accessible to lower-income people, then the most we can aim for is to cover costs and staff time."

Placing a lower priority on the profit motive is good for tourists but may jeopardize the long-term stability of a tour organization. This tradeoff plagues most groups, forcing them to search for creative funding possibilities.

"What many people don't realize," according to Joel Mugge of the Center for Global Education, "is the tremendous amount of work that goes into preparing one of our tours. If it's a new place for us, we always send a staff member down first to make the contacts and check everything out. Even if it's a country we've been to many times before, each group is different and has different interests and demands. To do the preparation and follow-up, and to do it well, requires tremendous costs that just can't be transferred to the participants without making the program even more elite than it is. So we must beat on the

foundations' doors and ask for contributions from former participants to keep the program going at affordable rates."

Individual or Group Travel?

While so far we've focused on group travel, many of the same
issues apply to individual travelers. To get the most out of a trip,
alternative travelers should learn about the place to be visited
beforehand. Instead of sticking to the tourist enclaves, tourists
can make an effort to stay in modest accommodations and talk
with local people—workers in the hotels and restaurants, street
vendors, bus drivers, children at school.

There are certainly advantages to individual travel—among
them, going at one's own pace, greater flexibility in scheduling,
and more one-on-one contact with local people. But there are
disadvantages as well. It may be more difficult for an individual
to process the experience and to come home and do something
about it. "It's hard for people to maintain their enthusiasm when
they get back," says Virginia Hadsell of the Center for Responsible Tourism. "They get a high on the trip, go home, and no one
listens. We've found that when two or three people from the
same community or the same church share the experience,
they're much more likely to do some kind of follow-up."

Alternative group travel has won converts from among some
of the most die-hard loners and rugged individualists. "I was one
of those people who always traveled alone," admits Kevin
Danaher, who participated in a study tour to the Caribbean. "I
thought groups were for people who were too afraid or too shy
to venture out on their own. But a friend of mine convinced me
to go on this trip, and I loved it. One advantage is that you don't
have to worry about the details of where to stay, where to eat,
how to get around—because someone else is worrying about
that for you. Secondly, you get to meet people—from government officials to poor peasants—whom you couldn't meet on
your own. But perhaps the greatest advantage is the group itself. Everyone brings such different perspectives—it was like
having twelve sets of eyes and ears."

Cara Taylor traveled with an ecumenical church group to
Haiti. "On these kinds of trips," Cara asserts, "being part of a

group is essential for processing and sharing the emotional impact. One of the men on our trip was terribly upset by the poverty, so upset that it made him physically ill. He's an engineer, so he's used to solving problems. Well, the magnitude of the problems in Haiti totally overwhelmed him. The realization that he wasn't going to be able to solve *anything* was a real psychological blow and left him totally helpless."

"Fortunately, the group was very caring. After twenty-four hours together, we were lifelong friends. What helped us get close was that the first night we had to write and discuss what arrangements we had to make at home in order to come on the trip. You wouldn't believe the traumas some people left behind. One couple's son had cancer, another woman's husband had been totally against her going and called her every night in Haiti to bawl her out. So the group was a vital support system."

Most alternative tour leaders make sure there are plenty of opportunities to spend time alone, as well as opportunities to do the kinds of things people normally do on vacations—swim, shop, dance. Tour activities are usually optional. It's always possible to skip the meeting with some government official and head out for the beach instead!

Alternative Tours for Families

One of the areas sorely neglected by the alternative tourist movement is family tourism. Most of the study tours are inappropriate for children. Abby Nelson, for example, took her eight-year-old daughter with her on a study trip to Central America. "I thought it would be a great experience for her. She speaks some Spanish and I thought the cultural exchange would be meaningful for her. The problem was that I ended up spending more time making sure she was happy than I did attending the seminars and meetings. I certainly wouldn't recommend it to anyone with young children."

The Center for Global Education is trying its first experiment with a family program to Mexico, combining sightseeing and "fun in the sun" with cultural and educational exchanges. "The tough part about family tours is that they take a lot of specialized planning and they are hard to pay for themselves," says

Joel Mugge. "But we are excited about this program and hope we will be sponsoring yearly trips."

The Travelers Society leads what they call "intergenerational tours" to the Soviet Union, and is now starting these tours to Ireland (both northern and southern) and to Kenya. The children get to meet and play with local children, whether in a peace camp in Ireland or a rural village in Kenya. On their last tour to the Soviet Union they had children, parents, and grandparents—with an age range of eight to seventy-five!

One of the greatest experiences for teenagers (usually eighteen and up) is working in international work camps. Volunteers for Peace in Belmont, Vermont, publishes a yearly listing of hundreds of opportunities to spend a few weeks working with foreign friends in the spirit of international cooperation. Some of the work camps are in the Third World—in places like Nicaragua, Ghana, Tunisia, and Turkey—but even many of the European camps are Third World-oriented. The range of activities is extraordinary: refurbishing tools and collecting school materials in Arhus, Denmark, to send to Namibian refugees fighting to liberate their country from South African domination; repairing roads in Soligen, Germany, with the wages used to buy an ambulance for Soligen's twin city of Jinotega, Nicaragua; working in Modena, Italy, on a national campaign to raise funds for the democratic opposition in Chile.

Dilemmas Confronting Alternative Tours

Alternative tours are certainly less intrusive than most, but there are still some who feel that the best tourism to the Third World is no tourism at all. At a 1986 conference on Third World tourism in West Germany, a native Hawaiian woman shocked the audience with the depth of her resentment towards tourists. "I don't want a single other tourist ever to come to Hawaii again," cried Haunany-Kay Trask. "We don't want you. We don't need you. Keep your money. I want you to stay where you are and tell all your friends to stay where they are. I don't want to extend my hospitality. It has been extended and it has been trampled on. We have been raped." She concluded by saying that the future will bring politically targeted violence against tourists. "There is no such thing as an innocent tourist," Haunany-Kay warned. "Everyone is culpable, and the violence that is done against my people, against my culture and my sacred land, will be returned in kind."[7]

This type of reaction leaves people like Virginia Hadsell, Director of the Center for Responsible Tourism, in a quandary. "I respect native peoples," says Virginia, "and I understand the tremendous destruction that tourism has wrought—pushing women into prostitution, kicking native people off their land to make way for high-rise hotels, stripping religious ceremonies and sacred sites of their meaning. But on the other hand I'm also realistic and I know that First World people will continue to travel. So I feel our job is to try to curb some of the worst excesses of commercial tourism, while providing an alternative that truly leads to greater human understanding."

The intrusive nature of tourism is exacerbated when alternative tours wear out their welcome by returning too often to the same place. How often can leaders take time from their busy schedules to meet with a group of foreigners? How much time can directors of successful development projects spare to show tour groups around without neglecting their own work?

"A good many Western aid and mission agencies are organizing church tours to Third World countries to look at aid programs, and the hospitality of the host communities is wearing thin," warns Father Ron O'Grady. "These people have their own work to do, and the presence of numerous visitors poking around, often asking elementary questions, is a distraction. It is ironic that some of the more successful aid projects in Third World countries now find it necessary to employ extra staff simply to take care of foreign visitors."

Joel Mugge of the Center for Global Education suggests developing a broad range of contacts as a way to get around this dilemma of going back to the same people over and over. "Many of the development groups that do tours to their own projects have realized this problem of 'overusing' people,"and are reorganizing their trips," says Joel. "Rather than putting the emphasis on the particular projects, they're putting the emphasis on the social conditions in the countries they work in."

Some groups in the Third World have addressed this problem by restricting visits to a certain time of year—determined in advance not by the visitors but by the hosts. Mondragon, a city located in the Basque region of Spain, is a much-touted example of a thriving alternative economic system, with one hundred worker-owned manufacturing and service industries and some two hundred retail stores. With visitors coming from all over the world, the workers at Mondragon had to do something to limit the flow. Until 1984, they posted a "gatekeeper" at the Caja Laboral, the financial heart of the system, in order to keep tourists out. Mondragon leaders have since come to realize the importance of a more reasonable tourism policy for public relations. Guided tours have now become one of the responsibilities of the Management Training Schools, and the classrooms are used to show videos and slides about Mondragon.

But for other groups, foreign visitors are tremendously important. The National Federation of Sugar Workers in the Philippines, for example, is eager to host visitors. Since the organizers are under attack from the military, members feel that increased visibility and support can only help. They have an entire division within the Federation to deal solely with visitors—both foreigners and Filipinos from the cities—taking them to stay in the homes of sugar workers in order to develop a deeper understanding of their plight.

Addressing the One-Way Flow

A critique common to both commercial and alternative tourism emerges from the harsh economic imbalance between the first and the Third Worlds. Although a small elite from Third World countries may have the money and leisure time to travel, the vast majority do not. Tourism is essentially a one-way flow.

We in the industrialized countries have come to think of vacations as a basic right of all working people, but for most people in the Third World "vacation" is a foreign concept. Father Ron O'Grady, who has lived among the poor in Asia for decades, explains. "Consider the poor. They are people who will never be tourists. When they speak of travel they mean going on foot, or in a crowded bus, to the next village or town. . . . Family incomes are barely sufficient for survival and there is no extra money available for luxury travel. Indeed, when they think of luxury, their minds cannot stretch far beyond a bottle of soft drink or a better meal. The concept of a paid holiday or expenditure on leisure travel or visiting a foreign culture is totally outside their conceptual framework."[8]

Some argue that the tremendous inequality between those with money and leisure time and those without makes Third World tourism deleterious. Peter Davies of the Center for Responsible Tourism, himself a seasoned traveler, feels that there is nothing wrong with tourism between countries of relatively equal economic status. "I'm living in Canada," says Peter. "Say I decide to go to San Francisco for my vacation. When I get to the airport I start talking to the cabdriver and I ask him what are the good spots to see. He says, 'When I get a few days off in a row, I go down the coast to Baja California and go camping in the state park there. I work my butt off during the week, but when I go down there I just kick back and relax.' The cabdriver and I have already established a rapport. We can relate as equals.

"But imagine the same scene in Sri Lanka and the cabdriver saying, 'Oh, I have a little cottage up in the hill country where I spend the summers.' He's lucky if he has a place to lay his head down after working twelve hours a day. 'Vacation' isn't in his vocabulary. That's why it's so difficult to relate on equal terms."

A group concerned with addressing the one-way flow of Third World tourism is the German Lutheran Church. Its Center for Development Education and Third World Tourism calls for (and helps finance) responsible tourism. It stipulates that each tour should fund a "reverse tour" in which the German group invites someone from the host country back to Germany to visit and continue the educational work. While it realizes that this will in no way redress the massive inequalities inherent in Third World tourism, it is a gesture that openly recognizes those inequalities and seeks to challenge them.

A White Middle-Class Pursuit?

The one-way flow in alternative tourism is further exacerbated by the fact that the tourists themselves represent an elite within their own countries. They are largely white, middle- to upper-class people. Many of the groups organizing alternative tours recognize this, but have trouble finding ways to overcome it.

"The criticism that alternative tourism is still for relatively rich, white people is a valid one and we are constantly looking for ways to make our tours accessible to minorities and people of low income," insists Joel Mugge of the Center for Global Education. "We were successful with one of our trips to Central America in which well over half the participants were low-income people of color from Detroit's inner city. We got some money to subsidize the trip, but the group itself spent an entire year fundraising to come up with matching funds. The trip had a tremendous impact on them, and made us even more aware of the importance of such exchanges.

"We are now steadily building up a scholarship fund and have already formed an advisory committee to work out the selection procedures. We hope to raise $25,000 a year in scholarships, $10,000 of which would be spent and the rest saved in a special endowment. Our goal is to raise enough money through that endowment fund to eventually spend a full $25,000 a year in scholarships."

Woman to Woman, which arranges tours to Mexico, also puts a strong emphasis on ensuring the participation of low-income people. "We price our tours so that each paying participant pays not only for her tour, but the in-country costs for one other person," explains Elaine Burns. "The low-income person then only pays the airfare. This way we guarantee that half the participants from the United States are low-income women."

Difficult as such fundraising efforts can be, they provide an opportunity for individuals to learn not only from their hosts but from each other as well. Says Alice Frazer Evans of Plowshares, "We believe that the community you learn *with* is as important as the community you learn *from*. There is no way that a group of twenty-five white American males can have as rich an experience as a mixed group. White tourists see with one set of eyes, while minorities see with another. They ask different questions. They push the group in different directions. The learning experience is then not only from without, but from within the group itself. So whether we have to get business executives to underwrite a minority person's trip, or fundraise through a church, or offer partial scholarships, our goal is that all our trips be multiracial."

Preaching to the Converted?

Tour operators who want the lessons of alternative travel to reach the widest possible audience believe that groups should also represent a range of ideological perspectives. "People that participate in these tours often have similar beliefs," says Virginia Hadsell of the Center for Responsible Tourism. "Many are already aware of the injustices in the Third World and the need for changes in U.S. policy. But if the entire group is of one mind, it is, in a sense, preaching to the converted. I think alternative tours should strive to take people of not only diverse incomes and colors, but also people of diverse political beliefs."

Cathy Sunshine, a tour director with the ecumenical group EPICA, agrees. "On a trip to Cuba I participated in, my roommate was a young woman who'd grown up with State Department parents and whose husband is in the military. She'd been surrounded with their views all her life and had no reason to disagree with them. She was constantly at odds with the rest of the group, but not in a confrontational way. I thought it was good to have someone like her in the group to keep the hard questions out in front."

Another question is how "objective" such tours should be, and how much emphasis should be given to getting many points of view. Some tours to Nicaragua spend equal time hearing the Sandinista and anti-Sandinista viewpoints. Others feel that North Americans get the anti-Sandinista viewpoint every day—in newspapers, on television, and from politicians. If a group has only a short time to spend in Nicaragua, they feel it is only fair to hear the voices of people not usually presented in the U.S. media.

"We want the tours to give people a sense of what conditions in the country are really like," says former tour leader, Becky Buell. "But then the question becomes, whose reality are we trying to convey? There's the reality as seen by poor peasants, by workers, by women, by development workers, by religious people, by businessmen, by large landowners, by government officials, by military leaders, by U.S. embassy personnel. When we only have a short visit to a country, it's impossible to give equal time to all the different views. Our rule of thumb is that if 90 percent of the people are poor peasants and workers, then 90 percent of our time should be spent looking at reality from *their* viewpoint and 10 percent talking to the more privileged people."

Reconciling Different Expectations

Conflicting economic and political realities among countries raise an additional dilemma for alternative tours: visitors and groups in the host country may have markedly different expectations of their encounters.

Sister Carol Coenen was a participant on a trip to Mexico for U.S. educators organized by Catholic Relief Services. She recalls one of the meetings set up with a group of Mexican teachers. "The Mexicans had arranged this incredibly formal meeting with headphones and translators. Teachers had come in from rural areas to make presentations to us—they all had basically come to ask for money! They thought that just because we were from the States, we had millions of dollars to give away. We were really taken aback, and had a difficult time explaining that we weren't there to give away money but to get a better understanding of their situation and to exchange ideas."

The Center for Global Education group that visited Haiti had a similar experience. "At most of our meetings with trade unions and peasant organizations, people understand that we were there to learn from them and express our support," recalls tour participant Christopher Kashap. "But we had one very uncomfortable meeting with a neighborhood committee in Port-au-Prince. This group was very suspicious of us and had a hard time understanding what we were there for. Their only contact with foreigners had been with missionaries or development types with money to hand out. So they wanted to know what we were going to give them. They said, 'We don't want to end this meeting until something concrete comes out of it.' Our group did not believe in relating through charity, but their group had no understanding of the concept of solidarity."

Tour leader Cathy Sunshine has found that the reception a group receives depends partly on the host country's previous experience with these kinds of tours. "An encounter like the one we had in Haiti would be much less likely in Cuba or Nicaragua, where the concept of solidarity is well developed. People in those countries know they can make alliances with sympathetic North Americans. But Haiti is a different story. Under Duvalier, the only visiting foreigners were missionaries, development experts, or government officials. It was a paternalistic relationship that many Haitians resented, and U.S. visitors today have to overcome that legacy."

Coming Home

While many of these alternative tours are intense learning experiences, participants often have problems using what they have learned after they return. Tom Peterson, editor of the anti-hunger magazine, *Seeds*, went on an Oxfam study tour to the Philippines. "Everyone came back changed; we were all inspired to become more involved. There is just no way you cannot be affected by this face-to-face intensive encounter. The problem is that when you get back to your own community and there is no one else who has experienced what you've experienced, you can go for a few weeks or a month but then you fizzle out."

The Center for Global Education has an extensive follow-up program. "We send people follow-up packets free for two years after the trip," says staffer Meredith Dregni. "We have a newsletter that keeps people informed of the issues in the region they visited and gives updates on what other participants are doing as a result of the trip. We also hold reunions and conferences so people can get together and support each other. For us, the follow-up is a vital part of the whole experience."

Plowshares Institute also puts a heavy emphasis on follow-up. Before going on the trip, Plowshare participants agree to a "covenant of interpretation, to share one's learning with colleagues upon their return to the United States in whatever events and situations are appropriate." During the trip, participants choose a covenant partner to help them decide on what action to take and to hold them accountable. At the end of the trip, the participants turn their written covenants in to the tour leader, but the participants themselves are responsible for carrying out their promises.

"The covenants cover an extraordinary range," says Alice Frazer Evans of Plowshares. "Some people pledge to give talks at churches and schools; some make lifestyle changes; some work on foreign policy issues; some decide to take on issues in their local communities. A lot depends on the place we visit. The groups that go to South Africa, for example, return with a strong commitment to help change U.S. policy towards that country. For groups that go to China, U.S policy isn't such an issue. People on the China trip are often struck by the excellent quality of childcare and realize how important good childcare is to improve the quality of people's lives. So three of the people on a recent seminar pledged to work on improving childcare facilities in their own communities."

A dentist from Oklahoma who went on a Plowshares seminar to East Africa pledged that within three years he would return to Uganda to teach for three months. Sure enough, before the three years were up, he was teaching at a dental school at Makerere University in Kampala, Uganda, and providing the school with its sole source of modern training materials. His work abroad also helped him discover the Third World in the middle of Oklahoma, and led him to set up an inner city health clinic for black and Native Americans in Tulsa.

As a mother of eight and a grandmother of ten, Barbara Watkins had a lot in common with the woman she stayed with during a trip to Nicaragua in the summer of 1986. "We had a lot to share about raising children," Barbara noted upon returning. Coming back to the United States, it was that level of understanding, not statistics, that Barbara Watkins shared in small meetings in churches throughout her home state of Mississippi. She attempted to find parallels between the black experience in Mississippi and that of the Nicaraguan people. "I tried to talk about the agricultural situation before the revolution with some parallels to tenant farming in the South, to show how labor is exploited," says Barbara. She was also struck by similarities between the civil rights movement and the Nicaraguan revolution, as two situations in which people put their lives on the line for change.[9]

This phenomenon of seeing the Third World here at home has affected the programs of some of the tour groups themselves. The Center for Global Exchange, after leading a number of international trips, felt compelled to "look in our own backyard." After leading a tour of poor Detroit residents and community organizers to Central America, some of the participants returned with the idea of hosting travel seminars to inner-city Detroit. "They took a close look at problems affecting Central Americans and while they thought that was wonderful—so much so that they are now organizing another Central America trip—they also decided it was high time for Americans to take a hard look at what's happening to our inner cities," the director, Joel Mugge, explains. The Center is now planning a series of U.S. travel seminars, including trips to U.S. farmbelts and to Native American reservations.

Seeing Ourselves Through Fresh Eyes

Peter Davies, with the Center for Responsible Tourism, believes the true purpose of alternative tourism is not to solve other people's problems, but to learn more about our own. "There are two types of 'alternative tourists.' One is a group of Americans who pack up the Statue of Liberty in their tote bag and go meet the huddled masses yearning to be free. In all sincerity and honesty, they say, 'You guys are really oppressed. You've got a big problem on your hands. How can we help you solve your problem?'"

"But there's another kind of exchange," Peter insists. "It's an exchange with visitors who are aware of the problems in their *own* countries and struggling to deal with these issues in their own lives. Say you are dealing with the issue of pesticides in your food system, and you go visit the Consumers' Association of Penang in Malaysia—an innovative group with years of experience in social struggle. You sit down together and discuss issues of mutual concern. You learn different ways people are dealing with similar issues. It's no longer a question of merely learning about other people's problems, but learning how to solve your own."

Tom Peterson of *Seeds* magazine concurs that travel can give us profound insights into our own problems. "I've discovered that going abroad to view someone else's reality teaches us a great deal about our own. I know a pastor from South Georgia who visited Christian-based communities in Latin America. He came back and said, 'The people in these communities are all asking how they can pull together to make their community a better place to live. But in my town everybody's asking what they can do to get out of here. I'm going to go back to my community and say that we have to work together to make this place better, instead of trying to get out.' That's just one of the small things we can learn. I've found that there are many, many lessons, if only we are willing to go and open ourselves to the risk of learning from others."

Virginia Hadsell of the Center for Responsible Tourism has led and participated in tours to Africa, Asia, and Latin America. "I've seen people totally transformed by these experiences," Virginia says. "I've seen people open their eyes and realize that we're all the same kind of people with the same life desires. Travel has dispelled the myth that we're the center of the world, that the universe revolves around our reality. I've also seen it change people's lifestyles, bringing people to the realization that they can live full, rich, and satisfying lives with few material goods. I've seen travel help remove people's fear and alienation, and replace their feeling of helplessness. I've seen people come back saying, 'Yes, the world is certainly more of a mess than I thought it was. There are certainly a lot of injustices and imbalances that need correcting. But if these poor people I have met, people with little education and so few resources, are trying to make changes, then surely I, too, must do my part.'"

Code of Ethics for Tourists

1. Travel in a spirit of humility and with a genuine desire to learn more about the people in your host country.
2. Be sensitively aware of the feelings of other people, thus preventing what might be offensive behavior on your part. This applies very much to photography.
3. Cultivate the habit of listening and observing, rather than merely hearing and seeing.
4. Realize that often people in the country you visit have time concepts and thought patterns different from your own; this does not make them inferior, only different.
5. Instead of looking for that "beach paradise," discover the enrichment of seeing a different way of life through other eyes.
6. Acquaint yourself with local customs—people will be happy to help you.
7. Instead of the Western practice of knowing all the answers, cultivate the habit of asking questions.
8. Remember that you are only one of thousands of tourists visiting this country, and don't expect special privileges.
9. If you want your tour experience to be a "home away from home," it is foolish to waste money on traveling.
10. When you are shopping, remember the "bargain" you obtained was only possible because of low wages paid to the maker.
11. Do not make promises to people in your host country unless you are certain you can carry them through.
12. Spend time reflecting on your daily experiences in an attempt to deepen your understanding. It has been said that what enriches you may rob and violate others.

Source: Center for Responsible Tourism (see Guide).

People from Decatur, Georgia have developed a sister city partnership with a town in Burkina Faso, West Africa. Here, a Georgia visitor grinds grain with her Burkinabe partners.

Photo by Gary Gunderson.

2

Partners With People

"I'm not afraid of Africa anymore. I'd be delighted if thirty years from now Africa was a strong, independent, and self-sufficient continent. And I'd like to help make it happen. That's because I now know some Africans. It used to be possible to walk away from the issue of hunger, to find some other diversion. But now I can't walk away from my friends."

—Gary Gunderson,
founder of the Decatur/Burkina Faso sister city program.

The city of Decatur, Georgia, is linked with the village of Bousse and the city of Ouahigouya in Burkina Faso, West Africa. Since 1985, delegations from Decatur have traveled to Africa to visit their partners. In return, Decatur receives visiting delegations from Burkina. These trips help establish avenues of communication across two very different cultures, and lend concrete support to the struggle in Burkina against hunger and poverty.

Hundreds of North Americans and Europeans have forged such partnerships with communities throughout the Third World. Pairings such as sister cities, sister unions, sister schools and daycare centers, and partner congregations offer multiple opportunities to learn about other cultures, to make new friends, and to contribute to development efforts in construc-

tive and lasting ways. Inventing ways to bridge the distances between people and places can open up a world of knowledge and
creativity. Partnerships can also be a vehicle for educational
work about poverty and social justice.

Gary Gunderson is one of the founders of the Decatur/
Burkina Faso partnership. His experience suggests the dynamic
potential of these projects:

"It began as a challenge, an adventure. Now it's more like a
beehive. The monthly meetings here in Decatur and visits back
and forth keep enthusiasm high, and new people continue to
become involved. The strengths of our community come into
play as more local institutions get involved. The medical association has linked up with the village's clinic. Others, working
with hunger organizations, are supporting projects initiated by
the villagers.

"But there is more. Much more. With a small group, you visit
the village, staying two weeks with a family. Your myths about
them (and theirs about you) are dispelled. Hunger is no longer
some impersonal appeal for money, but real families, people
you know. Letters flow back and forth. What was once an abstract concern is now a rich experience.

"Your group is exposed to a different set of values. You're
given friendships and, as in any true friendship, you change.
You're given the gift of participating in a village's struggle
against their problems, and in doing so, you learn new ways to
approach your own problems."[1]

Government-Sponsored Partnership Programs

Partnership programs in the United States flourished under
the federal government programs of the 1950s, when President
Eisenhower formally established sister cities to facilitate cultural and educational exchanges. From this legacy emerged a
number of different types of partnership organizations at the
city, state, and national levels.

Sister Cities International (SCI) is the largest government-
supported organization promoting sister cities. Founded in
1976, by 1988 it had matched 801 U.S. cities with 1,341 cities in 87

countries. According to organizational spokesperson Richard Oakland, SCI matches a new sister city almost every week.

In order to work under the auspices of SCI, individual city councils must recognize the partnership through an official decree or resolution, and city officials are appointed to oversee the program. Many of the activities are cultural—exchanges of musicians, ballet troupes, or theater groups. Others are based on economic and scientific interests.

Los Angeles, Seattle, and San Francisco, for example, are three of the most active sister cities in the country. Increasing trade with Asia and the Pacific has prompted them to "sister" with Pacific Basin cities. San Francisco alone now has six Asian sisters, including Shanghai. In that partnership, representatives from the Pacific Stock Exchange in San Francisco went to Shanghai to help set up a Chinese version of the stock market. Currently, solar energy specialists are gearing up for an exchange of ideas and technology with their Chinese counterparts.

While most government-supported programs concentrate on cultural and business affairs, some claim to address hunger and poverty in their sister city directly. Partners of the Americas, for instance, links U.S. states with Latin American countries in order to facilitate a transfer of material and technical assistance from North to South. "Partners" projects do not exclusively focus on the poor, but they do include such activities as training Honduran metalworkers in Vermont and exchanging teachers between New Jersey and Haiti.

Peace Corps Partners, another U.S. government-funded program, matches donor groups in the United States with Peace Corps projects in the Third World. Unlike the ongoing ties that a sister city program fosters, the purpose of a Peace Corps partnership is to elicit a one-time donation, either for a specific project (building wells, gardening, or beekeeping), or to a country (general funds to support Peace Corps programs there). Many of the participants in these programs are Peace Corps alumni who see the partnership as one way to maintain their commitment to the struggle against poverty.

Government-related partnerships offer the advantages of institutional support and greater funding possibilities than those available to independent partnerships. But government ties also impose some limitations. Perhaps the most fundamental disadvantage of choosing a government-supported program is that, to the people in the Third World country, the use of U.S. government funds is often construed as an endorsement of U.S. policy in that country. Where the U.S. government is not on the side of change for the poor, such ties effectively choke off the possibility of a meaningful partnership.

One example of the way government-sponsored programs become a channel for U.S. policy is Partners of the Americas. An outgrowth of the Alliance for Progress, Partners was set up after the Cuban revolution in 1959 to help the U.S. government stem the tide of communism in Latin America. Now one of the largest U.S. organizations sponsoring partnerships and development assistance through exchange programs, Partners of the Americas continues to rely on funding from the U.S. Agency for International Development (AID), the U.S. Information Agency, and multinational corporations. In Nicaragua, Partners of the Americas has earned the dubious distinction of distributing $1.5 million in nonmilitary contra aid, with AID hiring two CIA agents to help determine where the money should be channeled.

In the Vermont/Honduras Partners of the Americas project, AID involvement led to serious internal divisions. In 1983, AID persuaded the organization to sponsor an agro-export project, administered by the for-profit Food Pro Corporation, in exchange for a $750,000 AID grant—the largest in the Vermont group's history. This sparked a controversy that split the Vermont Partners into two factions: one favoring small-scale projects that emphasize self-sufficiency, the other favoring large-scale export-oriented production.[2]

Some of the Vermont Partners complained that for exchanges and training programs, U.S. government representatives or local politicians often nominated the participants—instead of leaving that process to the villagers themselves—and put participants through a screening process by the Honduran government's security force (DIN).[3]

Participants also noted the sheer weight of the AID bureaucracy. "It took us three tries to get our project proposals approved by AID," one Vermont participant told us. "We had to hook up with the right people, and we spent eighteen months learning how AID thinks before we got the go-ahead. Another disadvantage is that when the partnership has an official stamp, it's very hard to get beyond top-to-top communication with people."

Partners From the Ground Up

While the number of government-supported partnerships and sister cities has continued to grow in the United States, a new wave of partnerships is beginning to alter the traditional approach that links diplomacy and aid to U.S. foreign policy objectives. A plethora of citizen-run partnerships aim at building a more peaceful coexistence between the United States and the Soviet Union through education and cultural exchange projects. Many more focus on humanitarian and community development issues in the Third World.

These acts of citizen diplomacy are built from the bottom up. Though they may become official at some point through a city council vote or mayoral decree, they do not depend on such endorsements. Thus, they are much less likely to end up as elite-to-elite ties. They can absorb the energy and creativity of individual citizens, and they do not have to follow the boundaries and designs of U.S. foreign policy.

One way to create citizen-to-citizen partnerships is to work through other existing structures in the community—churches, universities, unions, and community groups. These can provide a focus and source of funds to get the partnership off the ground. In turn, many partnership programs serve to coordinate local activities. Organizing around Central America, for example, a number of existing solidarity groups in Wisconsin came together under the umbrella of a partnership.

Gary Gunderson believes that working through existing structures can be easier than creating new ones, but he warns that finding the right U.S. group to build a partnership with is no simple task. "Coming from a religious background, it was my assumption that the easiest way to start a partnership was to take a congregation in the First World and link it with a congregation in the Third World. We tried doing that at our church, but it never really worked out. We found that when you take an extremely homogeneous group from one culture and link it with an extremely homogeneous group in another culture, it's often hard for genuine, human relations to develop. Other churches might be able to pull it off, but in our case we were soon left with nothing but a wealthy church hooking up with a poor church to fund a project. And that wasn't my idea of a partnership."

Looking further in his community for common ground on which to build the partnership, Gary came across the work of Darl Snyder, a professor at the University of Georgia who had ties with the University of Ouagadougou in Burkina Faso. "What we stumbled upon was an institutional structure that was secular and non-ideological and could act as a bridge for a wide-ranging partnership."

Gary used Darl's knowledge of the country to make the initial contacts, and then Gary and Darl convinced the mayor of Decatur to make the ties official. The mayor agreed to form a sister city project, and in 1985, the three of them set out for Burkina Faso. "Perhaps because we were traveling with the mayor, the government of Burkina was very open and we met with five different government ministers. We explained where Decatur was, and that we were not interested in emergency relief but in forming a partnership. They recommended we work in Ouahigouya, one of the areas worst hit by the drought. We met with the mayor of Ouahigouya and decided to go ahead."

Gary got a taste of what it means to be a citizen diplomat when, just before departing for the United States, he had the opportunity to meet with Burkina's then-President Thomas Sankara (who was assassinated in a coup in 1987). "There were very severe tensions between the U.S. government and the Burkinabe government, due to the almost irreconcilable differences in world views of Presidents Sankara and Reagan," Gary explained. "But we were not in Burkina Faso representing the U.S. government. We made that clear to Sankara from the beginning and he was delighted by this citizen-to-citizen initiative. He compared politics to a compass and said, 'Your president only wants to see East and West, but a compass has many other points. I am glad we have found one of them to meet on.'"

Sister Rita Studer of the Network in Solidarity with the People of Guatemala (NISGUA) had a different experience in working with church-based partnerships. For her, Christian-based communities have been a natural bridge between the people of Guatemala and the United States.

Rita was a missionary in Guatemala for eight years. Upon returning in 1985, she wanted to work on a meaningful project with the religious sector in the United States. "I wrote to religious communities around the country that were already involved in peace and social justice issues, asking them if they'd like to form a partnership with a group in Guatemala. We had a number of positive responses, but we asked the churches to prepare a plan first, so we could get a sense of their commitment. That deterred some of the groups that were not as serious.

"So far, we have four active communities in the United States paired with Christian-based communities in Guatemala. We don't recommend that they send money, because we want them to base their partnership on deeper grounds. Most of them are focused on learning as much as they can about Guatemala, corresponding with their partners, and exchanging prayers. For me, the brightest part of organizing these partnerships has been being a witness to the broadening of world views for the Americans we work with. Their whole idea of Christian community has expanded. My dream is to get more groups involved, to see some of them arranging trips to Guatemala, and to see the groups become even more active in teaching other Americans about the situation in Guatemala."

Some groups get their start through campaigns using the structures of local government—whether it be the city council, town meeting, the mayor's office, or a ballot initiative—to declare an official partnership. This is not absolutely necessary for the survival of a partnership program. Some of the largest and most active partnerships have never bothered to get official recognition from their local government, in order to keep their people-to-people ties free from government influences.

Wisconsin provides an interesting example of this. In 1965, Wisconsin and Nicaragua became formal sister states under President Kennedy's Alliance for Progress. The original organization, the "Wisconsin-Nicaragua Partners," still exists. It is the one that is coordinated through Partners of the Americas, with the support of the federal government and private corporations. Its ties in Nicaragua are to the business community and groups opposing the Sandinista government.

Soon after the Nicaraguan revolution of 1979, a second organization was formed by people concerned about the U.S.

government's antagonism toward the Sandinista government. The new group, the Wisconsin Coordinating Council on Nicaragua (WCCN), is an umbrella for over forty peace and solidarity groups in the state focused on Nicaraguan and Central American issues. It organizes politicians, journalists, religious leaders, and farmers for educational tours of Nicaragua.

"We just declared ourselves a sister state," says Mirette Seireg of WCCN. "Since it was our umbrella that brought together the many Nicaraguan solidarity groups operating in Wisconsin, we felt we had a mandate to represent their interests and concerns about Nicaragua. And we are still the largest and most active partnership group in the state, perhaps in the country."

Other groups, however, find that working to gain official status can provide the impetus and clout needed to get a new partnership off the ground. The recognition, media coverage, or campaigning may help recruit participants and educate the community around the issues or region. Often the work to become a recognized partnership will lead the group into political battlefields that will challenge it to sharpen and define its convictions. Many city governments argue that they have no role in foreign policy, and therefore should not become involved. Under these circumstances, a partnership's survival depends on the strength and defense of its principles. These principles are reflected in the choice of a partner.

Criteria For Choosing a Partner

The group in Decatur did not choose to work in Burkina Faso for political reasons. They wanted to work with a poor country in Africa, and Burkina is one of the poorest. But they quickly learned that their choice of where to work had political implications, as the Reagan administration was at loggerheads with the government of Burkina Faso over Burkina's support for liberation struggles and its leader's outspoken condemnation of imperialism and neocolonialism. Gary Gunderson advises anyone contemplating such programs to carefully examine the political ramifications.

"I don't have a checklist of good and bad countries and institutions around the world," says Gunderson, "but I think we need to be aware that every time we relate outside the borders of the United States as American citizens, we're not just making a cultural or humanitarian connection, but a political one as well."

For some North Americans seeking partnerships, the political connection is primary. This is most striking in the case of Nicaragua. The growth of sister programs with Nicaragua in the 1980s is unprecedented. Never before have U.S. citizens en masse forged independent links to a country with which the United States was at war. While there were certainly individuals and small groups who visited North Vietnam to express their opposition to the Vietnam War, we never witnessed a situation like the present one where scores of mayors and city officials openly defy U.S. policy by creating an alternative citizen-based foreign policy.

In June 1986, the independent U.S.-Nicaragua Friendship Conference reported twenty U.S. cities with Nicaraguan partners. Two years later, the number had grown to nearly one hundred. Two U.S. states, Wisconsin and Minnesota, are sister states with Nicaragua. In addition, hundreds of churches, schools, daycare centers, agricultural cooperatives, and hospitals have "sistered" with their Nicaraguan counterparts.

Bernie Saunders, the mayor of Burlington, Vermont, explained why his city hooked up with Puerto Cabezas, Nicaragua. "Many of us in the city were absolutely disgusted about the president's illegal and immoral act of attempting to destroy the government of Nicaragua. We sat around here and we said, 'What can we do to show the rest of our country and the world that not everybody in the United States of America believes that the government of this powerful nation has the right to go to war and cause suffering against a tiny, impoverished nation?'"[4] Burlington decided that sistering with Puerto Cabezas, a Nicaraguan port that would be the likely staging ground for a U.S. invasion, would be a powerful foreign policy statement.

Maria Scipione, one of the founding members of the Rochester, New York/El Sauce, Nicaragua partnership, feels that her city was ready for a new way to act on foreign policy matters. "Many of us had participated in the Pledge of Resistance (a group demonstrating against U.S. intervention in Central America) and in the local sanctuary movement. We still do—but to be honest, we were feeling a bit drained from always having to come up against the courts, or the Immigration and Naturalization Service, or some other government bureaucracy in our work. The idea of a people-to-people tie was a relief! Even members of our city council signed our fundraising letters. The media began contacting us before we were ready to handle all of it. Rather than reacting to U.S. government policies, we were excited to be making some of our own."

The links with Nicaragua are not only at the city and state levels. Over a dozen U.S. hospitals and clinics, from Philadelphia to Denver to La Crosse, Wisconsin, have sistered with Nicaraguan clinics. Local 1199 Health and Hospitals Workers Union in New York City is drafting a resolution to twin New York public hospitals with Nicaraguan counterparts.

The U.S. group, MADRE, has twinned over thirty daycare centers. Judy Kahn, a teacher in one of the twinned daycare centers in Oakland, California, explained the difficulty and rewards of setting up such a program with a country at war. "We had two setbacks when the first two daycare centers we were twinned with were bombed by the contras. It forced us to bring up some sensitive issues with the children and parents, but we confronted those issues head-on. The children ended up writing letters to President Reagan, asking him to help stop the war in Nicaragua so the Nicaraguan kids could live. We never heard from the White House, but it's just as well because the kids came away from the experience feeling like, at two and three years old, they could be peacemakers. This started off a whole program on children as peacemakers. We talked about Anne Frank, and Samantha, the little American girl who visited the Soviet Union.

"Finally, MADRE twinned us with another daycare center in a safer part of the country. We sent our twin photos of ourselves and our parents, pictures we drew, and we've held some fundraisers with the community, allowing us to send about $800 worth of paper, pens, and other supplies. Recently, a representative from Nicaragua was visiting the West Coast and came to our center to thank us directly for our help. That made a big impression on the children. They really felt like they had done something to change things for the Nicaraguan kids."

Other Ties with Central America

Nicaragua is not the only country in Central America where sister ties have been forged as an antidote to U.S. policy. While the U.S. government has been sending over a million dollars a day to the Salvadoran government for its war against the Faribundo Marti Liberation Front (FMLN), U.S. citizens have devised more constructive ways of relating to the Salvadoran people.

New El Salvador Today (NEST) is a U.S. group working to help Salvadorans displaced by war rebuild their communities. Part of NEST's work lies in forming sister city relationships between U.S. cities and rural Salvadoran villages. By 1988, seven U.S. cities had paired with Salvadoran villages.

These villages, under constant attack by government troops in search of rebels, were abandoned in the early 1980s. Their residents were forced to live in refugee camps or urban slums. Anxious to return home, the refugees began resettling their villages in 1986.

"The Salvadoran government isn't coming out and saying they're against these repopulation efforts, but they continue to carry out *de*population maneuvers in neighboring areas, where they think there are rebel strongholds," according to Lisa Robinson of NEST. "The military bombs villages and the government cuts off humanitarian aid and Red Cross shipments to such areas. Who gets hurt by these policies? Hundreds of thousands of civilians. Our sister city program is a matter of survival for the people we reach."

Oregon State University is a sister with the University of San Salvador, El Salvador. The U.S. students have designed classes on Central America, raised money to bring speakers to campus, and declared the university a sanctuary for Central American refugees. In July, 1986, an entire issue of the student newspaper, *The Barometer*, was devoted to Central America, complete with in-depth interviews with teachers and students who had visited the region. In addition, the students collected and shipped twenty-five hundred books to the Salvadoran university's library.

U.S. workers have created the sort of ties with their

Salvadoran counterparts that exemplify the principle of mutual support through solidarity. "We are all jeopardized by policies which put down the struggles of working people," says Mary Ann Barnett, a San Francisco representative of the American Clothing and Textile Workers Union (ACTWU). That is why her union decided to become a "sister union" with the Salvadoran Textile Workers (STITAS).

"When we see a union in El Salvador being terrorized by its own government and by American corporations into accepting lower wages, then we sense that our own ability to better our conditions is being threatened," Mary Ann continues. "We are not joining forces with the Salvadorans for charity reasons, but to make all of our lives more secure."

In 1986, Francisco Acosta, the North American representative of the Salvadoran labor federation FENASTRAS, presented the problems of the Salvadoran textile workers to the California Joint Board of the ACTWU. He explained that the Salvadorans were on strike for better wages and working conditions in a factory which was licensed by Levi Strauss. The odds against the union were great, and they needed all the help they could get. The local ACTWU responded with a unique offer: to join the strike and pressure for improved relations between Levi Strauss and the Salvadoran workers.

ACTWU brought together several Bay Area groups concerned with workers in Central America, picketed outside Levi Strauss, and met with the press to publicize the situation in El Salvador. After one day of picketing, the strike was settled and the Salvadoran workers received the wage increase they were asking for.

Mary Ann Barnett shared her feelings about being part of a successful struggle. "In our industry, so many shops just close down and go to places where labor is cheaper that many workers in this country are just used to losing. I was so stunned when the Salvadorans won their strike. If what we did—pressuring Levi's and threatening its image—just helped them a little, then it made me feel that there was hope for our work in the United States."

The Communications Workers of America (CWA) Local 9415 also has a sister union, ASSTEL—the communications workers in El Salvador. "We use the relationship to keep our local members educated about what's happening in El Salvador, and to help out the Salvadoran workers when we can," says Fred Schwartz, a CWA member. "Comparing their salaries of $200 a month to our $400 a week makes the issues really stark. Also, when you're a union leader in El Salvador, you subject yourself to harassment, possibly even torture. Labor halls are bombed. We see how much is at stake for them, just for being organized.

"So sister unions are important. But it depends on what kind of sister union, and what you do. The idea of sisterhood is also used by the American Institute for Free Labor Development (AIFLD), a conservative labor organization that supports 'paper' unions in Central America—unions which are more on the side of the corporations than the workers. AIFLD focuses only on fundraising for charity, to get workers to donate money to help their poorer neighbors and co-workers. But we do more than that. We inform people of the political struggles that are going on to help workers become better off in the long term."

Fred Schwartz continues. "It's not just a question of what we can provide to our sister unions, because we do fundraising too, but what we learn from them. They have a lot to teach us about building really strong unions that can survive the most difficult times."

Ties With Other Regions

While the sistering concept has been a key tool in the struggle to change U.S policy in Central America, it is just getting off the ground in other areas of the world.

The United States-South Africa Sister Community Project, founded in 1987, links U.S. cities with black communities in South Africa that are under attack from the apartheid government. "These are communities that are being threatened with forced removal because of the government's policy of racial classification, in which certain areas are designated for whites only," says Project coordinator Ann Poirier. "By linking these threatened communities with U.S. cities, we are putting pressure on the South African government and at the same time educating North Americans about this policy of forced removals and other aspects of apartheid." By 1988 the Sister Community

Project had linked four U.S. communities (Louisville, St. Paul, Milwaukee and Berkeley); it is hoping to establish twelve such linkages by the end of 1989.

In other parts of southern Africa, U.S. groups are beginning to link up with communities in the Frontline States—the five countries in southern Africa (Angola, Mozambique, Zimbabwe, Zambia, and Tanzania) that are firm supporters of the struggle against apartheid. Africa Exchange was formed in 1988 for precisely this purpose. "The opportunities to form partnerships in that part of the globe are endless," says Kevin Danaher of Africa Exchange. "In Zimbabwe there are dozens of women's groups, peasant co-ops, schools, and community groups that are anxious to hook up with similar groups in the United States. We are also trying to link U.S. groups with towns, schools, and hospitals in Mozambique and Angola, countries where tens of thousands of people are starving due to South African aggression. It takes creative work to build these partnerships, but it's an essential part of changing U.S. policy from the bottom up."

Jim Cason of the American Committee on Africa is working with a number of Central America groups on a unique sistering concept which would create three-way ties. "For example, we're trying to hook up New Haven, Connecticut and Leon, Nicaragua—which are already sister cities—with a city in Mozambique. These three-way ties would bring the Southern African and Central American groups in the United States together, and would allow Mozambique and Nicaragua to learn from each other as well. We are trying to do the same thing with Harlem Hospital in New York City—hook it up with hospitals in Nicaragua and Mozambique."

Sister ties with Asia and the Middle East are fewer in number and in some cases, more controversial. During the height of the Palestinian uprising in 1988, Berkeley, California attempted to pair with Jabaliya, a Palestinian refugee camp in the Israeli-occupied Gaza Strip. The idea stirred up the heated debate over Israeli and Palestinian sovereignty. One proposed solution was to pair with the refugee camp *and* an Israeli town. Others argued against such a compromise, noting that Berkeley wouldn't consider a partnership with both a white South African town and a black township as a solution to the troubles in South Africa. The deeply divided community and city council eventually voted against making Jabaliya Berkeley's seventh sister city. Proponents then brought the proposal to the public in a ballot measure where it was also turned down.

"One of the reasons we were defeated is that the opposition outspent us $100,000 to $6,000," reflects Hilton Obenzinger, one of the measure's proponents. "But the question is not whether we won or lost at the ballot. The fact that the issue was being aired publicly was a great victory. There were debates on the radio and in the newspapers, and over five hundred people attended the city council meeting when the measure was being reviewed. Three other Palestinian ballot measures were held in other cities at the same time, and the one in Cambridge passed. The Palestinian question was suddenly thrust before the public eye as never before, and for us that in itself was a remarkable accomplishment."

From the war in Central America, we have learned the importance of openly struggling with these emotional issues. More ties with the Middle East—including exchanges of visitors—and more public debate can only serve to prevent the kind of debacles that arise when citizens turn their backs on controversial foreign policies.

The Dilemmas of Partnership

Whether or not sister relationships are forged for purely humanitarian or for both humanitarian and political reasons, they still face some common dilemmas.

• *Given the social and economic disparities between potential partners, can partnerships become more than a one-way transfer of resources? If not, what makes them any different from traditional charity?*

It's true that the economic disparities between partners are tremendous, especially if part of the criteria for picking foreign partners requires that they be impoverished communities. To bring those inequities home, Gary Gunderson observed that his four-year-old daughter has more books in her bedroom than all the books in their sister village's school!

The transfer of money and supplies is an essential part of any partnership with a poor, Third World community. But such aid is

not the only thing being transferred. Unlike the work of traditional charitable organizations, true partnerships' tasks involve
exchanges of people, cultures, ideas, and world views. In these
exchanges, the U.S. participants gain at least as much as their
Third World partners.

The villagers from Burkina Faso, for instance, gave their
Georgian partners a lesson in community organizing. "Americans hold onto the myth that we're the ones who get things
done," said Gary Gunderson. "We're the managers. Africans,
we say, are very nice and sincere people, but they can't organize. Well, our Burkinabe partners are highly organized, committed, and very clear about their priorities as a community.
Comparatively, we look like bumps on a log. So one thing we've
learned from them is the need to organize ourselves and to be
clear about our goals.

"They've also forced us to act on our convictions. For example, their first question when we sat down with them on our last
trip was, 'Last time we signed an agreement that we were both
committed to doing something about racism and oppression in
the world and we want to know what you've done.' They had
taught the children in the village about the civil rights struggle in
the United States, and they even erected a statue for Martin
Luther King! We didn't know what to say because we really
hadn't done anything. That's typical of them. They are committed to follow through on their promises, and they will press us in
a way that helps us maintain our integrity."

Raleigh, North Carolina's sister city is Shinyanga, Tanzania.
Participants in Raleigh have gotten the local TV station involved, so that while Shinyanga benefits from the seeds, health
equipment, and school and gardening supplies sent from
Raleigh, viewers in North Carolina have the opportunity to learn
more about the ecology, customs, and life of Tanzanians. The TV
station also helped launch a study guide for fourth graders, accompanied by video cassettes. Students learn about a hundred
words in Swahili, along with lessons on the importance of trees,
clean water, and basic health care—lessons of great importance
to our own society as well.

Paula Kline, one of the founding members of the New Haven,
Connecticut/Leon, Nicaragua sister city program, adds, "There
are always some elements of charity involved with this kind of

work, but we can also find ways of helping ourselves in the process. One example is a delegation we sent down to Leon to repair the roof on an art museum, which by the way was housing donated art from New Haven artists. Besides fixing the roof, the same delegation of people came home and joined a local housing rehabilitation project. Another example is a project we have to build a daycare center in Leon. We hold joint fundraisers, so some of the money raised actually stays in our community to build our own daycare programs. This way, we're not just helping the Nicaraguans, but we see ourselves more as collaborators with them in support of positive programs."

- **Even if partnerships do have some positive effect on both groups involved, aren't they still extremely limited in that they only affect such a tiny part of the total picture?**

Some partnerships, those that remain at the purely cultural or humanitarian level, may be limited in scope. But other partnerships do get at the heart of larger, structural issues. The partnership between Salvadoran and U.S. textile workers, for example, seeks to identify the common interests between U.S. and Third World workers. Such links across national boundaries are essential for creating a strong network of workers who can struggle cooperatively for common goals, rather than in a competitive, "protectionist" vein.

Gary Gunderson argues that the repercussions of Decatur's sister relationship with Burkina Faso go well beyond the relationship itself: "The Atlanta papers now run stories on Africa that they would have never run before. When our congressman voted against aid to Africa in a time of great need, the press noted that his vote came at the very time our delegation was in Burkina Faso developing a sister city relationship. And when the congressman came to speak at the Decatur high school, one of the first questions the kids asked him was, 'How come you voted against Africa?' It never occurred to him in his wildest imaginings that anyone in Georgia would care about hungry Africans. But now people do care."

The sister ties with Nicaragua certainly raise larger issues of U.S. foreign policy. Mirette Seireg of the Wisconsin Coordinating Council on Nicaragua downplays the material aid facet of the partnerships. "For us, the real beauty of partnerships with Nicaragua is their usefulness as a tool to raise consciousness about our foreign policy. For example, a group in Ann Arbor, Michigan, put the sister city resolution on the ballot and it became an issue that every voting citizen had to contend with. We've also seen that local partnerships can have an impact on the national level. Portland has a sister city in Nicaragua and when Portland's Republican congressman had to cast his final vote on contra aid, he said he couldn't vote for the aid because Portland and Nicaragua had sister ties."

Cambridge, Massachusetts, is paired with San Jose las Flores, El Salvador, through the NEST network. Ten days after the Cambridge city council passed the sister city resolution, the Salvadoran military occupied San Jose las Flores and captured eleven residents. In response, Cambridge city councillors, the Cambridge congressional representative, and community members wrote letters and sent telexes to U.S. and Salvadoran government officials, and published stories on the prisoners in local newspapers. Four of the eleven people captured were immediately released, and the Cambridge partnership planned to send a delegation to El Salvador to investigate and try to secure the release of the remaining prisoners.

When Madison, Wisconsin's sister city in El Salvador, Arcatao, was invaded by the military, the citizens of Madison took out a full-page ad in a major Salvadoran newspaper. The ad, signed by prominent Madison politicians, lawyers, priests, and union leaders, demanded that Salvador's President Duarte stop bombing and illegally detaining their sisters and brothers in Arcatao and neighboring villages. "We want you to know," the ad said, "that they are not alone. In light of the continuous persecution of our sister city Arcatao, we citizens of Madison will do everything in our power to assure them the right to live in peace."

Many developing communities in the Third World are in need of technical and financial support for their work. But many are also blocked by the anti-democratic policies of their government, often buttressed by U.S. policy. When partnerships work to counter such policies, they are helping to remove a major obstacle in the path of self-determination for Third World communities.

• *Where opposition to a controversial partnership exists, should you persist, drop the whole idea, or look for a partnership that is less controversial?*

There certainly is not one right answer to this question. Judging from the various strategies people have taken, there are as many options as there are possible partnerships.

Some community members will oppose the choice of working with Nicaragua or other countries that present challenges to U.S. government perspectives. Judy Kahn, whose daycare center is twinned with a Nicaraguan daycare center, feels that a compromise on the choice of a partner is better than no partner at all. "If there was opposition to a partnership with Nicaragua, I would sooner twin with Mexico, for example, than not twin at all. The bottom line is that there is so much to learn from the cultural exchange that it shouldn't be lost on a political battlefield. In my daughter's school, one of the families said they would rather put their efforts into helping poor Americans. So we did both. We twinned with a Nicaraguan daycare center, and with a community group in Mississippi."

Rich Weiner, a teacher at Mariposa Alternative School in northern California, helped link his school with two sister schools in Baja California: one is a small public school in a rural area, and the other is a private alternative school, much like his own, in a well-off Mexican community close to the border. Wary that choosing only the poor school might be labeled "too political," the teachers at Mariposa felt the combination of a rich and a poor school would be a good way to provide a balanced picture of life in Mexico.

"Students from Mariposa have visited both schools on the same trip," explains Rich, "and come home with very personal observations on the differences in lifestyle, family life, and culture between them and their newfound Mexican friends. The trip provided us with a basis for continuing our education on Mexican-American history, Spanish language, and other traditional subjects, but also created a forum for discussing social issues, such as the extreme differences in the way people live within the same country."

In Concord, Massachusetts, the partnership formed with San Marcos, Nicaragua created a storm of controversy. When a conservative group, the Concord Committee for Liberty, launched a vicious campaign to force the city to repudiate the partnership, those in favor of the sister ties refused to give in. They seized the opportunity to educate the community on Central American issues, and mobilized enough support to win the vote at a packed town meeting.

One piece of good advice is to always be prepared to meet opposition. Maria Scipione of the Rochester, New York/El Sauce, Nicaragua, sister city organization notes that although the idea of a Nicaraguan partnership was readily accepted by the local press and community in general, the sister city commit-tee was in no rush to get official recognition. "We did get a few council people to sign on at an early stage. But we really wanted to build an active, thriving organization before we asked for the city's rubber stamp of approval. That way, in case of a fight, we would be ready to take on the opposition with a clear notion of why we were doing this."

Katharine Stokes of Hingham, Massachusetts notes the disas-trous effects of not being well-prepared. "A group of us pro-posed a committee to consider the idea of a partnership with Nicaragua and we were booed and hissed practically right out of the town meeting! We weren't terribly surprised, given the re-cord of the town meeting, but we also weren't prepared to fight back with a clear vision and lots of facts. We should have done more of our homework first." Katharine's group is still planning to propose some kind of sister project for the town, but may pro-pose a different Central American country as a partner. "We aren't giving up on Nicaragua by any means. Our goal in this is to educate a population that is well-educated in the traditional sense, but ignorant about what's going on in the world. We feel strongly that any country we choose will help develop the po-tential for the community to become more aware of the issues in Central America."

Mary Voxman of the Moscow, Idaho/Villa Carlos Fonseca, Nicaragua, partnership has yet another idea on how to deal with opposition. "There is a group of us who for some time had been working on political action around Central America. We wanted to start an official sister city program but were aware that other people in the community were resistant to the idea of bringing a political organization into city government. We got around our opposition by stating a clear difference in purpose between the two groups: we created a sister city that is based on universal is-sues, such as peace and ending conflict. No matter what your political identity, you don't want to see our country go to war!

That was palatable to most people. We left the more political work to the original Central American group. But even so, once we got the sister city organization in place, more and more people have been reading about Nicaragua. The public education that we were able to do through the sister city project has helped strengthen the active participation in the other committee. And that education is what's so important."

"The key to avoiding conflict is finding common links between your city and the sister city," according to Alan Wright of the New Haven/Leon partnership. "For example, we took a prep school filled with kids who might ordinarily not care much about anything beyond getting into college, and we told them about a prep school in Nicaragua, built not just for kids from better-off families but for poorer kids, to give them a chance at getting a good education. We told them about the baseball team, and how the team had hardly any equipment. Well, of course the American kids thought that was a horrible predicament! So those who were most interested formed a group at school which planned fundraisers for the Nicaraguan baseball team at their sister school.

"We've also had the local garbage collectors union send rubber boots and gloves to the Nicaraguan sanitation workers. We sponsor an annual poetry competition for Nicaraguan and American poets, and we publish an anthology of the best entries. We have sister churches, sister daycare centers, and the latest idea is to get the *Law Review* at Yale to write about international law with regard to Nicaragua. There are so many opportunities for partnership, that no one roadblock should stop the group from finding other ways to make links."

• **Doesn't having a U.S. partner unfairly benefit one community over another? Can't partnerships actually disrupt a Third World government's efforts to allocate and distribute scarce resources?**

There *is* a danger that the sister community becomes privileged merely because some villagers happen to have connections with foreigners. Why should one clinic in Nicaragua have more supplies than another just as badly in need? Why should one town in Burkina Faso have a new high school simply because they know a group of people from Georgia?

Gary Gunderson recognizes this problem. "We have to make sure our sister program doesn't end up distorting the government's national plan of how scarce resources should be allocated. That's why it's easier if you have faith in the government you're working with so that your efforts fit in with their larger priorities. In some countries working with the government would mean working in the hometown of the president or the backyard of a cabinet minister."

The Nicaraguan government has complained about U.S. groups bypassing government agencies. One Ministry of Health official told us, "A lot of Americans come to Nicaragua, meet someone who works at a school or clinic, and say, 'Ah-ha. I think I'll hook up with that one.' But the communities most in need are often the remote ones that visitors are least likely to get to. So twinning in such an ad-hoc fashion may not be the best thing for the country as a whole."

To alleviate this conflict, the Nicaraguan government asked the U.S.-based National Central America Health Rights Network (NCHARN) to coordinate all the disparate sister clinics that had cropped up. Nicaragua, too, is trying to get more organized: towns and cities in the United States are urged to go through the Nicaraguan Embassy in Washington, D.C. to find an appropriate match, and a Nicaragua Sister City Program office has been set up in Managua to handle the growing family.

The Nicaraguans have also warned U.S. groups that they may have to redistribute some of the supplies sent down. A U.S. group may raise thousands of dollars worth of antibiotics and medical supplies for one clinic, but some of these scarce resources may be transferred if there is a dire need for those antibiotics elsewhere.

This is true in the case of the daycare centers as well. AMNLAE, the Nicaraguan Women's Association, oversees daycare twinning programs. They stress to the U.S. groups that while the bulk of what they send goes to their twins, there may be times when the packages are split up and sent to other daycare centers where the need is greater. "We know our twin gets some of what we send them because they send pictures and thank us," says Judy Kahn of Oakland, California. "It's possible that AMNLAE splits up the packages and allocates some supplies to other poor daycare centers. But that's fine with us, because they're the ones that know where the greatest need is."

The Bottom Line: A Partnership is a Commitment

The activities that transpire between partners will ebb and flow depending on the groups and individuals involved. Like all human relationships, these go in cycles: just when you think everything is going right, some other issue will emerge and challenge the relationship anew. Gary Gunderson's reflections on the early days of the Decatur/Burkina Faso partnership explain further:

"Six months after we started the partnership, we returned to Burkina with a delegation of ten people from Decatur. They greeted us with unbelievable hospitality—with a feast, and dancing way into the night. They even wrote songs for the occasion. They were hospitable in a way that Americans rarely are. It far exceeded the boundaries of what was economically justifiable.

"I was so American about the whole thing. I was sitting there thinking, 'This is such a loss for them. This is a bad waste of their money. They are a hungry nation; they should really be saving their resources. They're going to spend more money on this meal than they're ever going to get out of us.'

"It was a turning point for me personally. It forced me to realize that people who we relate to as 'the hungry' have a very great sense of humanity, even more than we do. I realized that for them, it was truly more blessed to give than to receive. We were showered all day with friendship, and that will resonate in our memories as long as we live. It will also resonate in their memories: after we left, the villagers danced and partied until four in the morning, celebrating.

"And they believed us when we said we wanted to be partners and gain from each other. I don't think we knew what that meant at the time, and we're still struggling to understand the full meaning of this commitment. But we've learned that a partnership is like a marriage—it takes a lot of nurturing, a lot of compromise, a lot of commitment. But when it works, as it has in our case, the rewards are phenomenal."

3

Aid: From Charity to Solidarity

The partnerships blossoming between the First and the Third Worlds tell us something about new trends in development assistance. But what forms should that assistance take? Anyone who has traveled to a Third World country is aware of the stark reality. Supplies, replacement parts, and repairs are in high demand—whether you're in a health clinic, a factory, a school, or a bus. Filling the gaps with spare equipment and supplies, or the funds to purchase them, can dramatically improve living conditions, and is a concrete way to support a Third World development project. Some people have taken direct aid even further by actually going to the Third World to provide their skills and technical expertise to burgeoning community development efforts.

While the concept of providing material and technical assistance is nothing new, the 1980s have witnessed two positive trends. First, in addition to the established, professional development associations, there are now hundreds of small, grassroots groups which have taken on the task of delivering direct aid or providing technical assistance. Second, the groups making the greatest contribution to this movement not only provide aid, but use aid as a vehicle for educating North Americans about the Third World and for changing harmful U.S. policies.

The Flow of Material Aid

Before World War II, most U.S. aid organizations—such as Catholic Relief Services and Church World Service—were an outgrowth of Christian missionary activities. During and after World War II, however, a new breed of secular organizations emerged. The largest of these, CARE, was founded in 1945 to send packages (yes, "care packages") to war-torn Europe. "Our first package actually went to France," according to Bonnie Long, director of CARE's San Francisco office. "We were sending food, agricultural tools, clothing, shoemaker kits—whatever we could to help rebuild Europe's economy. Individuals would sponsor or buy care packages, and could even specify where they wanted them sent—even if it was to an aunt in Italy."

As Europe recovered from the devastation of the war, these relief groups began to turn their attention to the Third World. They were later joined by new organizations that concentrated less on emergency relief and more on long-term development. Taken together, these groups comprise what is referred to as the community of NGOs, or Non-Governmental Organizations.

Some NGOs—such as Catholic Relief Services, CARE, and World Vision—have yearly budgets of over $100 million and hundreds of staff. While originally funded primarily by individuals, many NGOs have grown more and more dependent on U.S. government support. In 1987 Catholic Relief Services, for example, received a full two-thirds of its $273 million budget from government sources. Other well-known organizations receiving U.S. government money for their overseas work include CARE, Save the Children, Planned Parenthood International, and World Vision.

But since acceptance of U.S. government money implies acceptance of U.S. foreign policy, other NGOs have chosen to steer clear of government funds. Oxfam-America is perhaps the best known and the largest of the independent aid agencies. It was founded in 1970 as an offshoot of Oxfam-UK, which has been around since 1942. The American Friends Service Committee, the American Jewish World Service, the Unitarian Universalist Service Committee, and Grassroots International are some of the other U.S. groups funding a broad spectrum of grassroots development efforts with no government support.

Two new trends have emerged on the international aid scene. The first is the rise of the evangelical movement in the United States, and the consequent increase in the number of foreign evangelical missionaries. Most traditional Protestant and Catholic churches have reduced their emphasis on foreign missions. But born-again believers are increasing their prose-lytizing efforts, aided by food handouts and a strong anti-communist message.

The second newcomer in the 1980s is the "mega-event" like USA for Africa, BandAid, Live Aid, and Hands Across America. Mobilizing millions of dollars for hunger relief, these events were primarily set up to be short-term responses to crises. As a result, more attention has been paid to raising money through purchases of records or t-shirts than raising people's aware-ness about the *causes* of hunger and the long-term solutions. Nevertheless, these events have generated much-needed funds, and helped make the issue of hunger more visible to the general public.

People-to-People Aid Campaigns

The most exciting trend in material aid in the 1980s has been the proliferation of hundreds of small, direct, people-to-people aid campaigns. These groups, mostly staffed by volunteers, see the aid they offer not as charity but as a form of solidarity. The Southern Africa Medical Aid Project, a group of doctors and anti-apartheid activists, sends supplies and money to a hospital in Tanzania for political refugees from South Africa. St. Mary's Academy in Milwaukee, Wisconsin organizes a humanitarian aid campaign called "Trick or Treat for Nicaraguan High School Chil-dren", where students spend Halloween collecting clothes, medicines, toilet articles, and other supplies for Nicaraguan chil-dren orphaned by the contra war. The group, Caribbean Ex-change, sells Haitian art and uses the profits to support grassroots groups in Haiti that are part of a movement for demo-cratic change.

Many of the new material aid groups are raising money for less traditional resources than medicines, food, or clothing. This is most obvious in aid to Nicaragua. Bats Not Bombs and Baseballs for Peace send sports equipment; the U.S./Nica Printers Project raises money for parts and repairs for Nicaragua's printing presses; Jugglers for Peace donates juggling equipment and trains Nicaraguan jugglers. "While certainly the basic material goods are essential to life, food for the spirit is equally as important," claims Sue Severin of the Nicaragua Information Center. "Where the people are suffering the terrible grief of war and economic deprivation, they need more than ever to celebrate the joys of life."

Another innovative form of support is aid to families suffering extraordinary duress of one kind or another. A Swedish anti-apartheid group, for example, discovered the tremendous pressure placed upon the children at the Tanzania-based school of the African National Congress (the liberation movement of South Africa). Fearful of South African reprisals, the children are constantly under close surveillance and rarely get a chance to venture out. So Swedish families brought the South African children to Sweden to spend a summer. Their hospitality provided temporary relief to both the students and their families, and helped the Swedish children understand the hopes and dreams of their South African friends.

The Mexican earthquake of 1985 gave rise to another creative family aid project. Mexican women from garment shops hit hard by the disaster organized the "19th of September Union" to publicize the callous actions of factory owners who, immediately after the earthquake, hired cranes to salvage their sewing machines and cash boxes, leaving many women trapped inside the factories to perish. The Union tried to get compensation for the women's families, and to push shopowners to rebuild factories and provide much-needed jobs.

Operating on virtually no funds, the Union called on the international community for support. One of the most novel responses came from a union in Spain. In addition to sending financial support, the families of the Spanish union offered to host twenty of the garment workers' children for a summer in Spain—paying for everything, including airfare. "It was not only a fantastic learning experience for our kids," one of the Mexican union organizers told us, "but it was also an opportunity for us to spend more time organizing!"

Even groups that are U.S. focused are branching out to offer support to their counterparts overseas. The Northwest Labor and Employment Law Office (LELO) in Seattle is just one example. LELO is a multi-racial organization working to stop employment discrimination against low-income and minority workers in the United States. Some of the groups that comprise LELO include Filipino cannery workers, black construction workers, and Hispanic farmworkers. Recognizing the parallels between their struggles and those of workers overseas, LELO began building concrete ties with its Third World counterparts. In 1987, for example, LELO sent black American construction workers to provide technical assistance to construction workers in Mozambique.

What's a Good Group To Support?

For a U.S. organization wanting to support a group overseas, it is often difficult to distinguish one from another. While most groups claim to benefit the poor, in reality this is not always the case. And while most profess to be autonomous organizations, many have close ties to regimes that are far from democratic. The challenge lies in getting behind the rhetoric and ascertaining the group's true commitment to social change.

To complicate matters, in the 1980s the U.S. government began channeling part of its aid money through private groups, rather than solely through Third World governments. This was part of the Reagan administration's "privatization" philosophy which holds that private agencies, not governments, are the key to development. But instead of funding local agencies that have popular bases and a commitment to social change, U.S. aid flows mainly to more conservative business groups.

This is especially true, and takes on particular importance, in areas of conflict. In El Salvador, a country wracked by civil war and poverty, the U.S. channels over 75 percent of its economic aid through nongovernmental groups supporting private business. In 1987, some $30 million was allocated to just one business association that aims to solve the country's socioeconomic problems by promoting U.S. investment and increasing exports to the United States. Three million dollars went to Junior Achievement of El Salvador, which is using the funds to design business role-playing games for Salvadoran high school students.[1]

The Pentagon and State Department have also begun using private organizations in low intensity conflict (LIC) situations. LIC refers to unconventional wars, largely in the Third World, that combine overt military assistance with tactics such as covert aid, economic pressure, and psychological warfare. In these situations, such as in El Salvador and the Philippines, development aid becomes part of an alliance between the U.S. government and Third World governments to maintain a pro-business, pro-military, pro-U.S. hold on the country, regardless of the needs of the poor majority.

This is why U.S. groups trying to hook up with Third World organizations must do their homework beforehand. "It takes a lot of work to find good groups to support," says Chris Roszene, the Latin America field representative for the Canadian development organization CUSO. "You certainly can't rely solely on the word of the groups themselves, and just because they are staffed by local people doesn't mean that they are working for social changes that benefit the poor. You should get references from other respected institutions and individuals in the country. If you don't have these kinds of references, start with respectable U.S. aid groups—like Oxfam—that are already working there. It's worth taking the time in the beginning to make sure that the group you are supporting shares your philosophy and goals."

Creative Examples of Technical Aid

Furnishing material aid to Third World groups is only one kind of assistance. Another crucial type of aid is providing access to information. The distinction between "providing access" and "asserting expertise" is important. Rather than having outside experts tell them what to do—or do things for them—many

Third World organizations are asking for information they can use to make their own decisions.

The Appropriate Technology Project of Volunteers in Asia is responding to this need for information. Project workers gather the best written resources on appropriate technology, and catalogue them for Third World groups. "We're not saying it's the only need, and that with the information we provide they can solve all their problems," says project director Ken Darrow. "But we felt it was one practical way we could assist. We provide two services: one is the *Appropriate Technology Sourcebook*, which is a review of some 1,150 books, with information about how the books can be ordered. The other is a microfiche library of one thousand books, which comes in a container about the size of a shoebox. Together with a microfiche viewer and the shipping costs, the whole library runs about $1,000-1,200—which is a fraction of the cost of getting the books themselves." Volunteers in Asia has sold the library in about a hundred countries, and, according to their surveys, these libraries answer over fifty thousand questions every year.

Major drawbacks, however, limit the usefulness of this type of information. The users have to be literate, and literate in English, since most of the material has not been translated. "But perhaps even more limiting," admits Ken, "is that the user has to have a cultural orientation which says there is information in books that can be useful to our everyday lives. Most people—in the Third World or in this country for that matter—don't have that orientation, so our library is mainly used by professionals or by foreigners working abroad."

Another example of providing vital information occurred after the explosion of the Union Carbide plant in Bhopal, India. The Highlander Research and Education Center in Tennessee set up links with an Indian research group—the Society for Participatory Research in Asia—to provide information on the toxicity of the chemicals produced by the company, the way previous accidents had been dealt with, and the extent of Union Carbide's activities throughout the world. "Such information was essential to those working with the Bhopal victims," says John Gaventa of Highlander. "In India there is no legal obligation to make information available to the public. So we tried to provide that information, since people's access and control over knowledge is critical for ensuring any true public regulation over hazardous industry."

Jonathan Fox, a professor at the Massachusetts Institute of Technology who works with grassroots groups in Latin America, suggests a different kind of information Westerners can provide to Third World groups: information about potential supporters in the United States. "One function which outsiders can play is what in Spanish is called *interlocutor*," says Jonathan. "It's a kind of social interpreter—in this case someone who helps to translate the language of Third World grassroots groups into a language understandable to potential supporters in the United States. The *interlocutor* would explain who those supporters might be and how to approach them—both conceptually and practically."

Few would quarrel with the idea of providing a political, cultural, and institutional map to help guide Third World groups through the maze of U.S society. How detailed that map should be is the subject of much debate. Is it helpful enough to just give the names and addresses of potential U.S. funders and let Third World groups take it from there? Or should the idiosyncrasies of each funder be explained? Should U.S. supporters get involved in lobbying funders behind the scenes, and even writing grant proposals? Every *interlocutor* must be sensitive about crossing the fine line between making information available and making decisions which should be made by the Third World organization itself.

Working Abroad

The question of the proper role for outsiders is even more crucial when it comes to actually working abroad—directly providing our skills to aid Third World groups. Since 1961, more than 120,000 U.S. citizens have worked in the Third World through the best known and largest voluntary service organization, the Peace Corps.

The Peace Corps is a U.S. government organization and Peace Corps volunteers are part of the "country team" of the U.S. State Department, accountable to the U.S. ambassador in that country. As such, the Peace Corps is inevitably linked to broad U.S.

foreign policy objectives. This becomes clear upon examining where the Peace Corps concentrates its volunteers.

The growing regional conflict in Central America in the 1980s, for example, was accompanied by a dramatic rise in U.S. military aid—and a parallel rise in the number of Peace Corps volunteers in the region. By 1987 there were more Peace Corps volunteers stationed in Honduras (a tiny country of under five million people) than in any other nation in the world. Many of the volunteers work in the south, where over twelve thousand peasants have been displaced as a result of U.S.-supported military maneuvers along the Nicaraguan border.

This does not discredit the good intentions of individual Peace Corps volunteers. But where the U.S. government is fueling the militarization of a Third World country, U.S. policy diametrically opposes what many Peace Corps volunteers understand their role to be. One volunteer in Honduras told us, "You see the Honduran government spending $75 million to buy U.S. fighter planes while the children are increasingly malnourished. I feel that what I, as a Peace Corps volunteer, am trying to build is being destroyed—many times over—by my own government's militarized foreign policy."

Many who want to work abroad but feel uncomfortable about representing the U.S. government have sought alternatives to the Peace Corps. Thousands have ventured overseas with such groups as Volunteers in Technical Assistance, Plenty USA, Volunteers in Asia, and Partners for Global Justice. North Americans also contribute their labor working as short-term volunteers on projects ranging from reforestation brigades in Nicaragua to construction teams in Mozambique.

But whether working independently of the U.S. government or not, whether providing high-level technical expertise or volunteering with a work brigade, overseas work forces us to confront—to an even greater degree than for travelers or partnerships—some of the most controversial development issues of our time. Is our role as outsiders from industrialized countries one of going overseas and helping poor people "set things straight"? How can we be assured that our actions are truly helping, enabling the poor to continue the work long after we leave? Is it more important to stay home and try to educate the public and change U.S. policy?

Some say the role of outsiders is a purely technical one: volunteers should share their knowledge without getting involved in the political arena. Others believe that technical assistance has serious political and social implications—who you're helping, where, why, and how is just as important as the actual assistance rendered.

"It's not *what* you do, it's the way you do it," insists David Werner, Director of the Hesperian Foundation and author of *Where There Is No Doctor*, probably the world's most popular health manual for the poor. "I remember attending a conference in Ecuador sponsored by a U.S. health group. After the workshop was over and the U.S. delegates had basically finished telling the Ecuadorans what to do, one of the local schoolteachers, a kind of backwoods self-made trainer of health workers, got up and said, 'I don't want to offend anyone, and I really hesitate to speak. But if you want to know the truth, I think the biggest problem we have is the idiosyncratic need of Westerners to impose their ideas on other people.'

"I think that fellow hit the nail on the head. Westerners going abroad must look at themselves not as experts telling the local people what to do, but as a humble resource to be used as the local people see fit. We must recognize that we go with a certain body of knowledge which has positive and negative aspects, like any technology. For that knowledge to be applied in a positive fashion, it must be placed at the disposition and command of the local people to use—or not use—as they see fit.

"Our primary motivation for working abroad should be to gain an understanding of the Third World and the role of the superpowers in imposing their will on other people," David adds. "Our ultimate goal should be to reeducate people here at home and push our government to lay off the rest of the world, for that's the only way people will be able to make the necessary changes so they will no longer need our assistance."

Criteria for Deciding Where to Work

No group can work in every country, so choices have to be made about where to concentrate. Some groups feel they can make the most impact working in countries where the government is taking measures to improve the lives of the poor. Others narrow the field even further, focusing on countries that are not only struggling for their people's rights, but are under attack—the way Nicaragua is from the United States and Mozambique from South Africa.

Steve Sears is a member of Groundwork Institute, an association of planners, architects, environmentalists, and other professionals who serve as volunteer consultants on housing projects in developing countries. Groundwork's latest project is in Nicaragua, where Steve spends almost six months each year. He and his associates work on Nicaraguan cooperatives training peasants in housebuilding techniques. Steve shared some of his insights with us about the benefits of working with a government that is trying to meet the needs of its poorest citizens.

"I talked to my sister the other day. She and my father are supporting a religious-based project in Brazil, sending down $20 a month to help the poor. They're into seeing that the money gets to poor people themselves, not to the government. But the way I see it, independent church programs won't solve the development problem any more than bad governments will. At Groundwork we've learned that in order to educate people on a large scale, or in order to support their development projects, the government *must* be involved.

"What you see in Nicaragua is that every community has a government-supported school, a government-supported health clinic, and so on. A little boy stands up to read the liturgy, and his father stands over him, beaming, because he could never read. Only the government can help with those big victories, getting resources to the people so they can provide opportunities to their children. So outsiders working in that kind of environment can have a wider impact than if you are working at cross purposes with the local government."

In 1987 the Oliver Law Fund was established to provide technical assistance to the Frontline States—Mozambique, Angola, Tanzania, Zambia, and Zimbabwe—countries that are struggling to ward off aggression from neighboring South Africa. It was started by alumni of the Venceremos Brigade, an organization that sends annual work brigades to Cuba. The Chicago-based brigade members wished to link the black community of Chicago with southern Africa. They set up a program where recent graduates of technical training programs in the Chicago area spend one year teaching and consulting in one of the Frontline States.

"We named it the Oliver Law Fund after the first black commander of an integrated army. He was from Chicago and died in Spain while fighting with the Abraham Lincoln Brigade," notes Curtis Black, one of the founders of the fund. "Oliver Law went to Spain to fight for a cause similar to that of the Frontline States: he wanted to work against unfair aggression, to defend a democratically-elected government. One of the reasons we chose to link with the Frontline States is because we saw the similarities between the international solidarity efforts of fifty years ago and today's efforts to counter apartheid. On the other hand, we also want to show that international solidarity doesn't have to mean fighting in a war. In fact, it can be an important way of preventing one."

Working Under Repressive Conditions

Other aid groups have a different approach: rather than working in countries whose governments are striving to help the poor, they work where people are being repressed by their own governments.

Working under repressive conditions takes a lot of shrewd political maneuvering. Curt Wands of the Guatemalan Health Rights Support Project explains the evolution of their work in a country whose military has been one of the world's worst violators of human rights.

"In the late 1960s to early 1970s, a number of U.S. health care professionals began realizing the need to work in the Guatemalan countryside, since most health services were located in the cities and were inaccessible to rural areas. But controversies developed as soon as the network of rural health workers began to grow. When health promotors found themselves repeatedly treating people for recurrent health problems, they began to ask why. When they treated people for pesticide poisoning, they questioned the plantation owner about why he sprayed poisons with people in the field. After seeing case after case of malnourished children, they questioned the land distribution which left the majority of people without enough land to grow food on."

Guatemalan health care workers began to join forces with trade unionists, students, and teachers to press for change. They were quickly labeled "subversive," and their security was at stake. Doctors were found murdered on the roadside for all to see. They were forced to find more astute ways to work, so as not to disappear.

In 1980, they formed the Guatemalan Health Movement to serve people in the war-ravaged areas and to protect health workers. What started out as an emergency, short-term response to the counterinsurgency situation has become a full-fledged, parallel health structure. There are almost no other services for the people who have been displaced by the war—whose numbers now total well over one million.

The U.S.-based Guatemalan Health Rights Support Project was created in 1985 to support this indigenous health movement. "We support training of rural health workers, we send down delegations of U.S. health care workers to monitor the situation, and we do educational work here in the United States to stop the war and allow Guatemalans to build a healthier society. While it is certainly not easy to work in a country like Guatemala, we have seen how effective we can be, even in these repressive times, at supporting the Guatemalans in their struggle to build a new society," says Curt Wands.

For groups functioning under repressive conditions, the best aid might be simply the recognition and presence of outsiders. While this is not always the case, in some situations foreigners speaking out against government abuses can help protect local organizing efforts. In Honduras, for example, a U.S. friend of peasant and labor groups meets with foreign journalists to try to get them to write stories about some of these social movements. The articles increase the visibility of the movements and their leaders, making them less likely to be subjected to sudden arrest, torture, and imprisonment by the Honduran military.

A number of U.S. lawyers have lent their services to groups under attack by their own governments. The Lawyers Committee for Civil Rights Under Law sent a Federal appeals judge to monitor the treason trial of sixteen black South Africans in 1985. Twelve of the defendants were acquitted, an outcome that

South African defense lawyers attributed to the publicity surrounding the case. More recently, the United Auto Workers formed a panel of judges and lawyers to monitor the trial of Moses Mayekiso, a black union leader in Pretoria on trial for treason and subversion after organizing rent and consumer boycotts against his town council.

Hesperian Foundation's David Werner feels the decision about *where* to work is ultimately less important than the decision about *whom* to work with. "No matter where you're working, you must be ready to take sides, and to take the side of the poor. Because regardless of where you go, there will be different sides. And unless you are willing to stick your neck out, you shouldn't go in the first place."

What Kind of Aid is Appropriate?

Not only must we consider where and with whom to work, but what kind of help is most appropriate for that particular situation. Ken Hughes, director of the Institute for Transportation and Development Policy, sees repeated examples of inappropriate use of resources.

"Just look at our government aid programs," Ken points out. "Pakistan, for example, gets $200 million annually for transportation development projects from the U.S. government. But these projects are based on the idea that what Pakistan needs is a car factory, so that's what the money is spent on. Meanwhile, nine out of ten Pakistanis use the traditional tri-shaw, which, although archaic in design, makes good sense environmentally and culturally. Rather than spending the millions of dollars on building cars, we should be doing research on how to improve what most people already use."

In contrast, Ken's group sends bicycles and repair equipment to Third World countries. In 1987, Matteo Martignoni, one of the world's foremost bike builders, went to Haiti to look at ways to repair and construct more bikes. Thanks to his help, Haiti now has load-carrying tricycles, capable of hauling over one hundred pounds, and the Japanese Railway Association has pledged to donate a container of bicycles to the Institute for Transportation and Development Policy's Haiti project. To Nicaragua, in 1988 alone the Institute sent fourteen hundred bicycles and thousands of spare parts with an estimated value of over $150,000—more than double the number of bikes sent to Nicaragua since the project began in 1984. The Institute also sent all-terrain bikes to the Ministries of Health, Transport, and Agriculture in Mozambique.

In addition to providing material and technical aid, Ken and his organization are pushing for dialogue with the World Bank Urban Transport Group, and sponsoring conferences to educate policymakers about appropriate transportation needs in the Third World.

"All we want to do is build peaceful ties with Third World countries, and at the same time do so in a way that contributes to the sustainability of their transportation and energy systems," adds Ken. "So far, we've chosen to work in countries of great strife. In places like Nicaragua, Mozambique and Haiti, planners are barely able to go beyond the constant emergency situations to true development. It's hard for a government to allocate resources for bike repair training when there's a war going on, for example. That's where we can help."

Steve Sears of Groundwork issues a note of caution, warning that even the most sensitive professionals can be out of touch with reality. "We 'professionals' tend to have illusions about the perfect design project. We make plans in our offices. We talk about aesthetics, ecology, and so on. What we dream of is helping people build their 'crystal palace.'

"But then you realize that people don't want your crystal palace. Developmentally, this is the point where it gets very interesting. You see the same problems in our own country. Take low-cost housing. Planners want to know why the poor end up destroying their housing. What can you do? Walk away? Blame the poor?

"What we do is reassess. Who are these people? How can we involve them more in the process? We know that the people we work with are polite and don't want to offend us. They might go along with our plans, but not really believe in what we're doing. So how do we cut through the politeness? I've learned that to really solve these problems takes living and working with the people over time. There's no substitute."

The real test of a project's success is whether or not the local people take it over. "The goal is to get to a point where people are taking power from you," Steve continues, "and then you know you can leave. You can't just give power away, then people owe you something. But you can let people take it. For instance, I'm usually the problem solver when we come to an obstacle while building a house. I used to leave for awhile, and when I'd come back, the campesinos wouldn't have done a single bit of work without me there. More recently, they've kept on going without me. You have to step away to test it, to see if this process is at work."

Roland Bunch, whose organization, World Neighbors, provides financial and technical aid to agricultural projects overseas, agrees that the real test of whether your assistance is useful or not comes after you leave. "When you work in an area, you try to provide the best possible assistance based on indigenous knowledge, local systems, available materials, and resources. Then you leave, and hope people carry on without you. The best test for what constitutes 'appropriate aid' is when you return to that same area sometime later, and you see that the work has spread by itself."

Long-Term vs. Short-Term Commitments

Another issue that comes up when considering work abroad is whether short-term or long-term stints are more appropriate. Some organizations believe that short-term consultancies— from a few days to a few months—are preferable because you can perform a concrete task, but not interfere with the long-term work of the Third World groups. Short-term consultancies are also less expensive than long-term stays, they claim, and the Third World recipients are less likely to get "hooked" on outside help. Others feel that a commitment of a few years is imperative if you are going to make any lasting changes. They say it takes about six months to a year just to get oriented, to gain the trust of the people, and to understand how you and your skills can best fit in. Organizations treat this issue differently, according to their structure and goals.

In the medical fields, some groups take short-term stints to the extreme—literally flying in and out of poor Third World communities. Interplast, Inc. is one example. The idea for Interplast originated in 1965, when a fourteen-year-old Mexican boy named Antonio was sent to Stanford University Medical Center for an operation to repair his cleft lip. Six weeks later, Antonio was back in Mexico, in school for the first time, and even had a girlfriend. Dr. Donald Laub, the Stanford physician who performed the operation, had never seen anything like it. He learned that in the Third World children with cleft lips and palates often go into hiding out of shame, never learning to speak properly and never going to school.

In 1969 Dr. Laub established Interplast, Inc. to serve the poor, to give U.S. doctors overseas experience, and to train host country doctors and nurses in reconstructive techniques. Interplast now raises enough money for a pool of two hundred professionals to take twenty trips a year to about ten different countries. Once inside the host country, Interplast doctors and nurses join their counterparts to work together, often for twelve hours straight, performing as many as one hundred operations during a two-week stay.

But David Werner of the Hesperian Foundation is critical of this quick "in-and-out" approach to technical aid. "I don't deny that the highly specialized surgery such groups perform can make a radical difference in the lives of the people they reach," says David. "But this approach also has its drawbacks: it often creates hostility among local health personnel and, among the population, it instills a mentality of the 'great white doctors' coming in to save them. In terms of cost effectiveness, with the same material and human investment you could do a great deal more with fewer people working in one area for a longer period of time, because then you could really help develop a local team that could meet the community's needs on an ongoing basis."

Barbara Atkinson works with TECNICA, a group that sends hundreds of volunteers a year to Nicaragua and southern Africa. Most of TECNICA's volunteers go for short terms, but Barbara is currently part of a dialogue within the organization on the issue of shorter versus longer stays. "Two weeks is great if the project you work on is ongoing—in a way, it fosters self-help. On the other hand, there is also a sense of discontinuity on all sides. The most successful projects we've had are the long-term ones with a lot of follow-up."

A key factor in favor of short-term brigades is the need for educating the public about what's happening in Nicaragua. "As far as the Nicaraguans are concerned, the more North Americans who go to Nicaragua and then return to talk about the situation there, the better," Barbara explains. "Technical aid is a great way to get professionals down to Nicaragua. These people have credibility in professional circles, and can talk to others about ending the war and the economic blockade. And even if the short stints are less useful technically, they are better than nothing and they provide important channels for education."

Steve Kerpen of Architects and Planners in Support of Nicaragua (APSNICA), a construction brigade, agrees. "We consider ourselves a development organization, but for us the key is sending as many people down every year as we can. Volunteers come home and talk to everyone from the Lions Club to the PTA, and the financial support they can generate sustains our longer-term projects. People really relate to the idea of building rather than destroying. You don't have to even know whether you're for or against the Sandinista government to agree that humanitarian assistance is better than funding a war."

Learning Lessons, Not Following Models

Going to work in a revolutionary country or with an organization dedicated to social change often engenders illusions of the perfect society. "I wanted to use my technical skills abroad, and at the same time, I began learning a lot about the revolution in Nicaragua," Barbara Atkinson of TECNICA told us. "I thought about volunteering to pick coffee there, but when I heard about TECNICA I decided that would be the best way to really use my skills. Plus, I had this vision of an idealistic place of happy people making a revolution and a new life for themselves, and I wanted some of that hope.

"My vision of happy people crumbled when I saw how difficult life was there, with the war and the economic hardships. Almost everyone has a war story to tell. It was pretty sobering. One of my Nicaraguan friends went to his home village, and found out that half of the people he knew there were already dead. Despite experiences like that, I did find a lot of hope. The terrible conditions are balanced by the sense of family and community and by the common efforts to survive and rebuild."

Steve Sears of Groundwork also talks of the harsh reality of working on a development project in the Third World. "Working with campesinos, you realize the contradictions, you see the problems inherent in any development scheme. This is opposed to the fantasy you come in with about what a cooperative is, what a revolutionary society is. The reality can be harsh. The campesinos can betray your sense of how things should be— they get drunk, they can act interested in what you're teaching, but then turn around and do things the way they want to anyway. But they can also be creative, gentle, and loving, just like any American can. What keeps me going is that I've learned to see our progress not in giant steps, but in the little, everyday victories that we accomplish together—finishing a roof, making tiles, working on a floor plan.

"The shorter construction brigades probably get a bigger dose of the idealism and less of the real-life picture. In a sense, the short-run picture is more positive, but it's not really fair to make people into saints, just as it's not fair to put out models of development, ideologies for change, whatever, and be rigid about them. There are no models. Real progress is made by regular people doing the little things necessary to change their lives. It's easier to create heroes and quick fixes for problems, but from my experience, the real advancements for humankind are the daily struggles and victories."

The Risk Factor

Working abroad in conflict areas can mean taking risks, both abroad and at home. For instance, some TECNICA volunteers have experienced harassment in the United States upon returning from Nicaragua. Tax audits, firings from their jobs, and FBI interrogation are just some of the not-so-subtle ways the U.S. government indicates that volunteering in Nicaragua, though legal, runs contrary to official U.S. policy.

Safety is also an issue worth considering. Benjamin Linder, a TECNICA volunteer, was murdered by the contras in 1987. "After Ben's death, we weren't sure what was going to happen,"

TECNICA's Barbara Atkinson recalls. "Most volunteers are stationed in Managua, where there isn't so much a sense of the war. Ben, on the other hand, was in a remote, rural area. TECNICA announced immediately that we were going to continue our work. The Nicaraguans also chose not to restrict us. Only the U.S. government has attempted to block technical assistance volunteers going to Nicaragua.

"Ben was really doing what all technicians who work in developing countries wish they could do. He was developing a small hydroelectric power plant from scratch. He actually helped bring power to a town for the very first time. He said when he sat up on the hillside after they flipped the switch, he felt like God seeing the entire town light up. Ben's death really shook the professional community. Everyone thought, 'It could have been me.' It just shows that in some ways, the more effective you are, the more vulnerable you can be."

In April, 1988, the Linder family went to Nicaragua with $250,000 raised through a national speaking tour. The money went to continue the hydroelectric project that Ben had been working on. And since Ben's death, instead of losing volunteers as some had feared, the number of applicants for TECNICA positions has nearly doubled. According to program director, David Creighton, TECNICA has expanded both the number of delegations to Nicaragua and its staff size to accommodate the boom. Ben's death served as a warning to volunteers not to take their task lightly. But more importantly, it served as a challenge to take up where Ben left off.

Making Order Out of Chaos

The recent mushrooming of material and technical aid groups is a positive trend. But as we have seen previously, it also presents major challenges for the people in the recipient countries. Who is going to receive the aid shipments? Where is it going to be stored? Where are they going to get the transportation to deliver the aid to its final destination? And, most importantly, is the aid promoting or disrupting the country's national-level plans?

The plethora of aid groups supporting Nicaragua has placed

these issues sharply in the foreground. "At one point there was complete chaos," says Rick Lewis of the Nicaragua Network, an umbrella organization of some three hundred U.S. groups working with Nicaragua. "People would go down to Nicaragua on work brigades, for example, and then come back and start their own material aid campaigns to send things down to their co-ops. I myself was on a construction brigade in 1985, and someone in the brigade decided that when we got home, we should send blankets to all the co-op members. Well, the motive was good, but it raised a lot of questions. Why should this co-op get the blankets when there were a lot of poorer co-ops in the country who needed them more? And someone in Nicaragua had to put a whole lot of energy into receiving the blankets and shipping them up to this co-op. It would have been much better to just send the blankets to a central agency and let them decide who should get them.

"I saw another example of bad aid when I was up north in Estelí," Rick continues. "There were about fifty sewing machines that some North American had sent down and insisted they be sent to Estelí. But they were wired for 220 volts. Estelí doesn't have 220. So they were just sitting around gathering dust."

To bring some order to the chaos, the Nicaragua Network began coordinating its aid campaigns with the National Committee in Solidarity with the People (CNSP), a Nicaraguan group that helps coordinate international solidarity activities. In 1988 the CNSP organized an international campaign with groups from forty-three countries. Each of the countries was asked to focus on a different single item. Given the food shortages in Nicaragua and the fact that the United States is the world's largest producer of oats, the Nicaraguans asked the U.S. groups to provide forty-two hundred tons of oats—enough for sixty-seven million meals for children!

The Nicaragua Network does not say that all groups should drop their own campaigns to work only with the CNSP, but it does encourage groups to coordinate their efforts, and to make sure it is the Nicaraguans themselves who make the decisions about what they need.

The true test of the U.S. groups' ability to coordinate activities came after Hurricane Joan ripped through Nicaragua in October 1988. In response to Nicaraguan requests, North Americans mobilized to collect food, clothing, medicines, and money. Rather than each group conducting its own relief effort, joint actions sprung up throughout the country. The group, Quest for Peace, coordinated both air and shipping operations for material aid raised by scores of smaller organizations. Oxfam-America joined with groups of Nicaraguans living in the United States to airlift supplies to Nicaragua's devastated Atlantic Coast. The religious community got behind Pastors for Peace, a nationwide truck convoy driving supplies down to Nicaragua. While there is an element of chaos in all relief efforts, especially one made up largely of "seat of the pants" solidarity groups, the degree of coordination and professionalism proved that this movement had come a long way.

Assistance Flowing Two Ways

Most material and technical assistance programs suffer the same dilemma apparent in other solidarity efforts, from tourism to partnerships: the assistance tends to flow one way. More North Americans get to work in the Third World than Third Worlders have opportunities to come here, and material aid is routed from north to south. But there are examples of assistance projects that flow both ways. Careful planning and foresight can produce true exchanges of technical know-how, ideas, and culture.

The Canadian Farm Youth Exchange has worked hard to do this. Begun in 1984 as a joint project of several Canadian and Caribbean organizations, the Canadian Farm Youth Exchange brings young people from Canada and the Caribbean together to spend twelve weeks in technical and cultural exchanges.[2] So far, three such exchanges have transpired.

Darlene Henderson is part-owner of a grain farm and a member of the Canadian National Farm Union. She also served as the coordinator for the first two Farm Youth Exchanges. "First, the Caribbeans come here for six weeks, living in the homes of their Canadian partners and going through their daily routines with them. Then the same thing happens in reverse: the Canadians all go to the Caribbean, and live and work with the Caribbean farm families.

"Part of the time is also spent in discussion sessions with the participants. We talk about agricultural issues. It's funny, but what becomes most obvious to people is that in many cases, the Caribbeans and the Canadians have the same problems. One issue that they always talk about is how they have no control over the prices they receive for their commodities. They compare bananas from the Caribbean to wheat from Canada.

"They also talk about Canada's market controls on dairy products and poultry, to see if such a system is applicable in the Caribbean. In Dominica, the farm-to-market structure, where farmers bypass the middlemen and therefore retain more of the retail price, came directly from our exchange.

"Generally speaking, we've already seen success. Our goal is to develop young leaders with a broadened understanding of farm issues. Many of our participants are quite active in their local farm unions. Both here in Canada and in the Caribbean, we've seen some of these people rise to leadership positions in the national farm organizations. The most amazing transformations take place for these young people who participate, Canadian and Caribbean alike. Many of them come away with very strong impressions of how they perceive other cultures, about racism, about relative wealth, about how women are treated in different countries.

"Of course we still have some problems to work out. Since most of the funding comes from the Canadian side, we occasionally come up against power struggles. We like to think we're partners, but sometimes we do have questions about who should have the final power in decisionmaking. But partnership continues to be a goal."

The Highlander Center in Tennessee is another example of an exchange that flows in many directions. Through its Community and Environmental Health Program, Highlander has helped people in Appalachia meet with and learn from others around the globe who are grappling with the deleterious health effects of toxic chemicals. By hosting visits to Appalachia, people working in mines and tanning factories have met their counterparts from places as far away as South Africa, India, Mexico, Venezuela, Brazil, and Turkey.

"These people-to-people exchanges are vital," says program coordinator, Larry Wilson. "First of all, the foreigners are amazed to see that the Third World exists right here in the United States. They get a much better understanding of the global economic system. At the same time, a real bonding takes place between the visitors and hosts. This idea of global community is no longer an abstract philosophy. They realize they are affected by the same exploitative policies and most importantly, they realize that the only way they can make real changes is by organizing and speaking through one voice."

The exchange of ideas and information lasts way beyond the visits. When the residents of Yellow Creek, Kentucky were fighting the Environmental Protection Agency (EPA) for allowing a leather tanning company to pollute the area with dangerous toxic wastes, they called on their foreign friends for support. Letters poured in from Bangladesh, India, South Africa, Mexico. The front page of the local paper proclaimed "The Whole World is Watching Yellow Creek, Kentucky." "It was very embarrassing for the EPA," Larry Wilson recalls with a smile. "Imagine having people from Bangladesh writing to condemn the U.S. government for killing people in southeast Kentucky. It wasn't long before they announced a clean-up program and slapped a $3 million fine on the tanning company."

Linking Aid with Education and Advocacy

The most committed grassroots assistance groups consider their role as development educators in the United States to be equally as important as their ability to mobilize funds. "Through educational campaigns, we can do a lot to reverse the image of poor people in the Third World as hopeless and helpless people, and present them as they really are—very hardworking and innovative," notes Oxfam's Haleh Wunder.

One way to combine fundraising with education is to link community institutions with development projects overseas. The International Development Exchange (IDEX) encourages rotary clubs, schools, and church committees to co-sponsor small development grants to Third World communities. While these are not full-fledged partnerships on a par with the sister ties discussed in chapter 2, they do provide an avenue for educational activities. "The projects we fund have budgets under $5,000, so they're not out of reach of what U.S. community groups might be able to fundraise for," explains Becky Buell, IDEX's Executive Director. "This way a classroom, several classrooms, or an entire school can feel that it has a direct positive impact on the Third World community. We encourage correspondence back and forth between the partners, and have found that fundraising around a particular project has opened up a window on the world, enabling community groups to discuss broader political and economic issues inherent in their relationship to a Third World country."

The American Jewish World Service has local chapters that essentially "adopt" a project, raising some of the money to fund the project, and taking responsibility for local education. The San Francisco chapter, for example, adopted an agricultural project on the island of Negros in the Philippines. Their local events bring together Jewish and Filipino community participants to discuss how they can further support development efforts in the Philippines.

Some material aid groups go even further. Their goals are not only to provide much-needed funds to poor communities and to educate the public about conditions in the Third World. These groups realize that no amount of material aid is going to solve the problems of poverty and injustice. They realize that broader changes have to take place—changes in U.S. policy, and changes in international economic relations. For those groups, material aid campaigns are more than channels for funding Third World development efforts. They are a vehicle for helping U.S. citizens grasp the need for such changes *and* become advocates for change over the long run.

One of the most effective organizations combining material aid with education and advocacy is MADRE, a multicultural, multiclass group working with Nicaraguan and Salvadoran women. "Our material aid campaign is just one component of our work," says board member Vivian Stromberg. "We also link daycare centers in the United States with centers in Nicaragua. We organize tours throughout the United States to give Central American women an opportunity to talk to all kinds of U.S. women. We develop close ties with the Central American women we work with, so that our campaigns represent their true needs and interests. We join with other groups to protest such destructive foreign policies as U.S. aid to the contras. We publish a magazine to inform our supporters and inspire them to get more involved. And we speak out against many problems affecting women and children here in the United States, problems caused by the same policies that affect Central American women.

"For us, educating people in the United States and pressuring our government to change its policies at home and abroad are essential facets of our material aid work," continues Vivian. "We're not interested in charity, but in changing the conditions which keep people poor and disenfranchised. We are very serious and committed to building institutions, not just delivering aid or protesting policies in the short term."

The Quixote Center is another group that has masterfully combined material aid and advocacy. In 1985, when the U.S. Congress voted to send $27 million to aid the contras, the Quixote Center launched Quest for Peace—a campaign to counter contra aid with $27 million in genuine humanitarian assistance to the Nicaraguan people. "Since 70 percent of the people in the United States are against intervention in Nicaragua, we took the idea of matching contra aid with humanitarian aid as a mandate," says John Kellenburg of the Quixote Center. "We gather material aid donated from individuals, church groups, and other community organizations—everything from medicines to food to sports equipment—and ship it to Nicaragua. We also keep track of other organizations' shipments in our National Tally Office, shipments between sister cities and lots of other groups." To date, Quest for Peace has tallied and matched the $27 million and $100 million Congressional allocations for contra aid.

But material aid is just the beginning. "We start with material aid because the supplies are needed in Nicaragua and because that is something that most Americans can relate to," says Jeff Bissonnette, also with the Quixote Center. "But once people get involved, a politicization takes place. They see, for example, that while we are sending real humanitarian aid—food, clothing, medicines—our Congress is sending 'aid' to kill and maim the very people we're trying to help. They also become aware that there's an economic embargo that is preventing Nicaragua from importing supplies through normal channels.

"It's quite an amazing process. Since these people have seen the concrete impact of their material aid, they feel they can carry through and have a concrete impact in influencing U.S. policy. So we help them to become legislative activists— pressuring their representatives to end contra aid and lift the embargo. And little by little, we see a complete change in their thinking about U.S. policy which goes way beyond Nicaragua, beyond Central America, to question other areas of foreign policy and domestic issues as well. We've seen people who were never politically involved become advocates for change on a broad array of peace and justice issues."

That's the beauty of material aid. When done right, it can not only mobilize much-needed resources, but it can also engage people to make justice for the poor a priority, and can create a framework through which they continue to view the world for the rest of their lives.

Human rights abuses in South Africa have been the rallying cry for anti-apartheid protests throughout the country. Here Columbia University students demand that university funds be pulled from corporations working in South Africa.

Photo by Donna Binder/Impact Visuals

4

Championing
Human Rights

"There were two very important aspects which influenced the government to order my release. First, the workers' refusal to permit the continuation of rights violations. Second, the massive response from the international solidarity movement. I want to personally thank all those who worked to achieve my freedom."
—Humberto Centeno,
Executive Committee, National Unity of Salvadoran Workers (UNTS)

H uman rights" is a relatively young concept. The Universal Declaration of Human Rights was adopted by the United Nations in 1948. It set forth rights evolving from the Western political tradition, such as equal protection under the law, protection against cruel or unusual punishment, freedom of expression, and the right to participate in government through periodic elections. But it also established a series of economic rights, affirming that everyone has the right to a standard of living adequate for health and well-being, including housing, clothing, medical care, and food.

This official declaration reflects the inextricable link between different categories of rights. Political rights are meaningless when the majority of citizens remain economically disenfranchised. Likewise, exercising one's economic rights becomes impossible against a backdrop of political repression, and under a

91

government that remains unaccountable to the majority. People who speak out under these conditions risk their lives.

The Universal Declaration of Human Rights signaled to all citizens that they not only hold certain basic political and economic rights as human beings, but also that individuals are responsible for defending human rights for themselves and for other people. While the Declaration is not legally binding on governments, it provides a certain "code of ethics," and has been followed up by numerous declarations and laws that give the Declaration increasingly more clout in determining international standards for basic needs and rights.

The Declaration has also become the cornerstone for a movement that has grown to include human rights organizations in nearly every country of the world. Some, like Amnesty International, safeguard the rights of political prisoners. Amnesty works on behalf of over six thousand political prisoners every year, from Central America to the Philippines, from Libya to the United States, from the Soviet Union to South Africa. Other human rights groups like Survival International and the Food First Information and Action Network are working to ensure economic and cultural survival of indigenous groups and the poor who are struggling to organize and feed themselves. Groups like the Marin Interfaith Task Force on Central America and Peace Brigades International provide bodyguard services to threatened members of Third World human rights organizations.

Many of the U.S. human rights organizations—Human Rights Advocates, The Lawyers Committee on Central America, Americas Watch—are professional and legal organizations. They use their knowledge of national and international law to press for wider recognition of human rights, as well as punishment for human rights violators. The Lawyers Committee for Human Rights, for example, sponsored a fact-finding mission in 1985 to study human rights abuses against black children in South Africa. Its findings, published in the book, *The War Against Children: South Africa's Youngest Victims*, document the repression and violence used by the state against young people, and calls for stronger U.S. government sanctions against the apartheid regime.

One example of how the human rights law works for the poor in our own country comes from Sandra Coliver, a founding member of Human Rights Advocates, an organization providing resources to lawyers defending human rights cases in the United States. "One dramatic illustration of the use of international human rights law came about in 1986. The question raised by a certain case in Merced, California, was, 'Could a county cut back its welfare payments?' The court in Merced looked to international standards of what are considered basic needs, and ruled that Merced could not make the planned welfare cuts because it would reduce the standard of living for people to a level below these standards.

"Dozens of cities and countries around the world have incorporated human rights laws into their constitutions. One reason why [former Philippines President] Marcos doesn't want to stay in the United States is because we have precedents for being able to try him for his human rights violations in the Philippines."

But to believe that only lawyers can understand human rights—let alone defend them—would be a serious mistake. "What strengthens human rights is the mobilization of public pressure," says Sandra Coliver. "The grassroots campaigns on behalf of prisoners in the United States and other countries will tip the scales in favor of human rights. Economic and political oppression are the common enemies of all of us, whether in the advanced industrialized countries or in the Third World. We must therefore all begin to speak the same language, educating others about human rights, and actively working to make our voices heard."

Defending Individual Victims

No professional or grassroots organization in the world takes on the defense of all human rights at once. Amnesty International was founded in 1961, and is presently the largest human rights organization in the world. Amnesty's piece of the picture is very specific: it safeguards the rights of political prisoners, regardless of race, class, or politics. Amnesty seeks the release of prisoners of conscience, advocates fair and early trials for political prisoners, and opposes torture, the death penalty, and other cruel and inhuman punishment of prisoners. It works all over the world, not exclusively with the poor or in the Third World.

Since its founding, Amnesty has evolved into an international network of over 700,000 individuals. "The movement has grown tremendously since the early days," Curt Goering, Deputy Executive Director of Amnesty International's U.S. office, told us, "not only in terms of the number of individuals involved in international groups like Amnesty, but also in the number of indigenous human rights groups, working in their own countries to protect rights. Today there are over one thousand such groups, whereas before there were only a few.

"I attribute that growth to more and more courageous people standing up for their rights, as well as to an increasing awareness of the gulf between what the Universal Declaration of Human Rights says, and the way governments treat their citizens. What's fueled the growth, then, is a great deal of educational work, driving the point home to people in all political and economic systems that they have rights that should not be violated."

Letter writing is one of the most common forms of human rights advocacy on behalf of individual victims. As Ross Eccleshall, one of Amnesty's local group leaders, explains, "Writing letters on behalf of political prisoners is one way to effectively bring pressure upon a government to improve its human rights policies. It is an easy course of action for individuals wanting to improve the human rights situation for a person who has been arbitrarily arrested. It works, it doesn't take much time, it's nonviolent, and the protest exemplifies the freedom of expression citizens of every country should possess.

"We usually work for no more than two prisoners at a time, and we keep writing until they get released. In our community and in this country, we publicize the prisoner's case as much as possible, through country campaigns or issue campaigns, like abolishing torture. In the prisoner's country, we write to government officials, prison officials, the military, the judiciary, to labor leaders, to church organizers, to newspapers, to lawyers, to physicians—in fact, to anyone we think can assist the prisoner. When appropriate, we contact the prisoner and his or her family. We normally don't get replies, so after awhile we can feel disheartened and frustrated. What keeps us going is a strong sense of justice, and the knowledge that what we're doing eventually works."

Numerous other activist organizations work around particular countries—such as El Salvador, the Philippines, Korea, and Zaire—and see protecting victims of human rights abuses as one component of their work. The Committee in Solidarity with the People of El Salvador (CISPES), for example, is not an exclusively human rights-oriented organization but coordinates a Rapid Response Network as part of its broad mandate to support democracy in El Salvador.

On March 10, 1988, the Salvadoran Air Force dragged Humberto Centeno, a leader in the National Unity of Salvadoran Workers (UNTS), away from a demonstration in which workers were protesting the capture of fifty-three fellow workers. Centeno was thrown into the back of a treasury police truck, beaten, and hospitalized. The events that follow, as recorded by Sharon Martinas of CISPES, illustrate the power of a quick human rights response:[1]

"On Thursday night, March 10, 1988, the National CISPES office receives an urgent call from San Salvador. 'Centeno's been captured and beaten by the Treasury police. We're afraid they'll kill him!' The phones are buzzing—five regional CISPES offices are alerted as well as dozens of other labor, religious, human rights and solidarity organizations, supportive members of Congress and the national media.

"San Francisco CISPES, one of eighty Rapid Response networks in the country, goes into action: fifty telexes to El Salvador; five phone calls to the U.S. Embassy and Salvadoran military; fifty people mobilized within hours to demonstrate at the Salvadoran consulate; dozens of calls to local members of Congress and the media. Nationally, the network activates five protests outside Salvadoran consulates; a hundred phone calls to El Salvador; a hundred telexes; and sixty-five calls to congressional offices—all within twenty-four hours!

"Meanwhile, on Friday morning in San Salvador, thousands of workers demonstrated, defying police tear gas and bullets to demand Centeno's freedom. By Saturday afternoon, the phones were abuzz again with the news: Centeno was free!

"Although the repression in El Salvador is escalating, our work makes a difference. From January through March of 1988, the national CISPES office received information about 101 incidents of human rights violations, almost all involving more than one person. The Rapid Response Networks were activated sixteen times. Of the seventy-five people whose captures we protested, forty-eight were released, five imprisoned, three disappeared, and the whereabouts of nineteen are unknown. Our most successful efforts are for urban activists, for whom there are internationally coordinated forms of rapid response.

"We are less successful, however, in stopping military encirclement and denial of humanitarian aid to displaced and repopulated communities in rural areas, where fast international communication is prevented by the U.S. and Salvadoran governments.

"Can Rapid Response stop the death squads? Realistically, no. But who knows how many assassinations have been prevented by our relentless protest? The military high command has asserted that it will kill 300,000 if that's what it takes to stop the revolution. Facing that kind of will to slaughter, every life we save is a precious victory."

What About Individuals Who Advocate Violence?

One of the dilemmas facing groups doing human rights work on behalf of individuals is how to handle the cases of persons who advocate violence. Amnesty International chooses not to work for the release of individuals who have advocated or used violence against the state, even in the most repressive countries in the world. For this reason, Amnesty is sometimes criticized for not taking strong enough stands in nations such as South Africa or El Salvador. But as Amnesty's national refugee program coordinator Nick Rizza explains, the line is not always easy to draw.

"We are best known for our work on behalf of prisoners of conscience—Lech Walesa, Andrei Sakharov—but we are sometimes criticized when people do not realize the other groups we work for as well. Political prisoners who have used or advocated violence to overthrow a government are also part of our mandate. For these people, we advocate fair and prompt trials. We cannot pretend that governments do not have the right to imprison people who shoot at them. However, we can pressure that they be treated fairly.

"Where we get into sticky situations is in countries which have adopted a broad definition of actions that advocate the over-throw of the government. For instance, we differ with the gov-ernments of Israel and Nicaragua on whether simply being a member of the Palestine Liberation Organization or the contras, respectively, constitutes intent to overthrow the government, even if the individual has not committed any violent acts. We have been criticized for not advocating the release of Nelson Mandela, leader of the African National Congress (ANC), who has been in prison in South Africa for over twenty-five years. We can't work for his release because we do not take up cases of in-dividuals who advocate violence. But we do work to prevent his mistreatment in jail. During Winnie Mandela's periods of con-finement, we work for her release. Obviously there are gray areas, where people may feel we draw tough lines."

Local group leader Ross Eccleshall supports Amnesty's stand on the issue of violence. "We cannot be construed as advocating the overthrow of a government or being tools of a political or-ganization, whether it be a particular party, the CIA, KGB, or any other," says Ross. "This way, we hope that governments respect our work for being evenhanded and impartial."

Groups like TransAfrica, the American Committee on Africa and the Washington Office on Africa, on the other hand, main-tain a broader definition of political prisoners. "We see the work of Amnesty as very useful," says Cecilie Blakey of TransAfrica. "Their narrow definition of political prisoners, and their use of this definition across the board, gives them legitimacy that even some of the most conservative Congressmen like Jesse Helms would have a hard time arguing with. But we at TransAfrica have different ways of defining political prisoners and human rights abuses. We recognize the legitimacy of armed struggle to over-throw repressive regimes, just as people in this country took up arms two hundred years ago. So in the case of South Africa, we fully support Nelson Mandela and all other political prisoners fighting to overthrow apartheid."

Renata Eustis, a member of the Network in Solidarity with the People of Guatemala's (NISGUA) human rights campaign, ex-presses a similar view. "While we do not advocate the use of violence, in a place like Guatemala the term 'nonviolent' takes on a precarious meaning. The more I learned about Guatemalan history, the more I saw how the violence of the U.S. military has been involved in destroying what human rights existed. NISGUA works on many of the same issues as Amnesty would, and we employ similar methods. But our understanding of Guatemala has brought us to a point where we also support the different forms of struggle undertaken by the Guatemalan people, and that includes the legitimacy of the armed struggle."

Support for Indigenous Human Rights Organizations

Perhaps equally as important as working on behalf of individuals in foreign countries is strengthening a group's capacity to monitor human rights within its own country. In 1975, representatives from thirty-five nations came together to sign the Helsinki Accords. The Accords gave human rights issues a prominence in international relations that was lacking previously, and provided human rights advocates with a standard by which to measure the performance of their own and other countries. The Accords also stated that citizens have the right to know about and act upon violations of their rights within their own countries.

In the spirit of the Helsinki Accords, Helsinki Watch began in 1979 as a watchdog for human rights organizations in Eastern Europe, ensuring to the best of its ability that human rights monitors did not become victims of violence simply for their human rights activities. Subsequently, Americas Watch and Asia Watch were formed. In the works are Africa Watch and Middle East Watch. The Watch Committees have consistently monitored the freedom to defend human rights in other countries, and criticized U.S. foreign policies that perpetuate human rights abuses.

Another recent trend in protecting indigenous human rights groups is the physical protection of local activists through one-on-one or group presence. The Madres [Mothers] of the Plaza de Mayo risked their lives to protest the disappearance of thirty thousand men, women, and children during the reign of terror in

Argentina during the 1970s. Every Wednesday, the Madres marched around the Plaza de Mayo in front of the government offices, wearing white scarves embroidered with the names of loved ones, carrying placards with photographs of their children. The purpose of their march was to demand information about "the disappeared". From Canada, Sweden, the Netherlands, and other European countries came thousands of women to march with the Madres to show that they had international support and recognition, and to raise money to help find the Madres a meeting place to continue their organizing.

In the spring of 1988, at the height of Palestinian-Israeli clashes, the American-Arab Anti-Discrimination Committee provided scholarships to send U.S. teams of witnesses to the occupied West Bank. There, the teams talked with Palestinian organizers, health workers, and other residents, in order to take testimonies and provide more firsthand reports on West Bank human rights conditions to U.S. audiences.

Peace Brigades International (PBI) advocates and trains people for nonviolent conflict resolution throughout the world. One of PBI's tactics in the fight against human rights abuses is the personal escort. For three to twelve months each year, international volunteers (primarily European, but also North American) form teams of unarmed escorts and accompany members of local human rights commissions in El Salvador and Guatemala. They hope that just the presence of international observers will deter the death squads and military assassins. It's risky, but volunteers know that their protection lies in the repercussions— dramatic turnarounds in U.S. popular opinion and U.S. policy—that can occur if they are injured or killed by another government's military.

One of PBI's first assignments was to work for the Guatemalan Mutual Support Group (GAM) as a shield against attacks by government security forces. The GAM was organized in 1984 to provide information and support to some two thousand relatives of the disappeared in Guatemala. According to Chip Coffman, a member of one of PBI's escort teams, the GAM began to suffer the murder, torture, and disappearance of its leaders almost immediately after it was founded. But since the 1986 arrival of the PBI escort service, not one more person has been killed, though the threats to the GAM continue on a daily basis. "The experience can get very tense," says Coffman. "But in Guatemala I found it to be extremely rewarding. The GAM is the first human rights group to survive in Guatemala, and our accompaniment is part of that success."

Since working in Guatemala, PBI's escort service has also branched out to include striking Guatemalan labor unions. The military cracks down hard on striking workers, but PBI's presence has at least offered witness and protection. PBI escorts create a zone of safety within which people can meet and open dialogue on more equal terms.

In addition to the Guatemala and El Salvador escorts, PBI volunteers monitor border clashes between Nicaragua and Honduras, and consult with groups in Sri Lanka, Thailand, and Big Mountain, New Mexico about nonviolent confrontation tactics. PBI recently received requests for help from South African groups, and is considering work in the Middle East.

The Marin Interfaith Task Force on Central America (MITF) is another U.S.-based group that chose to act directly in another country to protect indigenous human rights efforts.

In the summer of 1986, all of the members of the Independent Human Rights Commission of El Salvador who could be found were arrested and tortured in San Salvador's Mariona Prison. That same year, another member of the Commission toured the United States to raise awareness of the tragic human rights situation in El Salvador. Bill Hutchinson is an active member of MITF, and heard the speech at his church. "After hearing him speak, I felt I had no choice but to respond to his call for help," Bill recalled. This was the beginning of a long and true friendship between the MITF and the Salvadoran Human Rights Commission.

MITF responded by sending North American volunteers to San Salvador to ascertain whether the Salvadorans wanted someone to stay in the office. They said they did, and MITF has supplied volunteers ever since. "We took testimony from people about the killings and disappearances of their relatives. Some of the disappeared were campesinos; most were urban-based people who were part of some organizing work. Those who disappeared included members of other human rights groups, labor unions, farm cooperatives, teachers, and truck drivers. Some were even members of cooperatives set up by the Duarte government itself. We kept food on the stove for the hungry who came to testify. We also accompanied Commissioners on their work, in order to thwart any further attacks against them."

While North Americans joined the Salvadorans to keep the Commission office running, the detainees in Mariona kept working. In prison, they interviewed every political prisoner they found, putting together a rare, firsthand report. On September 2, 1986, MITF members smuggled the report on the use of torture in Salvadoran prisons out of the country and published it in the United States under the title, *Torture in El Salvador*.

The relationship between local human rights workers and escorts can be tense. Accompaniment can be nerve-wracking for North Americans. Chip Coffman of PBI explains, "Being a personal escort to members of a human rights group under attack means accompanying someone all day. You literally relinquish control over your own life." On the other hand, some Salvadoran Human Rights Commissioners have expressed frustration over their work being recognized only because of the presence of some North Americans. And the stipend MITF provides to its escorts—$300 per month—is double the monthly salary of the highest-paid member of the Commission.[2]

The glue that keeps both sides together is the realization that human rights work has often proved fatal. On October 26, 1987, Herbert Anaya, the beloved leader of the Commission, was assassinated while taking his children to school. He was away from the office where North Americans stay. No Commission member to date has been killed while accompanied by a North American. "We like to think the protection we're giving them is one reason they're still there," says Suzanne Bristol of the MITF.[3]

Supporting Economic and Cultural Rights

Other human rights groups support organizations of the poor in their struggle for economic and cultural survival. Few organizations currently use this specific focus on economic and cultural rights for their work, but those that do—Survival International, and the European Food First Information and

Action Network (FIAN)—play a vital role in keeping this area of human rights alive.

Rolf Kunnemann, the International Secretary of FIAN, explains why his organization works for groups of poor people in the Third World who struggle for land and labor organizing rights. "All human rights are indivisible and interdependent, as anybody who works with violations of any basic rights understands. Most human rights organizations work on civil and political rights, and try somehow not to take a stand on economic, social, and cultural rights. FIAN is the first human rights group working on what we consider to be the most fundamental economic right: the right to food.

"One success we had was when we, together with local groups, halted two government programs in Ecuador that were taking peasants' land away. We have also helped peasants in Paraguay gain access to land, freed rural leaders from prison (in the Amnesty fashion), and provided the formidable force preventing land grabbers from taking over Indian lands in Paraguay and Venezuela. Another problem we worked on—helping rural workers in the southern Amazon area of Brazil—has been solved. The farmers won land from a cattle rancher, which had long been promised to them under the Brazilian agrarian reform. The manager of the ranch has been arrested for crimes connected to harassment and death of the peasants.

"To achieve these successes we carry out three types of activities: urgent actions, casework, and campaigns. In urgent actions we write letters and do publicity around problems of the landless or hungry. Casework is usually follow-up on urgent actions. For instance, in a country like Brazil we intervene on behalf of people trying to farm on privately owned, idle land. The casework requires that we research the laws that already exist to support these actions, including international statutes, but especially Brazil's own land reform laws that have not been implemented. And campaigns follow up on the casework, to further publicize and educate about the people's rights to land.

"Ultimately, our measure of success is really the feedback and encouragement we get from people concerned—from the victims of human rights violations and their support groups whom we've helped. If they think what we do is useful, that's good enough for us."

Tying Labor Rights to Trade Relations

A new focus for international human rights work has been tying workers' rights to trade agreements. The purpose of this strategy is to give preferential treatment to those countries that respect labor rights, and to sanction those that do not. At the forefront of this movement is Bill Goold, a congressional aide by day and an independent labor rights advocate by night. In 1984 and 1985, working as an aide to Congressman Don Pease, Bill helped draft laws conditioning U.S. trade preferences on compliance with labor rights.

Bill realized that passing the laws was only half the battle. The other half was trying to implement them. So in 1986 he founded the nonprofit International Labor Rights, Education, and Research Fund, to spread the word about these laws and get human rights, church, and labor groups involved in monitoring compliance with them.

"These laws give us the opportunity to build a new appreciation of the common interests between working people," Bill explains. "Unfair labor practices don't just hurt the workers in those countries; they force U.S. workers to compete with foreign workers who are systematically repressed, which creates a downward push on wages and labor rights everywhere. Take the case of South Korea. By repressing workers' rights, the government creates an artificial comparative advantage. So we're calling for sanctions against countries which fail to live up to internationally recognized standards, as outlined by the International Labor Organization of the United Nations."

With these laws, private groups can petition the trade commissioner, substantiating labor abuses in a particular country and calling for a public hearing on the issue. In 1987, eleven countries were challenged on workers' rights grounds, with petitions filed by groups like Americas Watch, the North American Coalition for Human Rights in Korea, the Council on Hemispheric Affairs, and the Electrical Workers Union. Other cases against Nicaragua and Rumania were filed by the Administration and the AFL-CIO. Of the eleven complaints filed, four countries were subsequently denied trade preferences: Chile, Paraguay, Rumania, and Nicaragua.

"The Administration instituted the trade sanctions against Nicaragua on purely ideological grounds," says Bill. "It didn't have much meaning either, because there is already a trade embargo against Nicaragua. But it did have an big effect on Chile which, by losing trade preferences and investment insurance, forfeited about $400 million in export earnings."

One case was brought before U.S. trade representatives by Americas Watch, which requested a formal hearing on labor rights abuses in El Salvador. "We petitioned in 1987, but our petition was rejected," explains Holly Burkhalter, who works as liaison between the Watch Committees and Congress. Americas Watch decided to build its case before petitioning again. It produced a full-length report on numerous abuses in El Salvador, resubmitted its petition in April 1988, and is waiting to hear whether a formal hearing will be granted.

"El Salvador now receives some trade preferences from the United States. What we'd like to see is U.S. trade representatives sit down with the Salvadorans and say, 'Look, we've got problems here that need to be corrected in order for these trade agreements to be honored,'" Holly continues. "But at this point we don't know whether that will happen. Congress is supportive, and the International Labor Rights, Research, and Education Fund is effective—given its small, volunteer staff. But it's ultimately up to the trade representatives whether or not we'll ever get to testify to all of these labor abuses that we're seeing, and implement some action against the Salvadoran government."

In another recent action to tie U.S. policies to human rights, the American Bar Association passed a resolution urging U.S. policymakers to consider the right to food in all foreign policy decisions, including trade, debt service payments, agricultural development, and land distribution recommendations.[4]

The Sanctuary Movement: A Local Perspective on Human Rights

A very personal connection to human rights emerges within our own borders. Refugees fleeing political repression—from Haiti, Eritrea, El Salvador, or Guatemala—bring human rights stories to life. Organizations in this country help refugees secure their status, support them in their struggle to survive here, and work with them so that their stories are heard.

The sanctuary movement is one of the best organized responses to the needs of political refugees in the United States. It began in a formal way on March 24, 1982, on the second anniversary of the assassination of Salvadoran Archbishop Oscar Romero. Almost simultaneously, churches in Tucson, San Francisco, Seattle, Los Angeles, and Chicago declared the legal process of seeking refugee status unjust, and became Sanctuary churches. By 1986 the number of public sanctuary sites had grown to three hundred. For every congregation that publicly declares sanctuary, there may be ten others working underground. Some twenty-seven cities in the United States have declared themselves cities of refuge. The cities of New York and Chicago have urged non-cooperation with the Immigration and Naturalization Service by asking city workers not to turn over undocumented workers from Central America.

Sister Maureen is one of the coordinators of the East Bay Sanctuary Covenant, a coalition of some thirty sanctuary churches in California. "We are confronted on a daily basis by people seeking refuge—mostly from El Salvador and Guatemala," says Sister Maureen. "Last night at 9 p.m. a group of nine Salvadorans showed up at our doorstep. You have only to talk to these people, to hear their stories and see the fear in their eyes to know that they are fleeing persecution and need our help. We don't feel that we are breaking the law by helping them. We are merely upholding the Refugee Act of 1980 that states that anyone who enters the country and demonstrates a well-founded fear of persecution has a right to temporary asylum.

"But our motivation to help those in need goes beyond the law; it is a moral calling to reach out to our fellow human beings in times of distress. This is a sentiment that cuts across religious lines, and in fact binds people of all different faiths. In our group alone we have congregations of Catholics, Presbyterians, Jews, Baptists, Unitarians, Methodists, and Lutherans."

The one-on-one contact that the sanctuary movement establishes between Central Americans and North Americans can be a powerful experience. "I was moved to get more involved in sanctuary after visiting Central America with a church delegation," says Irene Litherland, also of the East Bay Sanctuary Covenant. "I saw how people were persecuted by the military, and how the United States was involved in funding that war. What I had known in my head I then felt in my gut. But for those who have not had a chance to go to Central America, meeting refugees can can bring about the same type of conversion. It makes North Americans not only want to reach out to provide the refugees with safe haven, but to question our government policies that are causing these people to flee. This, of course, is why the U.S. government has found the sanctuary movement so threatening."

Measuring Success in the Short Run

All human rights organizations face the dilemma of striking a balance between short- and long-term goals—between helping those who are in immediate danger and advocating policy changes that would affect the longer term human rights picture.

Sandra Coliver of Human Rights Advocates feels this constant tension. "I was talking with a member of the House Foreign Affairs Committee about his human rights program. He told me that his greatest satisfaction was working on behalf of individual cases—say, freeing one Soviet political prisoner. I was appalled at the narrowness of his vision, but I also realized that that kind of fast action on individual cases is sometimes what we need to keep going. It is an indicator of how powerless we can feel at times in this area of work. Individuals may be able to take credit for individual cases, but in the long run it is the efforts and change of heart of many people that will make the real difference."

Amnesty staff also feels this pull between the short-term achievable goals and the long-term solutions. "At Amnesty we never lose sight of the individual," says Rona Weitz, Amnesty's area coordinator for Latin America. "But say we take up a campaign to release a hundred prisoners and we get ninety-eight out. Sure it's a tremendous victory, but not if the next day we turn around and see that another ninety-eight have taken their places. Particularly in Latin America, we have seen this kind of revolving door, and have realized that we have to go beyond individual cases to tackle the pattern of repression."

This is why Amnesty has recently expanded its approach to include campaigns that cast individual abuses in a larger context. "Our first campaign was against torture," Rona Weitz explains, "and later we organized separate campaigns around political killings by governments, the death penalty, and disappearances. We are also now doing country campaigns. For example, we're starting a campaign that looks at three states in Brazil where human rights abuses stem from land issues. These new approaches have basically evolved from the recognition that short-term successes on individual cases are essential, but they're not enough."

Many activist groups have found that focusing on human rights abuses can be a way to move people to examine the bigger picture: why such abuses exist in the first place. NISGUA's Renata Eustis has witnessed this in her own work around Guatemala. "Guatemala is so far away from most people's everyday lives that we really have to personalize our education campaign to make more people aware of what's going on, and hopefully to get them to care.

"We organized a campaign in Los Angeles by setting up house meetings. People would invite their friends to talk about the situation in Guatemala. In particular, we would talk about the disappearances and the need to support the human rights work of the GAM. It has been pressuring the Cerezo government for information on the disappeared, and punishment of those involved in human rights abuses. The GAM's story is very compelling, it reaches people on a human level. We talk about what it would be like if someone in the room suddenly disappeared. How would we feel?

"What we found is that human rights has been a tool to get people involved in learning more about Guatemala. Of course our work specifically on human rights has been successful in itself: in Los Angeles we got people to write twelve thousand letters to President Cerezo on behalf of the disappeared. For people who were not really acquainted with Guatemala, they can't help but be touched and compelled to learn and do more."

The Long Term: Changing U.S. Policy

The Marin Interfaith Task Force hopes its work has both short- and long-term effects. "We work in the short run to offset the human costs of an undemocratic Salvadoran government," says Bill Hutchinson of MITF. "But in the longer run, we hope our efforts to bring news about human rights will lead to a wider recognition of the meaning of U.S. foreign policy in El Salvador." It is not an easy agenda, especially here in the United States, where the Commission's report on torture—with some testimonies implicating U.S. servicemen—fell on mostly deaf ears. (The report's blatant evidence of torture in El Salvador was later nominated as one of the twenty-five most under-reported stories of the year by Project Censored of Sonoma, California.)

Peace Brigades International also tries to build a long-term commitment to human rights issues. At home, PBI returnees share the impact that their trip had on their lives. "Our work does not end once a team of escorts comes home," Chip Coffman explains. "We do a lot of speaking, and we recruit new people to join the escort teams. If we do not speak out against the death squads, which are armed by the U.S. government, then we are complicit in the crimes against the Central American people."

The sanctuary movement, too, looks beyond the immediate needs of political refugees in assessing its success. Mike McConnell, who has documented the growth of the sanctuary movement, noted, "With refugees on their doorsteps, the terror in El Salvador and Guatemala is no longer a mere litany of statistics for North American religious people. They have been forced to choose between moral and secular law, and between the people of El Salvador and Guatemala and the U.S. government. That congregations have chosen to side with the Central Americans in Concordia, Kansas and Treadwell, New York, as well as in San Francisco and Chicago, indicates how deep and widespread opposition to U.S. policy really is.

"The objectives of sanctuary work now include opposition to the military buildup in Honduras and the efforts to overthrow the Nicaraguan government. Thus through the sanctuary movement, many have learned of the regional nature of the crisis and understand that the actions of the U.S. government are a continuation of a long history of intervention."

The Watch Committees also see changing U.S. policy as a central part of their work. "We try to make human rights more of an aspect of U.S. foreign policy," says Holly Burkhalter of the Watch Committees. "We have put together a committee of twenty-nine senators and 133 House members who sponsor specific actions on behalf of human rights monitors who become victims of violence. But we also play a role in the efforts to change U.S. policy towards human rights-abusing governments. The truth is that what the U.S. government does matters for human rights throughout the world, so we as Americans have a special obligation to keep working."

Robert Duval, a Haitian businessman and founding member of the Haitian League of Former Political Prisoners, knows the truth of the matter firsthand. "I am a businessperson, and my family has been in Haiti for over one hundred years," he told us. "The Duvalier government tried to force me into exile, because I was an outspoken critic of their policies. When I refused exile, I was tossed in jail for almost two years. I went from 220 pounds to ninety pounds while imprisoned. I saw 180 people die of malnutrition and other causes in those years.

"In 1977 I was released along with 103 other prisoners, when Jimmy Carter threatened to cut aid to Haiti because of its human rights abuses. But what happened? In 1980 when Reagan was elected President in your country, the Tontons Macoutes (Duvalier's police force) rode through the streets shouting, 'The cowboys are in power, the cowboys are in power!' and rounded many of us up again. If you Americans think that politics in your country don't matter to us down here, think again."

Holly Burkhalter's approach to human rights at the policy level provides a response to Robert Duval. "Recognizing that U.S policy in a country or a region may be one of several forces at the root of human rights abuses, we measure success in terms of changes that come about in our own policy, or how the perceived threat of a change in U.S. policy is pressure enough to affect change in a foreign country's policies. We have several recent examples from Central America. Publicity about contra abuses in Nicaragua became a prominent part of cutting aid to the rebels. In El Salvador, political assassinations have been reduced from thirteen thousand in 1981 to forty-five in 1986, in part as a result of U.S. government threats to cut back on aid if death squad activity continued.[5]

"Another example from El Salvador is the aerial bombardment of the countryside from 1983 to the present, costing hundreds of lives and displacing thousands of families. The Salvadoran government wouldn't admit to doing it. Through Americas Watch pressure and Congressional scrutiny, the Salvadoran air force finally admitted to the bombings. The bombings have almost stopped, but of course part of that success is due to the fact that so many areas have been depopulated. Keep in mind that in each of these examples, there are a variety of forces domestically and internationally that have contributed to the success of a campaign. Nevertheless, we see ourselves as a vital piece of the picture, working to make U.S. foreign policy more humane.

"It's also true that the administration in power can make a difference. Under Carter, Latin American and Caribbean countries were more carefully scrutinized with regard to aiding repressive regimes. Reagan has reversed all of that. On the other hand, the Carter and Reagan administrations—through the State Department and Foreign Service—have had almost identical positions toward Asia, befriending and aiding repressive leaders in Korea and the Philippines.

"Perhaps the most encouraging way to look at human rights work is to recognize that our job is to keep the issue alive, since there are no perfect governments. We must take on any administration, with regard to any group or country—the Sandinistas and the contras, the Duarte government in El Salvador and the FMLN. We never feel that our work is done, or that we're going too far.

"Let me say finally that the Watch Committees cannot take all the credit for the successes we've seen over the years in policy changes regarding human rights. Our work, Congressional support and action, and grassroots activism are equally important forces in pressuring for change."

The Future of Human Rights is Humans

Nick Rizza from Amnesty International reiterates Holly's sentiments. "What's most important is that the public be involved with human rights, since governments will always be imperfect and we can't rely on them to monitor themselves."

Already thousands of individuals are writing letters and telegrams, making phone calls, participating in fact-finding missions, hosting house meetings. "There's so much work to be done," notes MITF's Bill Hutchinson. "I recommend joining an existing organization, strengthening its work and learning the ropes. From there, other opportunities and needs become apparent. Those of us who aren't traveling to El Salvador help raise funds and write letters for prisoners. We also continue to do outreach and education in our community.

"We can only rely on ourselves," Bill continues. "We nourish each other to keep going. We develop friendships and become dedicated to working for what we feel is just. In this business, the bottom line is your heart, your faith, and your concern for other human beings."

Chip Coffman of PBI doesn't expect to see the world's human rights problems solved in his lifetime. But he does feel that he is part of an historical tide, keeping a check on the use of violence against people working for change. "The struggle for civil rights in the United States is an example of a long-term struggle that has its successes, but must also be ongoing. In international human rights work, we must consider our efforts over the long haul. Day to day we measure success in terms of 'prisoners freed' or 'decreases in killings.' But really we hope that we are protecting the seeds of change—the grassroots initiatives in which people take power and gain greater control over their lives. If we can give people some ground to stand on where they never had any before, there is hope."

Curt Goering of Amnesty International points to some long-term trends challenging human rights activists to work even harder. "Human rights is a harder struggle as the tools of repression become more sophisticated. We see indications in Latin America and elsewhere, where we have traditionally been effective, that governments no longer opt for long-term imprisonment. Instead they disappear or extrajudicially execute individuals who pose a perceived threat. That's a dangerous trend. We saw that happen to Herbert Anaya in El Salvador, to Hector Gomez in Colombia, and to literally hundreds of others.

"But on the positive side, more and more people are joining human rights groups and speaking out, taking over the leadership when their leaders disappear. Another encouraging trend is that young people in the United States are becoming increasingly more active. The number of high school-based groups has doubled; we expect to involve two thousand high school groups in 1989. Through this growth, and through the Global Concert Tour's highlighting the Universal Declaration of Human Rights, we expect that fewer human rights activists will fall victim to government repression.

"Human rights has a fundamental, central place in all struggles. We saw the power of increased awareness of human rights in Haiti, the Sudan, and the Philippines in overthrowing dictators. We also saw it in the case of Iran. Our hope is that human rights will continue to be a catalytic force for change in repressive governments all over the world."

Making Domestic Connections

North Americans may falsely assume that human rights abuses only take place elsewhere, far from our own borders. Discrimination on the grounds of color, race, and sex continues to be an all too common form of abuse. The gross violation of the rights of Native Americans is both an historic and ongoing blight on our country's human rights record. And if we agree that human rights encompass an economic dimension, then the lack of housing, jobs, and health care in the richest country on earth constitutes a flagrant offense.

The death penalty is another contentious human rights issue in the United States. While rights groups insist that capital punishment is "cruel and unusual," Congress recently enacted legislation expanding its use. Police brutality is also a common occurrence, and is particularly striking when police assault demonstrators who are simply exercising their First Amendment rights. In 1988, for example, Dolores Huerta, vice president of the United Farm Workers, was so brutally attacked by police at an anti-Bush demonstration in San Francisco that she suffered two broken ribs and a ruptured spleen.

Foreign policy that perpetuates human rights abuses overseas has concrete ramifications on democratic rights here at home. For sixty years, the American Civil Liberties Union (ACLU) has witnessed the connections between U.S. foreign policy and domestic rights. "One of the most striking recent examples is the denial of asylum for Salvadoran and Guatemalan refugees and the prosecution of U.S. sanctuary workers," says Elaine Elinson of the ACLU. "U.S. church people are being accused of breaking immigration laws, when really they're trying to help victims of U.S. foreign policy in Central America. Fifty percent of Nicaraguans who apply for asylum get it, while only 3 percent of Salvadorans who apply are granted asylum. If the U.S. government were to grant asylum to more Salvadorans and Guatemalans, essentially it would be admitting its mistakes in the region. So instead, the government prosecutes North Americans who provide sanctuary to political refugees.

"Foreign and domestic rights are also linked in the case of denying people visas to travel in the United States and speak. Mrs. Salvador Allende, Gabriel Garcia Marquez, and other prominent Latin Americans, for example, are denied access to U.S. audiences on the basis of the McCarran-Walter Act—which is in essence an infringement on our right to hear points of view that are critical of our government's foreign policy.[6] Another example was the group of Palestinians rounded up and imprisoned in Los Angeles. They were accused of circulating a newspaper advocating the PLO position. They're not in prison anymore, but their case is pending and they may face deportation.

"Over 120,000 Japanese Americans were imprisoned because of similar hysteria during World War II. The Redress Bill, passed in 1988, is important because it acknowledges that the U.S. government unreasonably denied Japanese Americans their civil liberties.

"The rights people take for granted here are very quickly undermined when our government needs to stir up support for its foreign policy abroad. These abuses not only open our eyes to conditions in other countries, but they also show us the toll our foreign policy takes on us."

David Lerner works with the Center for Constitutional Rights (CCR), a New York-based professional organization that fights anti-democratic practices of the U.S. government through the legal system. David Lerner agrees that working for higher standards of rights abroad is inextricably linked to strengthening democracy at home. "On one level, we care about human rights overseas for the simple fact that our tax dollars support torture and other abuses. In our name, suffering continues.

"But on another level, human rights abuses are not just happening 'somewhere over there,' but at home, too. Poverty, homelessness, and hunger are likewise elements of oppression that persist in the United States, even with our system based on democratic principles. We also experience limits on our rights when we speak out against human rights abuses. FBI surveillance of Central American solidarity organizations, and limiting the flow of people and information into the country through the McCarran-Walter Act, for example, is the flip side of funding the contras, or sending military equipment to El Salvador—policies that perpetuate human rights abuses in the Third World. These limits to people's economic and political rights in our own country are sometimes harder to see. Often they're not even viewed as abuses, but as aberrations or unfortunate outgrowths of our political and economic system. But they are consistent abuses, and part of the system.

"When we think of human rights abuses, we immediately think of Argentina under the junta, or of Franco in Spain, or some other dictator. But human rights broadly defined should ensure people of life, liberty, and the pursuit of happiness wherever they live. Our own Constitution falls short, because without guaranteeing housing or jobs, people are not free to pursue life and liberty. We need to keep pushing the meaning of human rights beyond torture, and beyond what's happening in other countries. We need to continue to identify the links between U.S. foreign policy, human rights abuses in the Third World, and limits to rights at home, in order to raise the standard of human rights for all people."

The bottom line for alternative trade groups such as Pueblo to People, whose San Francisco store is shown here, is not to maximize profits but to provide a decent income for Third World producers such as those making pots in Guienea Bissiau.
Photo credit: Jeff Walker (store), Medea Benjamin (woman)

5

Fair Trade:
Buying and Selling
for Justice

"I was in graduate school studying music in Wisconsin. During vacation my husband and I went on a trip to Peru. I'd only been out of the country once before, and what shocked me most about what we saw was how hard the women work. That's not to say the men don't work, but suddenly the old adage 'Men work from sun to sun but women's work is never done' took on new meaning.

"One day in Cuzco—which is this breathtaking site of the old Incan ruins—I suddenly had what I thought was the most brilliant idea in the world. I'd import some of the beautiful clothing and crafts the Peruvian women made, sell them in the United States, and send the money back down to the women. At the same time, the crafts would be an entree for me to talk to Americans about the lives of Third World women.

"When I returned to the United States and did some homework, I discovered that there were already a number of groups doing the same thing in other countries. Tapping into their expertise and experience, in 1986 I set up the People's Exchange International."
—Jessica Lindner

"One day I heard about a woman who was importing Tanzanian coffee and sending the profits back to the producers in Tanzania. It sounded like a terrific way to go beyond the charity approach to hunger by supporting fair trade. So I started going around to some of the larger churches here in Canada and encouraging them to do this sort of thing. They all said, 'Good idea, but. . .' or 'We'd love to Peter,

117

but. . . .' After getting a heavy dose of 'buts,' my wife—who is her-self a pastor of a small church—finally turned to me and said, 'I guess that leaves us.'

"So in 1981 we turned our spare bedroom into an office, our ga-rage into a warehouse, and our old beat-up station wagon into a delivery truck. By 1984 we were selling $500,000 worth of coffee, tea, cashews, and vanilla beans, and sending most of the money right back down to the producers. That's how Bridgehead Trading was born."

—Peter Davies

"I grew up in a small rural town in southern Indiana. I had a reli-gious upbringing and was always sensitive to people's needs, but my first real exposure to poverty was during the college semester I spent in Kenya. That's where I learned not only the outrageous extent of human suffering but also the systemic injustice that per-petuates that suffering. The other thing I learned was the incredi-ble power my country, the United States, has in the world. And this knowledge compelled me to come home and do something about it.

"At first it never occurred to me that selling crafts could be a ve-hicle for venting my outrage. I thought of trade as exploitative and crafts as apolitical and indirect. I was more fired up about direct political actions like divestment and boycotts—actions I still wholeheartedly support. But I wanted to do something positive that would give Americans a greater understanding of struggles in the Third World. Working with Jubilee Crafts, I realized that for the people I wanted to give a voice to, crafts could be a powerful mode of speaking."

—Melissa Moye

"As a Catholic priest in Holland, I had a lot of ties with the Third World through the missionaries in our order. But I later left the priesthood and went to work with the Eduardo Mondlane Foun-dation, a Dutch group supporting the independence struggle of the Portuguese colonies of Mozambique, Angola, and Guinea Bissau in Africa.

When these groups received their independence in 1975, they turned to their former supporters for help in their even more daunt-ing struggle—the struggle for economic independence. I didn't know the first thing about importing and exporting. I certainly was no businessman. But I also knew these countries were desperately poor and had few places to turn. Commercial enterprises were only interested in profits, not in helping these newly independent nations build up their war torn economies.

I was living in a houseboat in one of the Amsterdam canals at the time, and turned it into the headquarters of a non-profit import company called Stichting Ideele. Ten years later, with a staff of twenty, we were doing about $7 million worth of trade with Third World countries.'

—Carl Grasveld

J essica Lindner, Peter Davies, Melissa Moye, and Carl Grasveld are part of a growing movement for fair trade with the Third World. Their groups are known as Alternative Trade Organizations, or ATOs, and their goal is to create a more equitable system of trade with the Third World. For Third World producers, ATOs offer a rare opportunity to export in a non-exploitative fashion. It also offers them the confidence and sense of self-worth that comes from earning their money instead of relying on gifts or handouts. For consumers, ATOs provide an opportunity to support the poor in a way that goes far beyond charity, and to generate respect and understanding for people of other cultures.

Origins of the Alternative Trade Movement

The international alternative trade movement is an amalgam of three distinct trends. One is church-related, another is an outgrowth of development efforts, and the third is based on political criteria.

In the United States, the church-related groups are the oldest and largest. Two of the major groups are SELFHELP Crafts, which is affiliated with the Mennonite Church, and SERRV Self-Help Handcrafts, which is run by the Church of the Brethren. Both began buying crafts from European war victims after World War II and later turned their attention to the Third World. In

1987 SELFHELP operated 110 retail stores and SERRV was selling its goods to some fifteen hundred churches around the country.

ATOs with a development focus began in Europe in the 1960s. The first Third World shops—stores selling goods produced by Third World cooperatives—were started by the Dutch branch of the development group Oxfam. They later spread throughout Europe, Australia, and New Zealand. By 1987, Oxfam-UK, for example, was selling $14 million worth of Third World goods in five hundred retail stores. And Switzerland, a country with only six million inhabitants, has more than five hundred Third World Shops.

Jim Goetsch discovered these Third World shops while visiting Europe and brought the idea back to the United States. "It seemed like a great way to not only support Third World producers," Jim explains, "but also to begin creating a clearer understanding among the American people of the need for basic structural change in the world's marketplace." In 1970 Jim founded Friends of the Third World in Fort Wayne, Indiana and later helped start other stores around the country.

The third trend in ATOs, the political support groups, also have strong roots in Europe. One of the main groups in this category is Stichting Ideele in Holland. Stichting differs from both the development and church groups in that it does not work directly with producers but with governments. "We work with some of the poorest countries in the world," director Carl Grasveld explains. "They are poor for many reasons, but one is that trade has tended to work against them. For many, trying to make gains from trade is like trying to walk up a 'down' escalator. There is, however, usually no alternative to trade—apart from permanent dependence on loans and aid, and thus permanent vulnerability. Therefore, a number of countries are trying to put their commercial relations on a new footing by seeking new partners and a better deal."

Before working with a government, Stichting looks carefully at its policies to see if they are aimed at lessening inequalities within its society and providing its citizens with decent education, health care, and jobs. Based on these criteria, Stichting works with such countries as Zimbabwe, Mozambique, Angola, Cuba, Nicaragua, and Vietnam. Stichting has worked closely with a number of parallel groups in North America, including Bridgehead Trading in Canada and Equal Exchange in Cambridge, Massachusetts.

These three distinct trends in the ATO movement are by no means mutually exclusive. Pueblo to People, a Houston-based group selling food and crafts from Central America, focuses on both development and politics. It works with cooperatives to help them develop technical skills, but it also sees itself as part of a broader movement for social change. Jubilee Crafts, based in Philadelphia, combines the religious and political aspects. It is firmly faith-based, but it is also one of the most politically outspoken trade groups in the United States.

Compared to Europe, the alternative trade movement in the United States is in its infancy. "The European movement is much more developed, but it isn't necessarily a model for us," Rink Dickinson of Equal Exchange explains. "Europe has a long social democratic history, and ATOs can often get substantial institutional support. Stichting Ideele in Holland started with a big loan from a union. Traidcraft in Great Britain, one of the largest ATOs with a staff of over one hundred, benefits from government subsidies. Unfortunately, we haven't been able to get that kind of government or union support here in the United States.

"What's different about the United States, and ironically this works to our advantage, is that our government is directly involved in so many places around the world—but not usually on the side of bringing greater economic and political justice to the poor. More and more Americans are learning about that. Thousands of people have been to Nicaragua, for example, and now drink Nicaraguan coffee as a statement. There are a lot of people who are looking for creative ways to support Third World economies. That's a big challenge, but we're excited about being able to take up our small part of that challenge."

What Distinguishes ATOs From Commercial Importers?

While the philosophies and strategies of the alternative trade groups are quite varied, they share a number of characteristics which distinguish them from commercial importers:

- *Unlike other businesses, their goal is to benefit the poor, not to maximize profits.*

Most ATOs struggle to keep expenses and salaries as low as possible, so they can return the bulk of the money to the Third World. Staff members of Friends of the Third World go so far as to live on incomes of under $2,000 a year so they don't have to pay taxes that would support the military. Members of Pueblo to People work as a collective, earning less than $1,000 a month. "While we hope to increase our salaries as the business grows, we certainly didn't go into this work to get rich," said Jim McClure, who took a $15,000 pay cut to join Pueblo to People. Groups such as SELFHELP Crafts and SERRV keep their costs low by relying heavily on volunteer staff.

By keeping expenses low, most ATOs are able to pay their producers substantially more than commercial importers pay. Pueblo to People returns an average of 40 percent of the retail price to the producers, compared to about 10 percent for commercial retailers. Some ATOs buy from their producers at the going market rate, but then channel their profits into development projects in the producers' country or into educational activities in their own country.

ATOs also try to ensure that much of the final processing of the product is done in the Third World itself, so more money will remain in the producer country. Commercial importers usually reserve the labor-intensive activities for the Third World where labor is cheap, while the processing and packaging are done in the industrialized countries. In the case of cashews, for example, many U.S. companies import raw cashews from India, and then roast, process, and package them in the United States. In contrast, Pueblo to People helps villagers learn to do the processing and packaging themselves so they can double the value of the cashews. New Wind in Finland developed a simple tea bag machine so the Tanzanians it works with can export the higher-priced tea bags instead of loose tea.

- *ATOs see the education of consumers as an essential part of their work.*

Groups that sell through mail order often use their catalogues to explain where and under what conditions the products are made. Some groups, like Pueblo to People, explain the political conditions within the countries from which it buys. Jubilee Crafts goes even further, using its catalogue to call for a change in U.S. government and corporate policies that hurt the poor. "We want to present the crafts in such a way," the catalogue states, "that they might become a stimulus for Americans to begin thinking about the role that our life-styles and government play in keeping many people poor and powerless."

Some wholesale distributors put a tag on the product itself, explaining where and how it is made. The Boston-based group, Equal Exchange, which is a wholesale distributor of Nicaraguan coffee, sends out educational material on Nicaragua with every order.

Many of the ATOs sell at fairs, churches, and schools, and use these as prime opportunities to do educational work. "We see every sale as a chance to talk to people about what we're doing and why," says Melissa Moye of Jubilee Crafts. "Say I'm selling crafts to a women's group at a small rural church. The women are usually fascinated by the Guatemalan weavings, since lots of them do embroidering and quilting themselves and appreciate the manual dexterity. They're often amazed that people in these 'uncivilized' countries can do such fine work! From there I try to explain the conditions under which the Guatemalan women work. I explain how many of them are the sole support- ers of their children because their husbands have been killed by the military. I explain how many women can't do this kind of weaving anymore because they have been pushed into 'model villages' where traditional activities are considered subversive. For us, educating the U.S. public is certainly as important as sell- ing the craft."

Not all groups, however, take their educational role this far. "For some of the larger church-based ATOs," Melissa ex- plains, "it is difficult to have an educational component that goes beyond an explanation of who makes the products and under what conditions. They have a broad-based constitu- ency and can't afford to alienate anyone. While we are church- based, we are not church-funded, which gives us a lot more latitude in our educational work. We can—and do—discuss the political situation in the producer countries, the role of the U.S. government there, and what we should be doing to make things better."

• ATOs *often work with producers shunned by commercial distributors.*

"The people we work with are often the poorest, the least educated, the least skilled in things like keeping books and quality control," explains Jim McClure of Pueblo to People. "On top of that, we work in areas of tremendous social upheaval. The people we're working with in El Salvador and Guatemala, for example, could be killed tomorrow by their militaries. Who would want to operate under such conditions? It's certainly not the best atmosphere for maximizing profits, but it's under such conditions that you find the people in most need."

ATOs also tend to be more sensitive to the needs and problems of producer groups they work with. Randy Gibson of SERRV says that unlike commercial importers, ATOs work with producers to iron out problems rather than cutting them off if they make mistakes. "Say we start working with a new group in India that doesn't have experience in packing and shipping their goods. Well, suppose they did a lousy packing job and when the first shipment arrives, half the crafts are broken. A commercial buyer wouldn't speak to them again. We'd subtract the losses from their inventory, but we'd give them another chance. That's the difference."

Carl Grasveld of Stichting Ideele gives another example of how ATOs are willing to work through problems with the producers. "Before independence from Portugal, Mozambique was a large exporter of sesame seeds. But when the Portuguese owners fled the country, the machinery began to break down and none of the Mozambican workers had been trained to fix it. The seeds were not cleaned properly, and the commercial distributors refused to buy them anymore. So we began to buy the seeds and clean them in Europe. At the same time we helped the Mozambicans revamp the machines and train the workers to maintain them."

ATOs also work to strengthen the marketing capacity of their client groups, and they urge the groups to market through as many channels as possible. "Unlike commercial distributors," says Paul Leatherman of SELFHELP Crafts, "we don't care who else the groups work with. In fact, we encourage and help them to find other marketing outlets—other nonprofits or even commercial outlets. We also encourage them to sell as much of their products domestically as they can. We certainly don't want the groups to be dependent on us as their sole outlet."

Deciding Where and With Whom to Work

While ATOs are united in their concern for people above personal profit, they differ in the criteria they use for determining which groups or individuals to buy from.

Most ATOs prefer to work with cooperatives rather than individuals, but some will deal with individuals when they cannot find suitable cooperative structures. The People's Exchange International, for example, intended to deal solely with cooperatives, particularly women's cooperatives. But in some countries it found so many of the cooperatives weakened by internal divisions that it has resorted to buying from individuals instead.

SELFHELP Crafts, the Mennonite organization, strives to maintain the co-op criteria. But director Paul Leatherman warns that when you get out into the real world, you have to be prepared to make compromises. "While ATOs may have a list of 'ideal criteria' for the groups they want to support, few groups fulfill all the criteria. Many groups call themselves cooperatives—since they know that's what we want to hear—but they don't really work like cooperatives. They might have just one person making the decisions, or a few benefiting more than the others. We try to check out the groups as much as we can, using the contacts we have with churches or other development groups. We have stopped buying from a number of groups when we felt the workers were not treated fairly."

SELFHELP considers itself nonpartisan, and doesn't choose co-ops based on political considerations. "We worked with producer groups in Vietnam during the war and we're still there now," says director Paul Leatherman. "We worked in the Philippines under Marcos and we're still there. We work in South Africa and Chile. And we'd work with Nicaragua if we could find a suitable product to import. Our criteria is not what kind of national government there is, but the needs of the people."

Other groups, like Stichting Ideele, regard political criteria as foremost. Stichting does not work directly with cooperatives but works through local governments, and only with governments that have proven their commitment to the poor. If there are changes at the national level away from a commitment to greater equality, Stichting will pull out—as it did in the case of Sri Lanka and Madagascar. "It's impossible for us to help all the poor, everywhere," says Stichting director Carl Grasveld. "We must choose where to focus our energy, and for us it is on those countries that can provide some inspiration and hope for the possibility of a more just world. While in many ways it is more satisfying to work directly with the producers, we recognize the need to help governments struggling to build more equitable societies."

There are those who share Carl's political perspective but disagree with his analysis. "Sure, it would be great to only work with 'good governments,'" says Jim McClure of Pueblo to People. "And we're happy to be supporting Nicaragua by selling Nicaraguan coffee. But the reality is that some of the neediest people live in countries with repressive governments. In Guatemala there are some thirty-five thousand widows, over one hundred thousand orphans whose parents have been murdered by the military. So what do you do? Can you refuse to work with them because it's not 'politically correct?' No matter what the government, people need to eat."

Jim does agree with Carl, however, that it is impossible to help everyone and choices must be made. That is why Pueblo to People tries to work with those co-ops that are part of some larger social movement. They hope to strengthen not only an individual co-op but a broader momentum for change. For example, in Honduras Pueblo to People works with co-ops that belong to one of the national peasant organizations pressuring the government to implement land reform.

Where broad-based community organizations don't already exist, ATOs like the British One Village see the producer group itself as an agent for change. "What begins as a craft cooperative," says director Roy Scott, "can be a nucleus from which other community development takes place." Roy believes that profits made by alternative traders should be funneled back to the community to tackle wider community needs.

While this criteria of supporting cooperatives as part of a larger community or nationwide struggle seems straightforward, in practice it is not so simple. What if you are working with some terrific local co-ops, but the national group with which they are associated becomes co-opted? Do you abandon the local group because it is no longer a vehicle for larger social change?

Pueblo to People faced this situation in Honduras. "We'd been working with a campesino group for years when there was a change at the national level and some of the leaders were corrupted," explains Jimmy Pryor. "But we didn't feel we could abandon the villagers because of problems at the national level. Besides, we've learned that all campesino organizations go through cycles and that corrupt leaders eventually get replaced. So after much discussion, we decided to hang in there and hope for the best."

ATOs intent on strengthening popular organizing faces another critical dilemma. What happens if the groups they are working with become so successful at community organizing that they are seen as a threat by the powers that be?

Producers working with ATOs in Guatemala, for example, have been tortured and murdered by a ruthless military that labels all attempts to organize the poor as subversive. Some groups have pulled out, fearful that their work was putting the lives of indigenous groups in jeopardy and convinced that development efforts cannot thrive under such repressive conditions. Others have stuck it out, but with a much lower profile and extreme caution. Still others who left during the height of the Guatemalan death squad activities have trickled back inside the country to test the waters under the new civilian leadership.

Despite the risks, some ATOs argue that their presence is required in precisely those places where the social struggles are most volatile. "We work with political prisoners in Chile, Palestinian refugees in Lebanon, widows in Guatemala—people who face the fiercest obstacles," says Melissa Moye of Jubilee Crafts. "We understand the stakes, but we also understand that these are the places where we can have the most effect. Jubilee worked with political detainees in the Philippines under Marcos, for example. Years before the Philippines made the U.S. headlines in 1986, Jubilee was speaking out against Marcos and educating people about the tough political issues facing the Filipinos."

One issue on which ATOs are clearly divided is whether or not to trade with co-ops in South Africa. Some of the groups, like Stichting, insist that since the majority of South Africans have called for breaking all commercial ties with the racist regime, no Western groups should trade there. They argue that even though ATOs work with poor blacks and not with the government, they still pay export taxes that go to support apartheid. The same arguments that hold true for corporate divestment, they insist, hold true for ATOs.

Melissa Moye disagrees. "I have been very active in the divestment movement for years, and here I am purchasing crafts from South Africa. I've thought about it long and hard. I talked about it with the producers themselves, and even consulted with a number of South Africans whom I trust.

"What distinguishes our trade is that we work with people who are not connected to the government; in fact, they are people who are not just fighting for survival but fighting for change. The groups we import jewelry from offer legal services for blacks who are detained by the government. They also operate a cooperative black-run, black-owned farm, where people are learning the kinds of leadership skills they'll need for a post-apartheid system. And selling South African crafts gives us an opportunity to talk about South Africa. For us, divestment is much more important than selling crafts, but selling the crafts gives us the chance to urge Americans to work for divestment."

Regardless of where they stand on this issue, most ATOs agree that an ideal way to support the victims of apartheid, while avoiding the dilemma of working directly in South Africa, is to work with South Africa's majority-ruled neighbors. Jubilee trades with groups in Zimbabwe, Zambia, and Botswana, and is anxious to forge links with Mozambique, a nation under constant attack from South African-sponsored aggression. Friends of the Third World has taken the initiative to educate other U.S. groups on the situation in southern Africa and made increased trade with the area a special focus of the 1988 ATO conference.

European ATOs have gone much further, putting pressure on their governments to allocate substantial resources to the countries of southern Africa. Stichting Ideele is at the forefront of the push in Holland. "We are trying to get the Dutch government to promote trade between the nine members of SADCC, the Southern African Development Coordination Conference," says

Carl Grasveld. "Right now it is easier for the southern African countries to trade with Europe than with each other. So we are trying to help build up the infrastructure needed to strengthen intraregional trade. We are also trying to find substitutes for products that the southern African countries are currently getting from South Africa."

Working With Third World Governments

ATOs that have chosen to work directly with Third World governments have had their share of trials and tribulations. Most revolutionary governments have suffered brutal civil wars which, coupled with their colonial legacies, leave a dearth of skilled labor, crumbling infrastructures, and depleted government coffers.

Trade with countries like Mozambique, Angola, and Nicaragua is further complicated by unrelenting sabotage from within and abroad. Stichting's Director, Carl Grasveld, gives an example. "We were asked by the Mozambican government to help it export oranges to Europe. We agreed, but the only way to ship the oranges from Mozambique to Western Europe was through the port of Durban in South Africa. South Africa saw Mozambique's efforts to break into the Western European market as competing with its own citrus exports, and held the shipment in the port for three months before sending the rotten load on to Europe.

"Although it was more expensive, our only other choice was to send the oranges by plane to Paris, and then pick them up in our truck and take them to Holland. In Holland, we marketed the oranges as a socially just alternative to South African oranges, and we found that consumers were quite willing to pay a bit more for them. The first five loads they sent were great. But the quality of the sixth load was very poor. 'Well,' we thought, 'they must have had some temporary technical problem.' The seventh load was even worse, so we had to go to Mozambique to find out what was happening.

"It turned out that the technicians in charge of quality control were all South Africans, and they had been giving a Grade AA stamp to third or fourth quality oranges as a way to sabotage the operation. We finally straightened things out, but it took much more time and expense than a commercial distributor would ever agree to absorb."

For U.S. ATOs, working in countries at odds with the U.S. government poses problems of a different nature. Take the case of Nicaraguan coffee. In 1985, Friends of the Third World and other U.S. ATOs got together to buy Nicaraguan coffee. They had just bought their first load when the United States imposed a trade embargo, making it illegal to import directly from Nicaragua. To comply with the terms of the embargo, the ATOs were forced to import Nicaraguan coffee that was roasted, processed, and packaged outside Nicaragua, since the embargo allowed for the importation of Nicaraguan products only if they are "substantially transformed" in a third country. U.S. groups turned to Holland and Canada for Nicaraguan coffee, a move that implied a substantial increase in costs.

In March 1988 the ATOs selling Nicaraguan coffee got another jolt when they discovered that, in the midst of the peace negotiations being held between the Nicaraguan government and the contras, the Reagan administration decided to try to tighten the screws on Nicaragua by broadening the embargo. When the ATOs learned that the Treasury Department was planning to ban all Nicaraguan products—including those like coffee that were processed in third countries—they sprung into action. "We called everyone we could think of—newspaper reporters, the wire services, our representatives in Washington," recalls Jonathan Rosenthal of Equal Exchange. "And collectively we stirred up such a fuss that the administration backed down—at least temporarily."

Asking the Right Questions

While ATOs see themselves as the seeds of a new world trade system, they are still plagued by the inequities inherent in the present system. For example, the world market prices for commodities like coffee and sugar are outside the control of ATOs and the producers they work with. ATOs are also criticized for trading products like coffee and caffeinated tea, which are neither very ecologically sound nor healthy for the consumer.

"We import coffee—and potentially other export cash crops such as sugar, tea, and cocoa—because that is what people have to sell," says Jonathan Rosenthal of Equal Exchange. "When possible, we will work with producers to promote a more balanced array of crops. However, at least until the long-term imbalances inherent in the current unequal international trade relations are rectified, the producers will continue to be dependent on the income from exporting those crops. Centuries of lopsided development cannot be turned around in a few years."

Stichting Ideele faces the dilemma of importing food from countries where people go hungry. "I know it seems crazy for us to be selling oranges and cashews from Mozambique while millions of Mozambicans go hungry," says Grasveld. "But Mozambique desperately needs the foreign exchange so it can buy staples like corn and rice. Besides, thanks to rebel attacks, the country's internal infrastructure is in such a sorry state that the locally produced food would literally rot instead of getting to people who need it."

Paul Leatherman of SELFHELP is sensitive to the criticism that its work reinforces dependency on foreign markets. "We do encourage the co-ops we work with to produce as much as possible for the local market. But the reality in most of the places we work is that people are too poor to constitute a significant local market. So part of our goal is to put more money in the hands of local people so they'll be able to buy more locally produced goods."

ATOs which distribute crafts face another dilemma: Are they contributing to the "bastardization" of traditional art? "The beauty of crafts is that they are a manifestation of traditional cultures. They are works of art, and no two are the same. But when you put a craft in a catalogue," says Jim McClure of Pueblo to People, "you then have to start cranking them out all the same. Otherwise the customer receives the product and says, 'Hey, that's not what I ordered. The tablecloth I ordered was blue and red and it matched my dishes. This one doesn't match.'"

ATOs have realized that the mass production of crafts can contribute to environmental destruction. "We were concerned that by exporting hardwood products from Central America we might be adding, in some way, to the region's already severe deforestation," explains Jimmy Pryor of Pueblo to People. Pueblo to People, therefore, set up a fund whereby profits from the sale of hardwood products would be donated to organizations working for the preservation of the region's rain forests.

ATOs face the additional dilemma that some of their products—made by people in poor countries—are affordable only to rich people in rich countries. "We'd like to support both the Third World poor and our own working people," Carl Grasveld of Stichting comments. "But some of the products we import, like lobster or Havana club rum, are out of reach for the Dutch working class." The same is true of Nicaraguan coffee which in 1987 sold in gourmet U.S. coffee shops for over $7 a pound.

Some ATOs are also trying to grapple with the "Third World here at home." Says Melissa Moye, "Jubilee Crafts now trades with Native Americans, Hmong refugees, Appalachian women, and black senior citizens here in North Philadelphia. We believe that ATOs should try to link with oppressed people wherever they are. The more we try to link issues and build understanding among people's movements, the stronger we will be."

It's not enough for ATOs to guarantee that producers get a fair return for their work. There are many more issues involved—environmental factors, the health of the producer and consumer, cultural and political implications of their work, how the exchange affects women's roles, appropriate ties between domestic and foreign groups. "New considerations come into play that just don't enter the picture when your sole concern is profit," Jim Goetsch of Friends of the Third World points out. "But what's so beautiful about this movement is that we're constantly debating these issues and trying to come up with new, innovative ways of dealing with them. We certainly don't have all the answers, but at least we're asking some of the right questions."

What Impact Do ATOs Have?

Total sales of the international ATO movement amounted to about $75 million in 1987, some $8 million of which were U.S.

sales. Given that this represents only a tiny portion of Third World imports of food and crafts, do ATOs really have much of an impact?

The impact of ATOs goes beyond the dollar figures. "First of all," explained SELFHELP Director, Paul Leatherman, "we work with groups that are too poor and unsophisticated to have access to commercial buyers. So while we may not be reaching large numbers of people, we're reaching some of the neediest. Secondly, by buying directly from the villagers and eliminating the local middleman, we often have a ripple effect by raising the price the middlemen pay. I've seen this happen in Saharanpur, in northern India, where our purchases of carved wood at 10 to 20 percent above the local price forced the middlemen to up their prices, too. So our influence is greater than the figures suggest."

Pueblo to People has witnessed the same effects in Honduras. "We're now buying up 30 percent of Honduras' cashew crop," says Jim McClure. "So the remaining 70 percent also goes up in value. And when we go into a Guatemalan village and buy a few hundred pieces of clothing, the producers are in a better position to demand more from other buyers."

ATOs have also seen that increasing people's incomes by marginal amounts can have a dramatic effect on their lives. In Guatemala, Pueblo to People is starting to foster the production of coffee and herbal teas—hibiscus, lemon grass, and chamomile. It's working in an area where farmers can't make enough money on their own small plots, so are forced to migrate to the coast every year to pick cotton and coffee, for low pay and under horrendous conditions. It is hoped that the extra income the farmers will gain from producing herbal teas for the ATOs will provide an alternative to migrant labor.

While ATOs are certain of having helped thousands upon thousands of Third World producers, they are also painfully aware of how much more they could be doing. In the past, many ATOs have been plagued by an identity crisis. While they were small businesses, they shunned the business world. But to really grow and help the greatest number of producers, they had to become more professional and "hard-nosed" in their dealings.

Equal Exchange, an example of one of the up and coming

ATOs in the United States, feels strongly about the need to be more businesslike. "The three of us who founded Equal Exchange previously worked at a cooperative food warehouse that distributed food to over 450 co-ops in the Northeast," Jonathan Rosenthal explains. "Experience taught us the dangers of being lax about the business end. We may not be out to get rich, but we are out to run a successful business. And the only way to do that is to be aggressive about getting capital, about marketing, about advertising.

Stichting Ideele also sees the need for expanding and professionalizing the ATO movement. Stichting itself is anxiously probing the possibility of entering into joint ventures with progressive governments. To get access to new technologies and markets, many Third World governments have to rely on multinational corporations, or, in rare cases, joint ventures with multi-nationals. But ATOs could forge a model for a new type of joint venture that would look out for the best interests of the producer country. Such ventures would enormously increase the impact of ATOs.

Stichting has begun such an arrangement with the government of Cape Verde in West Africa. Although it is an island, Cape Verde had no fishing industry. Stichting and the government of Cape Verde have started a tuna business in which the government owns 51 percent and Stichting 49 percent. Unlike relationships in which the multi-nationals call all the shots, this type of joint venture is based on equality. The contract states that in ten to fifteen years Stichting will sell its shares to Cape Verde at their present value plus inflation. It also states that all profits are to be reinvested in the business. The three-person board of directors is comprised of one government representative, one representative from Stichting, and one representative of the Cape Verde workers. It is a truly unique experiment that may open up an entirely new role for ATOs.

Stichting also feels that ATOs could significantly aid Third World countries in developing and marketing new products. "In Cape Verde and Angola we are helping to develop the fishing industry," says Carl. "In Cuba we are helping to link some products—from rum to candy to lobsters—with commercial distributors in Europe. In Mozambique we are designing new products like sesame and cashew butter. If poor Third World countries are ever to break out of the dependency of a few un-stable products, we must assist them in finding new ones."

Cooperation Among ATOs

ATOs are not anxious to imitate the cutthroat manner in which commercial businesses relate to each other. "We may be competitors in the strict sense, but we feel more like cowork-ers," says director Jim Goetsch of Friends of the Third World. "We're all aware that our goal is to strengthen the movement as a whole, and not to be the biggest ATO on the block." The groups are so concerned about networking that there is now a steering committee that organizes an annual conference where ATOs around the country gather to share ideas.

The mutual support among the different ATOs is unheard of in traditional business circles. SELFHELP and SERRV often swap information on the producer cooperatives they buy from. Friends of the Third World provides technical assistance to Third World Handarts. Jubilee encourages SELFHELP to strengthen its educational component. And Co-op America has created a national marketing vehicle through which many of the ATOs are already selling their products.

"The strength of this movement lies in its diversity and the fact that we're willing to work together," says Melissa Moye of Jubilee Crafts. "The groups that have taken marketing more ser-iously push the less professional groups along. Those who are in the forefront of innovative educational work are a reminder to the others of the key role education should play. Among us, we're searching for the right balance between selling products and selling ideas."

Helping to Push the Movement Forward

"I drive all the way across town to buy Nicaraguan coffee here," says Mary Baron while shopping in Pueblo to People's San Francisco store. "And whenever I have to get a gift—for weddings, birthdays, Mother's Day—I come here first. I figure the least I can do is spend my money where it's doing some good."

The most general way to support the growth of ATOs is to buy from them. Alternative traders—and their Third World producers—can only thrive if there are more and more educated consumers buying their goods.

"We have producers who could easily double their output," says Paul Leatherman of SELFHELP Crafts. "But we have to build up the demand first. We've been growing steadily in the past few years, but our limitations are still on getting enough customers."

The biggest boost to the ATO movement in the 1980s has been the Central American movement. Thousands and thousands of Americans outraged by U.S. policy in the region have been searching for concrete ways to both voice their outrage and forge ties of friendship with our Central American neighbors. By 1986, despite the U.S. economic embargo of Nicaragua, Nicaraguan coffee was the ATOs top selling item. As Rink Dickinson of Equal Exchange notes, "People know that every pound of Nicaraguan coffee they buy is in open defiance of our government's policy."

Even groups like SERRV, which do not see their work as politically motivated, have had a hard time keeping up with the upsurge in demand for Central American goods. "Two things have coincided here—one is the increased U.S. interest in Central America, and the other is the fact that Central America is a region with some of the most beautiful crafts in the world," says SERRV's Randy Gibson.

The challenge for the ATOs is to convert the new Central American awareness into a broader consumer consciousness. "We want to take those customers who are buying Nicaraguan coffee and get them in the habit of being educated consumers in general," said Rink. "For example, we are now beginning to import tea from Sri Lanka, and by doing so are supporting a large grassroots movement in Sri Lanka which works in poor villages. For some, it will take a mental flip to look at Equal Exchange beyond just standing up to U.S intervention overseas. But it's a way to broaden their understanding about economic and political issues that go beyond direct U.S. intervention."

But the alternative trade movement needs more than

consumers—it needs more people to get actively involved. Jim Goetsch of Friends of the Third World suggests that people interested in putting their energies into building this movement attend the annual ATO conference. It's a perfect way to meet the players, seek advice, and learn how best to fit in.[1]

Helping to sell ATO products is one way to get involved. Many groups, like SERRV, SELFHELP, and Jubilee Crafts, are looking for people to sell their goods on consignment at churches, schools, fairs, and community gatherings. "Some churches do an amazing job selling our crafts," says SELFHELP Director, Paul Leatherman. "One church in the small rural town of Fairfield, Pennsylvania—a church of only seventy-five members—sold $60,000 worth of crafts in three days of Christmas sales! That's much higher than most groups sell, but no matter what it is, every little bit helps."

For those interested in delving deeper, a next step could be setting up a retail store, and selling goods purchased from some of the larger ATOs. SELFHELP and Friends of the Third World, for example, encourage people to set up retail stores and provide technical assistance to develop sound business plans.

Kathie Klarreich, an artist from San Francisco, visited some Pueblo to People cooperatives while traveling in Central America. She was so impressed that she returned to San Francisco to open a Pueblo to People store—its first retail store apart from the Texas headquarters. "I can't say it was easy, since I'd never done anything like this in my life. Just when the store was about to open, I was struck by the fear that I had suddenly taken on this incredible responsibility without really knowing how to set up a store, how to do bookkeeping, how to get customers. I was so afraid I might fail, but fear is part of doing something new. Now that the store is open and thriving, I know it was well worth the effort. Just about every day someone comes in the store and says how glad they are that we're in San Francisco."

For those interested in ATOs as a career, Rink Dickinson of Equal Exchange advises spending some time as an intern with one of the existing groups to avoid "reinventing the wheel." "Then go out in the world, take what you've learned, and help push this movement forward."

The Time is Ripe For ATOs

In Europe an exciting movement is underway to unite the ATOs in a federation that would streamline their activities by facilitating contact with producers, reducing the cost of developing new products, saving money through economies of scale, and creating a banking facility for member organizations with temporary cash problems. The ATOs also envision that the federation would give them greater political clout to lobby for fairer trade at meetings of the General Agreement on Tariffs and Trade (GATT) and the European Economic Community (EEC).

The United States is also buzzing with ideas about ways to boost the ATO movement. Paul Freundlich is the founder of Co-op America, a mail order organization which sells a broad range of products made by socially responsible businesses in the United States and abroad. Paul has launched a daring proposal that calls on the various U.S. ATOs to collaborate in setting up a Third World trading corporation called Fairshare Foundation. The goal would be to create a national network of stores in every major U.S. city and a joint Third World catalog that would generate hundreds of millions of dollars in sales.

Paul sees Third World traders as part of a larger movement in the United States to create a socially responsible marketplace—a marketplace which also encompasses food and housing co-ops, employee-owned businesses, alternative media, and socially responsible investment funds. "Third World traders are part of a larger vision of a marketplace where consumers can find what they need and want—from food to clothing to daycare to health insurance—without sacrificing their values," says Paul.

"There's a whole generation of people who grew up in the 1960s struggling with a new vision about how the world should be. Some were drawn in through the hippie movement, others through the anti-war movement, others through the civil rights and the women's movement. But while most went back into the mainstream, they still yearn for something better.

"That's why I feel the time is ripe for alternative trade to really take off, because it's a credible way for people to state their values. It's a way for people to take part in designing a new type of society. Right now our society rewards the middleman—the banks, the insurance companies, the distributors. Up to a point, that's okay, because distributing products and services is useful in a large economy like that of the United States. But the power and money that has accrued to middlemen is not okay. Through Co-op America, we're proving in a small way that a 'middleperson' can serve producers and consumers, and the best interests of society—without compromising the bottom line.

"By building an alternative, we are challenging the basic economic assumptions that presently regulate our economy and world trade. We're creating an alternative that is accountable to workers, to communities, to the environment. And if enough of us support these alternative structures, who knows? Maybe one day we won't have to call ourselves 'alternative' anymore."

Dramatic street protests, such as this one staged by the Rainforest Action Network, can sway consumer choice and be a powerful tool in changing corporate behavior.

6

The Buck Stops Here: Consumer and Corporate Accountability

The twentieth century is marked by the astonishing reach of transnational corporations. Del Monte in the Philippines, Castle and Cooke in Central America, Shell in South Africa—all are examples of corporations based in the industrialized countries whose dealings stretch deep into the economies of Third World nations.

Some transnationals have become so omnipotent in the Third World that they can make, break, and shape governments. In 1954, the United Fruit Company in Guatemala orchestrated the overthrow of the reform-minded government of President Jacobo Arbenz. In 1951, after Iran's leader, Premier Mohammed Mossadegh nationalized the oil industry, the CIA—at the behest of Western oil companies—replaced him with the repressive, but pro-Western, regime of Shah Reza Pahlevi. In 1973, ITT and Kennecott Copper helped topple Chile's democratically-elected government headed by Salvador Allende and install the dictatorship of General Augusto Pinochet.

Why do transnationals—many of them U.S.-based—flock to Third World nations to begin with? Most are looking for a source of cheap labor and raw materials, and favorable government trade policies. Others view the populous Third World as a profitable market.

While foreign corporations can provide much-needed jobs, the trade-offs are often severe—low wages and benefits, no job security, and environmental destruction. Moreover, new jobs may be created at the expense of traditional livelihoods. The banana companies in Central America threw thousands of peasants off their lands to make way for vast plantations. Japanese fishing companies destroyed the incomes of small Filipino fishing communities. The introduction of U.S. clothing manufacturers in Mexico doomed thousands of independent Mexican seamstresses.

Transnational corporations have also been caught callously dumping banned and contaminated goods—particularly medicines, pesticides, and toxic wastes—on unregulated Third World markets. Many Third World governments, desperate for marketing techniques to encourage mothers, regardless of their economic means, to bottlefeed rather than breastfeed their infants. These techniques included free samples to doctors and mothers, mass advertising, and "milk nurses" dressed in professional-looking uniforms who visited hospitals and advised new mothers to bottlefeed. As women began to bottlefeed their infants, their own milk dried up. They became dependent on infant formula, but lacked money to buy adequate supplies and clean water to mix it with. Nestle's hardsell approach resulted in the death of thousands of babies in poor Third World countries.

The enormous international campaign launched to curb these practices made boycott history. At its peak, the campaign involved some one hundred groups in sixty-five countries. One of its greatest achievements was working with the United Nations to establish an ethical code for the promotion of baby formula. The World Health Organization (WHO) passed the code in 1981 by a vote of 118 to one, with the United States casting the lone negative vote.

"The passage of this code was an incredible victory. It set a standard by which all infant formula companies could be judged," says Nancy Cole of Infant Formula Action Coalition (INFACT). "But its significance went beyond the infant formula industry, for it was the first time that an international standard had been set to judge the behavior of *any* industry. That's why it was fought tooth and nail by not only infant formula companies but by others, like the pharmaceutical industry. They saw the writing on the wall and knew they would be next."

After reaching a settlement with Nestle, INFACT lifted the boycott in 1984. In keeping with the organization's mission to stop the abuses of transnational corporations, INFACT next turned its attention to what it saw as the gravest threat to global survival—nuclear weapons. In 1985 INFACT launched an aggressive campaign against the Pentagon's third-biggest weapons contractor, General Electric.

Those involved in the Nestle boycott, however, realized that it was necessary to continue to monitor Nestle's compliance with the WHO code. For that purpose, the group Action for Corporate Accountability was founded. In October 1988 Action declared that Nestle had failed to live up to the code and called for a renewal of the boycott.

There are about one hundred boycotts going on in the United States at any given time, although few of them are Third World related. In 1985 Todd Putnam founded the *National Boycott News* to document and publicize consumer boycotts. Professional in appearance, the newsletter is put out on a shoestring budget by a volunteer staff who have set up shop in Todd's apartment.

As a sophomore in college, Todd read all about corporate abuses—from the dumping of hazardous products to the overthrowing of governments. He was so shocked by what he learned that he decided to drop out of school and do something to challenge the corporations directly. "I was convinced that we could stop these corporations through an organized boycott movement," Todd recalls. "So I started the *National Boycott News* as a springboard to alert consumers to boycotts and their potential. Some people see corporations as insuperable forces and don't realize we can influence their behavior. We have to remind the public that we are the ones who put corporations where they are; if it weren't for us, the consumers, there'd *be* no corporations."

When is a Boycott Appropriate?

A few key questions help determine whether a boycott is appropriate. Is there a significant abuse that the company could correct if it wanted to? Is the boycott winnable? Will the elimination of the abuses in one company induce others to improve their practices?

People often have the misconception that *all* companies working in poor Third World countries are abusive and should therefore be boycotted. Todd Putnam insists that such assumptions are shortsighted and too simplistic. "In the case of Central America," Todd notes, "many people seem bothered by the mere fact that U.S. corporations are active there. They are concerned that the presence of such economic interests gives the United States further reason to meddle in that region's affairs.

"But many U.S. firms operating in Nicaragua have favorable relations with the Sandinista government and allegedly oppose any U.S. attempts to overthrow it. The Sandinistas, striving for a mixed economy, have repeatedly negotiated with IBM to keep its Nicaraguan offices open, and have occasionally allowed both IBM and Exxon to repatriate their profits in U.S. currency. Coke and Pepsi franchises employ a large number of Nicaraguans, as do other U.S. corporations."

So Todd suggests that before deciding to boycott a particular company, consumers do their homework to understand just what role that company is playing. Fortunately, there are now a number of excellent groups around the country which can facilitate that research, such as the Interfaith Center on Corporate Responsibility (ICCR) and the Council on Economic Priorities. Boycott organizers should also stay in close touch with the Third World groups calling for and/or affected by the boycott—labor organizers, consumers, and others. The boycott is essentially a response to *their* needs, not just a tool for Western consumer activists.

Another key question for determining the appropriateness of a boycott is its prospects for success. Some groups use boycotts to raise awareness but have little hopes of actually winning. Nancy Cole of INFACT disagrees with this tactic, and feels that boycotts should only be undertaken if they can be won. "Conceiving of boycotts as merely educational tools dilutes the power of boycotts as a whole. Sure, they are great educational tools, but there are a lot of other ways to do educational work. We should really save this powerful economic strategy for the issues where it *will* work. The other thing to remember is that corporations are now taking the threat of boycotts seriously. But if we undertake boycotts in an ill-conceived way, the threat will lose its sting."

Measuring Success

A common fallacy assumes that a boycott will be successful only if most of the population participates. While it's true that to win a boycott you need a critical mass of supporters, that critical mass may be quite small. Cesar Chavez of the United Farm Workers coined the rule of thumb that a boycott that garners support from 5 percent of the population is very effective. With 10 percent support, it's devastating.

Another fallacy is that the only way to measure the economic impact of a boycott is to see how it affects sales. Sales are hard to monitor because most companies do whatever they can to disguise changes in sales and claim they are feeling no impact. But more importantly, there are other 'costs' to a company that may be harder for the public to see but can be even more destructive than decreased sales. The greatest punch of the Nestle campaign, for example, was delivered in the slowing of Nestle's growth plans in the United States. The increased advertising budget necessary to improve the company's public image added further costs.

The Nestle boycott was so damaging that Nestle set up an entire public relations firm in Washington to fight it. The head of Nestle's Washington operation, Rafael Pagan, later established a consulting firm called Pagan International, Inc. to help "beleaguered corporations." John Mongoven is on the staff of Pagan International. "Very rarely is the impact [of boycotts] purely at the cash register," he says. "You have problems with employee morale. Employees don't like working for a company that is being attacked." Mongoven tells the story about a Nestle executive coming home one day to his eight-year-old daughter's query, "Daddy, is it really true you kill babies?"

"You have problems recruiting the top students from colleges and universities because they don't want to get involved in a company with that kind of reputation," Mongoven continues. "Also, you find that top-level executives spend an inordinate amount of time on the issue when they should be doing other things."

Sometimes just the threat of a boycott is enough to get a company to take action. Environmentalists were up in arms when they learned in 1985 that Coca-Cola had purchased thousands of acres of pristine rain forest land in Belize to grow oranges for export. (Coke was part of a deal that bought up one-quarter of all privately held land in this tiny Central American nation.) In 1986, protestors in Germany staged sit-ins in Coke bottling plants; Swedes demonstrated in Stockholm; and the Rainforest Action Network in the United States orchestrated a letter-writing campaign and threatened to launch a boycott.

"Coca-Cola is very concerned about its image," says Denise Voelker of the Rainforest Action Network. "They flew a representative over to England to talk to Friends of the Earth there. And when we threatened a boycott, the company's vice president came to a conference we had organized and announced that they would not use rain forest land to grow oranges. Not only that—they also announced that they would be donating some of their land for a natural wildlife preserve and contributing funds to a local conservation group."

But such successes are unfortunately not the norm, and most boycotts remain difficult to win. In fact, Todd Putnam of *National Boycott News* estimates that only about half of all boycotts affect a company's products or policies.

One of the major drawbacks is that boycotts are not a "quick fix." Because they take a long time to show results, the groups that call them often don't have the staying power to win. The Nestle boycott and the United Farm Worker boycott of California grapes took nearly a decade to have an impact. Corporations are well aware that people often get discouraged before boycotts become effective. They know that if they hold out, in the long term the boycott will probably collapse.

"When we discussed taking on the GE boycott," Nancy Cole recalls, "we were very clear about what kind of timeline we were talking about. We said it would take seven to ten years to beat GE. Well, that takes a tremendous personal and organizational commitment. Who in this country these days is ready to make a seven-year commitment to anything? So you must have staying power, and you must break the campaign down into short-term achievable goals to keep the commitment alive. You've got to realize from the start that when you're talking about boycotts, you're talking about the long haul."

Not only do boycotts take a long time to make inroads, but sustained victories can be elusive. This has been true even in the highly successful Nestle campaign, where a renewal of the boycott was deemed necessary in 1988 to force Nestle to comply with the agreement it had signed when the first boycott was lifted in 1984.

But a boycott against one company can have a ripple effect on an entire industry. The Heinz Corporation was only too eager to sit down with Midwest farmworkers, for example, after the farmworkers' union staged a successful seven-year boycott against the Campbell Soup Company. And the Nestle boycott certainly affected the marketing practices of the entire infant formula industry. The ability to control the abuses of an entire industry, however, must be carefully weighed before launching a boycott. Some skeptics of the GE boycott, for example, wonder how effective the boycott can be. Even if GE does stop producing weapons, might that only serve to make the weapons industry even more of an oligopoly than it is now?

On some occasions, the gains have been short-lived. A coalition of Australian workers and churchgoers launched a boycott against an Australian tuna company, Safcol, for mistreating its workers in the Philippines. The boycott garnered tremendous support among the Australian population by publicizing the plight of Filipino workers, thus forcing Safcol to improve wages and conditions. But the workers' hopes were cruelly dashed just a few months later, when Safcol closed the factory down.

Some boycotts not only call on companies to stop their abuses, but ask them to take responsibility for repairing the damage they've wrought. Environmental activists, for example, were boycotting Burger King to stop it from purchasing Costa Rican beef grown by turning rain forests into cattle ranches. (Burger King's purchases accounted for 70 percent of Costa Rican beef exports.)

In September 1987, Burger King succumbed to the pressure and announced it would stop buying Central American beef. But the environmentalists realized that they weren't really helping the Costa Ricans simply by stopping Burger King. The damage to their environment had already been done, and the watersheds and forests were sorely in need of repair. The U.S. groups discussed this problem with their allies in Costa Rica— environmental and small farm groups—and decided to ask Burger King for reparations.

"We're now demanding that Burger King donate money to Costa Rica's national park system," explains Denise Voelker of the Rainforest Action Network. "It's a way of saying to the companies, 'You just can't cause all sorts of damage and then walk away. No, you're responsible to do something about the mess you've made.'" Burger King refused to negotiate with the environmentalists, so in 1988 the boycott was reinstated.

An Empowering Experience

Despite the odds, activists insist that boycotts are a powerful tool we must learn to wield ever more skillfully. Todd Putnam is amazed at how many individuals who pursue progressive goals fail to understand their power as consumers. "I attended one peace conference where the keynote speaker hailed the successes of the anti-apartheid movement while intermittently sipping from a can of Coke Classic. [Coke is being boycotted by the anti-apartheid movement for its investments in South Africa.] We have to be consistent. We can't fight aid to the contras while drinking Coors beer on the side, giving Joseph Coors more money to buy contra bullets."

In a store, a restaurant, or at a potluck, Todd always looks for an opportunity to mention a particular boycott casually. "My experience is that when people hear of a boycott, they will always ask you 'why?' Imagine trying to bring up the issue of migrant farm workers and labor laws without referring to a boycott, much less trying to get the person to do something about it! At least with a boycott there is a set direction. You aren't left just saying something depressing or making people feel guilty, knowing they won't go home and write their legislators. You can educate and activate at the same time, without having to lecture and moralize."

"The beauty of boycotts is that they are very concrete, very tangible," agrees INFACT's Nancy Cole. "The other great characteristic is that everybody can do something if they want to, and everybody can do more. You can start by simply refusing to buy a product. Then you can go further and talk to your store manager about stocking alternatives. You can talk to your friends and convince them not to buy. There is a series of progressive steps you can take."

Because boycotts are consumer-oriented, the constituency tends to be more middle class and female. The Nestle campaign galvanized scores of homemakers and working women who'd never been involved in any political activity in their lives. Some would put a list of Nestle products on the refrigerator to remind themselves every week not to buy them. Others went a step further and got more actively involved.

Nancy Cole has seen many of these women transformed by their boycott work, finding personal strengths they never knew they had. "I remember one time during the Nestle campaign, we were trying to get Taster's Choice coffee (another Nestle product) off the grocery shelves. People were going out every day, meeting with store managers or leafletting consumers. There was one woman who had never done anything political in her life, but she was moved by the issue and decided to join us. When she was outside the store, the manager came out and tried to shoo her away. Instead of being totally intimidated, she stood her ground. 'No way,' she said. 'I have every right in the world to be here.' This time it was the store manager who was intimidated—so intimidated he didn't even call the police. And when she returned to the store a few weeks later, he'd changed his mind and decided not to stock Taster's Choice. It was a great victory for her."

Some people allege that boycotts are too confrontational, too negative. They say they'd rather be involved in something positive. Such comments make Nancy Cole bristle. "We don't have many tools that allow us to chip away at the structures of injustice. Boycotts can do that. In a society that works to disempower people in so many ways, boycotts can be an empowering experience. That seems pretty positive to me."

Union Solidarity

As transnational corporations extend their reach all over the globe, so, too, have workers begun to build transnational ties to demand better working conditions and the right to organize. In 1969, for example, British, Finnish, Swedish, and Norwegian dock workers refused to unload table grapes in support of the California farmworker boycott. When union leaders at the

Coca-Cola factory in Guatemala were gunned down by company thugs, the Geneva-based International Union of Food and Allied Workers launched an impressive international campaign which helped force Coca-Cola to the bargaining table.

Union solidarity is not solely from north to south: workers in the Third World have also taken enormous risks to show their support for workers in industrialized countries. In 1986, in an unprecedented display of international labor solidarity, more than three hundred workers at 3M plants in South Africa staged sit-ins to protest the loss of jobs at 3M's Freehold, New Jersey plant. According to Emma Mashinini, General Secretariat of the South African union, the layoffs and plant closure in Freehold were very similar to layoffs at three 3M plants in South Africa. For their support of U.S. workers, the South Africans faced arrest, loss of jobs, and intimidation, but according to Ms. Mashinini, "That's the price we must pay to show solidarity with other workers."

As a result of the South Africans' effort, 3M workers in South Africa and New Jersey issued a joint statement and a bill of rights for plant closings. The 3M New Jersey plant did eventually close and move. Freehold workers sought employment opportunities elsewhere but, through the organization Hometowns Against Shutdowns, remained tied to their South African co-workers. In 1987, New Jersey workers participated in a letter-writing and publicity campaign on behalf of Amon Msane, the chief shop steward at 3M's plant near Johannesburg, who was arrested and held without charges in South Africa.

Why should workers get involved in issues beyond their own workplaces? One response comes from the Labor Network on Central America, an affiliation of numerous labor committees in the western United States concerned about U.S. policy in Central America.

"The attacks on labor in the United States and other countries are closely related," says Fred Schwartz, a member of the Communications Workers of America and a volunteer with the Labor Network. "For example, many multinational corporations are shutting down plants in the United States to profit from cheaper labor in Third World countries. Conservatives within labor see the solution in protectionism. They support tariffs being placed on goods from other countries. They want to protect U.S. jobs by insulating U.S. workers and trade. But others of us disagree. Rather than support trade barriers, we seek to promote the conditions in places like Central America that enable people to gain better wages and more economic security. We'd like to see increased organization and unionization here and abroad, and increased wages. That way, we're protecting *all* of our jobs by bringing the people on the bottom up to our level, not simply protecting or insulating the people already on top."

Key to this strategy, Fred explains, is educating workers about their real interests. "We are saying that to provide job security here, you must ensure the security of all workers. The domestic economic crunch we are now in means workers need direction: we need to understand the obstacles we confront to keep our jobs. When the U.S. economy was good, some workers could be convinced that their interests were the same as their employers' interests, and that they'd benefit from sticking with U.S. policy as set by the government and the corporations. But when times are tough and these companies quickly abandon workers for cheaper labor in other countries, U.S. workers will not be easily convinced that they should align with their employers on foreign policy issues.

"Some union members still support the old guard AFL-CIO types. Their frame of reference is not to support unionism, but to confront communism. They accept a lot of information about which unions are communist and which are not, some of it from the AFL-CIO International Affairs Department, without checking it out. So we help provide an alternative source of information."

Reflecting on the goals of the Labor Network, Fred Schwartz adds a personal note. "I think it's equally important to include moral questions, and not deal only with the 'mutual self-interest' question, when you're talking about labor solidarity. Every week we receive reports of Salvadoran trade unionists who have either been arrested, beaten, or assassinated. Some of them are hard to believe, they're so gruesome. Usually, the victims' only 'crime' has been their willingness to speak out for peace and justice in a country where one is as scarce as the other. Can anyone, union member or not, read these reports and still only wonder, 'What's in it for me?'"

Exercising Shareholder Rights

Along with boycotts and worker solidarity is a kind of activism that works to change corporate policy from inside the corporate governance structure itself: shareholder activism.

A shareholder—and this can be anyone with as little as $20 or $50 invested in a company—has the right to vote on policy issues. Put enough shareholders together, and they can introduce resolutions to be voted on by all shareholders. These shareholder resolutions, which appear on a corporation's annual proxy statement, serve to educate shareholders and corporate managers about shortcomings in corporate policies and can hopefully change those policies.

Individuals can also become involved in shareholder issues through such institutions as churches, unions, pension funds, and universities. All are major corporate investors, and people connected with them can play a vital role in pushing them to sponsor socially responsible resolutions.

The churches have been in the forefront of this shareholder movement. Since 1971, their efforts have been coordinated by the New York-based Interfaith Center on Corporate Responsibility (ICCR). By 1988 ICCR was serving as a clearinghouse for 220 Catholic orders and twenty-two Protestant denominations and agencies.

ICCR Director, Tim Smith, has been working on shareholder resolutions for the past two decades. "The church's first resolution was by the Episcopal Church, calling on General Motors to withdraw from South Africa. In 1971 this was a very courageous action. People in both the business and church communities believed we were out of line challenging business. These first resolutions received under 3 percent of the shareholder vote, and considerable ridicule."

In those days, the notion that corporations had a "social responsibility" was considered incompatible with capitalist principles. Conservative economist, Milton Friedman, called it a "fundamentally subversive doctrine." At a stockholder meeting of Gulf+Western, chief executive, Charles Bludhorn, vehemently attacked the church activists, calling them dupes of Fidel Castro's Cuba. When ICCR contested Castle and Cooke's abusive labor practices in the Philippines, chief executive Donald Kirchoff labeled it a Marxist-Leninist front.

But the churches were undaunted, and the movement grew in size and scope. In 1987, for example, church groups submitted 165 resolutions, almost two-thirds of them about South Africa. They asked companies to stop all sales to South Africa and to withdraw and terminate all license and franchise arrangements. They also called on banks to end loans to South Africa.

Socially responsible resolutions deal with a wide range of other issues as well. In 1987 these included asking Exxon to prohibit further investments in Chile until the restoration of full democratic rights; calling on banks (such as Citicorp and Bank of America) to stem unlawful capital flight from Third World countries and to disclose "how social, economic, political and human rights factors are considered in making loans"; and proscribing Philip Morris and Nabisco from advertising and promoting tobacco in Third World nations, where tobacco consumption is growing three times faster than in industrialized nations.

It is one thing to sponsor a resolution, however, and quite another to win it. Because of general reluctance by investors to vote against management recommendations, it is virtually impossible to win a shareholder resolution that management opposes. The time it takes to get a resolution passed can also pose a "catch-22" for shareholder activists. For example, shareholders felt victorious when they successfully persuaded the U.S. company, Pizza Inn, to sign the Sullivan Principles, a corporate code of conduct for companies operating in South Africa. But by the time the company agreed to sign in 1986, South African activists had already criticized and disavowed the Sullivan Principles for not going far enough to strengthen black workers' rights.

Despite the odds, ICCR defends the resolution strategy as a hopeful one. The average vote in favor of socially oriented shareholder resolutions has risen from 5.4 percent in 1983 to 12.4 percent in 1987. ICCR also contends that the real impact of resolutions is masked by the voting record, because almost one-third of the resolutions are negotiated with management before they even make it to a vote.

"Since 1980, church groups have negotiated between twenty-five and thirty of approximately one hundred resolutions they file each year," Tim explains. "Negotiated settlements are a concrete accomplishment of the shareholder resolution process. Through them we have convinced infant formula companies like American Home Products to change their sales practices; we've gotten banks like Chemical Bank to consider human rights criteria in their international lending; and we've prompted pharmaceutical companies to stop selling hazardous drugs abroad."

In some cases, the companies have actually worked in partnership with the shareholder activists. Dr. Audrey Smock oversees investments for the United Church of Christ. She recalls that when Sears bought the investment firm of Dean Witter Reynolds, many church groups protested its new subsidiary's sale of bonds for South Africa. "At first, Sears would not respond," Audrey says, "so we filed shareholder resolutions. The company then agreed to undertake a policy review and, after the study, not only changed the policy but went further and asked the churches to help write the policy."[1]

Amy Domini, in her book, Ethical Investing, calls shareholder activists "corporate gadflies."[2] "The dictionary says gadflies include horseflies, botflies, and others which bite or annoy livestock," says Amy. "Critics claim that corporate gadflies are an ineffective, expensive annoyance. But over the last ten years, corporations have spent millions on lobbying, lawsuits, and regulatory actions attempting to limit the gadflies' influence. They must have bitten someone."

Divestment From South Africa

"In the past ten years there has been a fundamental change in people's conception of corporations, and the notion of accountability or socially responsible investing has become fairly mainstream," asserts INFACT Director, Nancy Cole. "The Nestle boycott helped, so did the United Farm Worker boycotts. But the real catalyst has been the divestment movement."

The divestment movement grew in response to a call by major black and nonracial organizations in South Africa to curtail all economic relations in or with South Africa. Divestment activists are unified in their goal to force U.S. companies to stop supporting the apartheid system, although they employ three

different tactics—divestment (selling off stock from and preventing the purchase of corporate paper in companies doing
business in South Africa); bank pressure (asking that there be no
new deposits or investments in financial institutions making
loans to the South African government); and selective purchasing (adopting criteria to determine whether a company's products or services should be purchased because of its ties with
South Africa's apartheid system).

This movement for public control over investment decisions
has its roots in the anti-apartheid movement of the 1960s. The
1960 Sharpeville massacre, in which South African police massa-
cred sixty-nine people protesting pass laws, triggered U.S. student, church, and community actions and awakened many
North Americans to the extent of U.S. corporate support for
apartheid. Religious orders and pension boards with shares in
U.S. companies began to question company directors about the
morality of such investments.

The divestment movement gained new momentum in the
wake of the 1976 Soweto uprising, a nationwide youth rebellion
that rocked South Africa. In 1977, the governing board of the
U.S. National Council of Churches called on private U.S. industries to end all economic collaboration with South Africa and
urged the churches to withdraw all funds from financial institutions with South African investments. Community activists,
trade unionists, and university students joined in the effort to
sever the U.S. links with the apartheid regime.

Milo Anne Hecathorn has been involved in anti-apartheid
work since 1973, and was coordinator of the $top Banking on
Apartheid ($BOA) movement in California. "After the 1976
Soweto explosion, U.S. banks began shoring up the South African economy to keep it from collapsing. So we started the $BOA
campaign to get individuals to withdraw their money from
banks with South African connections. We'd go into low-income
areas, for example, and leaflet outside Bank of America. We'd
give people questionnaires to ask the bankers about their activities in South Africa, as well as their redlining in local communities. And we'd give people a list of alternatives, like credit
unions and smaller savings and loans, where their money would
be better invested.

"The response was overwhelming, for it was very empowering

for people to realize they could have a say about how their money was used. Soon we began getting calls from churches, pension fund beneficiaries, and unions asking us which financial institutions should be used. So what started out as a campaign to advise individuals about their bank accounts grew into a campaign that even worked with cities and pension funds on how to invest and spend their money in more ethical ways. What was once merely a hassle factor for banks and corporations became a question of the bottom line for them."

Due to grassroots pressure, U.S. cities began to pass selective purchasing legislation. Willie Kennedy, a San Francisco city supervisor, sponsored one of the toughest pieces of divestment legislation. It prohibited the city from working with any bank doing business in South Africa, from contracting with any firm doing business in South Africa, and from buying any products from anyone doing business in South Africa. "I always heard that if you hit a man in his pocketbook it hurts the most," Willie told us. "I watched those South African children being gunned down on television. It was just hideous. Being black myself and knowing that what they were going through was much worse than what we went through in the South during the civil rights movement, I couldn't stand it any longer. I felt, 'Hey, we've got to do something to help these people.'"

By early 1988, laws prohibiting investment of public monies in South Africa existed in nineteen states, thirteen counties, and seventy cities. Institutions with investments totaling $500 billion—including states, cities, universities, churches, and foundations—were pressing companies to divest from South Africa.

But anti-apartheid activists soon realized that many corporations were claiming to divest but were continuing their business deals through other channels. While one hundred companies had sold their South African operations by 1988, many retained financing and distribution contracts, and therefore were still profiting from apartheid. In other cases, U.S. companies pulled out only to watch Japanese investors fill in the gaps and keep the foreign capital rolling into South Africa. Even so, the strength of the divestment movement in Europe and the North America had its own ripple effects: Japanese activists have launched their own protests against Japanese corporations doing business in South Africa.

"The great thing about the divestment movement is that it creates a climate of accountability," Nancy Cole adds. "It puts a spotlight on the usually dark world of transnational corporations. And that's the only way we're going to start seeing some real changes in corporate policy."

Socially Responsible Consuming and Investing

On the other side of the coin is a new movement to support companies with *good* corporate practices. "Perhaps there are no perfect corporations—completely nonexploitative, nondiscriminatory, environmentally responsible, democratic and charitable—with excellent union records," says Todd Putnam of the *National Boycott News*. "But there are certain companies which are preferable to others. These relatively good corporations are not only alternatives to the 'bad guys,' but a virtual vanguard for the movement toward economic democracy and they deserve our support."

The Council on Economic Priorities, a New York-based group monitoring corporate activity, agrees that it is important to give praise where praise is due. Every year it presents "Corporate Conscience" awards to the best firms (and dishonorable mentions to the worst). The Council has also compiled a consumer guide called *Rating America's Corporate Conscience*. The guide analyzes 130 U.S. corporations that dominate the consumer market, ranking them according to such criteria as investment in South Africa, weapons contracting, and labor practices.

Steven Lydenberg, co-author of the guide, sees its usefulness on two different levels. "On one level it can help consumers decide which toothpaste or which peanut butter to buy. On another level it's meant to sensitize consumers to the fact that different companies have very different histories and practices—and that we should be aware of those. We certainly scrutinize every aspect of a politician's record. So why not scrutinize corporations' records as well? Sure, it makes life more complicated, but it also makes it more interesting and gives us an immediate, everyday voice in how we'd like our society run."

For those who want to use their financial resources to promote a more just society, another option has become increasingly popular—investing in one of the many and growing socially responsible investment funds.

Some socially responsible funds—like the Pioneer, Dreyfus Third Century, and the Pax World Fund—have been around for many years. But ethical investing really took off in a big way in the 1980s, with investments jumping from $40 billion in 1984 to $300 billion by 1987. Working Assets, Calvert, Parnassus, New Alternatives—the list of alternative investment funds is now long and growing. Even individual brokers at such traditional investment firms as Merrill Lynch and E. F. Hutton have chosen to offer their clients some socially responsible investment services.

Socially responsible investing involves two complementary approaches: avoiding companies whose practices you dislike, and seeking out those with products, services, and policies you agree with. The latter might include businesses developing solar energy and recycling, or companies supporting community development.

Investing in your principles does not necessarily mean sacrificing returns, either. On the contrary—socially responsible companies often show superior investment returns. You also don't have to be rich to be a socially responsible investor. Some groups do require a minimum investment, but this is often as low as $500 or $1,000.

If, however, you can't afford such investments, you can still take simple actions like moving your savings account to a socially responsible bank. The South Shore Bank of Chicago is one example. It makes small loans available to low-income residents, and has a policy of allocating half of its assets to community development loans. "People who really care about the way banks use their money should go to their banker and say: 'I want to see the way you lend your money and where you lend it,' says South Shore Bank Vice President, Joan Shapiro. "Banks have literally millions of dollars—your dollars—that could be marshalled for alternative investments. There are over 14,500 banks in the United States. Just think what the banking industry could do with all those assets. But they won't unless they feel the consumer pressure to do so."

Part of the work to make international capital more accountable to local communities revolves around making more of it accessible to the poor. A unique innovation in U.S. lending to poor communities has come, ironically, from the Third World itself. The Grameen Bank, a bank in Bangladesh which lends small amounts of money (an average of $60) to the "poorest of the poor," has turned commercial banking on its head. With an amazing repayment rate of 98 percent, Grameen proved that poor people with no collateral are indeed creditworthy.

The Grameen model has spread not only to other Third World countries, but to the United States as well. The South Shore Bank has initiated a Grameen-type lending program and another model has been started in rural Arkansas. Muhammad Yunus, Grameen Bank's founder, hopes to see such banks cropping up all over the world in the coming decade.[3]

The significance of the socially responsible investment movement is enormous. Investment consultant, Jill Violet of Progressive Assets Management notes, "This movement recognizes that, like it or not, in our present society power is money. Up until now, the conservative forces have mastered the rules of the game and used them to realize their beliefs. We progressives are finally recognizing the power that *our* money can yield to realize *our* beliefs."

Pension funds are a good case in point. Public and private pension funds control enormous pools of money—about three trillion dollars in 1988 and probably as much as four trillion dollars by 1995! This is the equivalent of one-third of all domestic capital. The tragedy is that this money, which comes from workers, is controlled by management committees which invest it in companies that often have little regard for the workers themselves. "Think of the teacher or the nurse who works hard day in and day out to serve society, to instill people with certain ideals," says Jill. "It's his or her money that's being invested in companies that bust unions, tear down rain forests, exploit cheap foreign labor, or build weapons to destroy our planet. Think of the power we can wield once we take back control of these funds."

John Harrington, Director of Progressive Assets Management, agrees. "The crux of the issue is who *controls* capital, and how it's manipulated. When corporations raise money to expand their operations overseas, where do you think that money comes from? It comes from pension funds, deferred wages, money market funds that you and I invest in. We've lost control over our own money and it's now being used against us. We're essentially allowing our money to subsidize all the evils of the world. The key issue, then, is to gain control of capital. That's the whole ball of wax."

What is the Ultimate Goal?

All of the strategies discussed in this chapter—boycotts, shareholder activism, divestment, worker solidarity, socially responsible investing—are pointing in one direction: to redefine the very accountability structure of corporations. Ironically, this transition harkens back to our country's earlier notions about corporate rights and responsibilities.

Historically, U.S. corporations were public entities, directly accountable to local and state governments. Corporations were chartered to serve the public interest, and their charter could be withdrawn if that interest was not served. It was only a century ago, in the post-Civil War era, that corporate governance was transformed to include private corporations accountable solely to shareholders.

Now that today's corporations have so much impact on our lives—and the lives of people all over the world—such public accountability must be reinstated. Perhaps we must go back to the notion of federal and local charters for large corporations, spelling out their rights and responsibilities. And certainly we must strengthen government regulatory agencies so that corporate activities are carefully monitored. Another essential ingredient is greater worker control, through the worker ownership movement and such union gains as having worker representatives on corporate boards.

Working on all fronts—as consumers, workers, shareholders, and voters—we must build a movement that not only counters the most egregious corporate transgressions, but charts a new kind of corporate structure which is accountable to the workers, to the community, and to society at large.

Former Berkeley, California Mayor Gus Newport visits Palestinians in the West Bank as part of the growing movement to influence U.S. foreign policy through "citizen diplomacy."

Photo by Adam Kufield.

7

Government By the People

For the general public, U.S. foreign policy in the Third World conjures up images of U.S. military assistance bolstering democratic governments or U.S. economic aid feeding starving people. But North Americans who have had the opportunity to study or witness firsthand the effects of U.S. policies abroad often come away with a very different impression. Many believe that the primary goal of U.S. foreign policy is not to safeguard democracy or nourish the hungry, but to ensure the dominance of pro-Western regimes—often at the expense of human rights and equitable development.

The examples we discuss in earlier chapters represent alternatives to traditional U.S.-Third World ties. Through new trade and corporate relations, socially responsible tourism, human rights activism, more effective material aid, and so on, people have begun to create a framework for a new type of foreign policy. Our ongoing ties with Third World communities help strengthen democratic social change already underway, and enhance the ability of Third World people to keep more of the wealth that they themselves produce.

But there is a flip side to the coin. In order to support democratic social movements abroad, parallel efforts must exist to halt official U.S. government and multilateral policies that block the kinds of changes these groups are promoting—changes such as land reform, literacy programs, public health care, progressive tax structures, and initiatives to redistribute wealth.

163

Efforts to directly influence government policies are taking place on a number of fronts—from demonstrating against U.S. intervention overseas to lobbying against environmentally un-sound World Bank loans to pressing for the creation of alternative foreign aid institutions. Some groups work within the existing structures of government, pushing for reforms and improvements. Others seek to build entirely new institutions, better able to respond to the needs of the poor in the Third World.

Stopping U.S. Intervention Through Demonstrations and Civil Disobedience

Whether in Guatemala in 1954, Chile in 1973, or Vietnam in the 1960s and 1970s, the U.S. government has repeatedly shown its willingness to intervene in the internal affairs of other nations. Unlike the Vietnam War, in which the draft and the body bags provided clear evidence of the U.S. role, today's wars are primarily fought by proxies—the contras in Nicaragua, for example, or UNITA in Angola. Classifying these wars as "low intensity conflicts," the United States fuels them by giving training and equipment to the fighters. On the non-military side, it employs a variety of other tactics—funding civilian opposition groups, manipulating the media, dispensing "humanitarian" aid, imposing economic embargoes—to try to win the hearts and minds of the locals over to the pro-U.S. position.

The present challenge for anti-interventionist groups is how to make these "hidden" wars real—and objectionable—to the U.S. public. The most common strategies are demonstrations and other forms of civil disobedience, and lobbying government officials.

Street demonstrations are a time-tested method of keeping an issue fresh in the public mind. Leslie Cagan works for the National Mobilization for Survival and has helped organize coalitions for numerous demonstrations, ranging from protesting the wars in Central America to supporting the Third UN Special Session on Disarmament.

"Demonstrations perform three critical functions," explains Leslie. "First, they provide a vehicle to voice opposition and demand change, or to show support for a particular set of issues.

Public, coordinated, national pressure is critical. Even though we don't get a 'next day' response from Congress or the White House, we know they're aware of our position on the issues. Second, when we're able to break into the mass media—and we often are—we can help redefine national priorities. We believe that our statements help U.S. citizens rethink the issues of the day. Third, demonstrations really do serve to energize the front-line activists. Those of us in the bigger cities forget how hard it can be to educate people on the issues, day in and day out. So when we pull together a large group, activists from all over the country get a chance to meet other people with the same concerns and pressures, and they get a tremendous boost to their spirits.

"Of course, demonstrations are not the only way to reach people, and planning a demonstration carries with it a whole set of concerns. A major one is the cost. Should local groups spend the money to send delegates to demonstrations, or should they continue the work they're doing locally? Judging the timing and the best use of scarce resources is a challenge. We also face the challenge of bringing together a critical mass of people, or we risk looking like we have no support. So far, we've been successful in bringing out large groups of people in the New York and D.C. areas."

The June 11, 1988 demonstration in support of the Third UN Special Session on Disarmament is one example of the difficulties in achieving a balance between people and resources. On that day, one hundred thousand people marched down the streets of New York City. "Raising money to pay off the debts we incurred is our next job," adds Leslie Cagan, who coordinated the national coalition that planned the event. "Because it was an election year, we weren't able to mobilize the funds we needed, since many of our potential donors were putting their money into the presidential campaign. People gave us their physical presence, and turned out in larger numbers than we expected. But we're still looking for the funds to pay our bills."

Other people wish to make a more dramatic statement, and combine demonstrating with acts of civil disobedience.[1] Civil disobedience relies heavily on the persistent commitment of individuals to risk serious fines and prison terms to show their condemnation of government policies.

The Pledge of Resistance, a network of organizations that came together in 1984 to oppose the escalating U.S. involvement in Central America, believes that nonviolent civil disobedience is an appropriate grassroots response to government-sponsored violence. From unfurling a banner at the Iran-contra hearings emblazoned with "Ask About the Cocaine" to lying down on runways so military planes bound for Central America can't take off, Pledge participants continually risk arrest in order to raise awareness of U.S. military involvement in the region. When the United States sent thirty-two hundred National Guard troops to Honduras in March of 1988, daily protests rocked the country during the guard's entire two-week stay. In San Francisco alone, five hundred protesters were arrested.

Brian Willson is a Vietnam veteran and a founder of Veterans Peace Action Team, another group practicing civil disobedience to protest U.S. policy in Central America. Moved, as many veterans are, by his own explicit memory of the sordid U.S. involvement in Vietnam, he began formulating a response to the escalating U.S. intervention in Central America. "I had become intellectually curious about nonviolence—to find an alternative way of talking about peace other than through 'just war theory.' I couldn't see how we could get anywhere with military solutions," Brian says.[2]

In September 1986, Brian and three other veterans staged a forty-seven-day fast on the steps of the Capitol building in Washington D.C. to protest U.S. arms shipments to the Nicaraguan contras. The following year the Veterans Peace Action Team joined another civil disobedience group, Nuremberg Actions, in a vigil—this time at the Concord Naval Weapons Station in northern California. Their plan was to fast and remain on the tracks for forty days, hoping to stop the trains carrying bombs destined for Central America.

The veterans gave clear advance notice of their intentions to officials at the station. Nevertheless, a Navy train, moving down the track at accelerating speed, ran Brian Willson over, severing both his legs and injuring his head. Brian's amazing recovery and brave comeback as an outspoken critic of U.S. military policy in Central America is indeed an extreme example of individual commitment. His experience has succeeded in moving more people to make a personal commitment to change U.S. policy.

Since Brian's injury, the Concord Naval Weapons Station has become the site of a peace encampment, with protesters on the tracks every day to stop the weapons shipments. Concord also hosts periodic demonstrations, the largest attracting some ten thousand supporters. As a result of these actions, weapons shipments from the base have slowed from an average of thirty to two munitions trains per week, and there has been a similar decrease in explosives trucks leaving the main gate.

"We're going to have to start taking risks to stand up for the truth," says Brian. "Those of us speaking the truth are going to be intimidated, jailed, injured, and killed. But when you start living what you really believe in, the risks don't matter anymore. It's not that you do stupid things—in fact you do things even more thoughtfully and carefully—but you are pushing the system. You are giving those in power an alternative, which to them is perceived as a threat to their national security. But their national security is a threat to my personal security, and the world's security."

Civil disobedience provides a means for individuals to vent their disapproval of U.S. policy. It also serves to draw media attention, thus educating and hopefully galvanizing other individuals into action. But civil disobedience does have its drawbacks. There are just so many times the media will give coverage to protesters being dragged off by the police: after a while, the actions may lose their impact. Much time and money is also spent on dealing with courts, lawyers, and bail. And the risks involved often make such actions prohibitive for people with family commitments and financial responsibilities.

But Bill Nygren of the Pledge of Resistance feels that as one strategy in a larger movement, civil disobedience adds a much-needed, dramatic impact. "Civil disobedience has always been a major force in social change, like in the civil rights movement or the peace movement. It provides the 'heat in the street,' and we desperately need that."

Lobbying to Halt U.S. Intervention

Another activist strategy for halting U.S. intervention is lobbying Congress. Neighbor to Neighbor (N2N) was formed in 1985 with the goal of halting U.S. government support for the wars in Central America, particularly support for the contras in Nicaragua. District by district, N2N organizers set up lobbying networks to convert "yes" votes on contra aid into "no" votes in Congress. Unlike most lobbying efforts, N2N's strategy is not to work through high-powered lobbyists in Washington D.C., but through grassroots campaigns. "We reach people through local campaigns, including standing on street corners to get petitions signed, phonebanks, and TV ads," explains Robyn Macswain, a N2N organizer.

Kit Miller, also of N2N, adds, "The contra aid votes have been so close that even turning around a few votes counts a lot. But this kind of lobbying takes persistence. We know that we generated one hundred thousand letters in one campaign, for example, but we didn't see the representatives respond to the pressure for six months. Our goal is really to build a climate in which a 'yes' vote on contra aid is unacceptable to the constituency. But the real responsibility lies with people who write their representatives, and take personal responsibility for changing our foreign policy."

The Nicaraguan contras are not the only U.S.-supported guerrilla force. UNITA is another rebel group—in this case with close ties to South Africa—that is trying to overthrow the legitimate government of Angola. From 1986 to 1988, the Reagan administration supplied UNITA with at least $15 million a year in covert funds. Fearing that a new administration might cut off the covert aid, UNITA leader Jonas Savimbi came to the United States in July 1988 to rally congressional and black community support for his war in Angola.

The Washington lobby group, TransAfrica, mobilized all its resources to expose Savimbi's ties with the racist regime of South Africa. "When we heard Savimbi was coming to the United States, we called on leaders in the black community, mayors, and members of Congress to issue statements condemning Savimbi," explains staffer, Ibrahim Gessama. "Since it was the time of the presidential elections, we forced all the candidates to take a stand on aid to UNITA. We also targeted the media, and even managed to get our director, Randall Robinson, to debate Savimbi on "Nightline." It was an extremely successful campaign in that we exposed Savimbi for what he is, and under-cut his support in Congress."

Grassroots lobbying efforts have had a profound impact on another negative U.S. foreign policy—that of implicitly support-ing the white minority regime in South Africa by refusing to im-pose economic sanctions against it. In 1986, TransAfrica, the Washington Office on Africa, the American Committee on Africa, and others organized an impressive lobby to gain Congressional support for comprehensive economic sanctions against South Africa. The bill passed, and had such solid support in Congress that it survived President Reagan's veto.

The resulting 1986 comprehensive as is Anti-Apartheid Act was the most powerful anti-apartheid law ever passed by a U.S. government, and it was implemented by the most pro-apartheid administration in U.S. history. What explains that par-adox is the tremendous power of the grassroots U.S. movement.

Dilemmas of Washington-Focused Campaigns

Lobbying, civil disobedience, and other government-targeted actions are time-honored means for changing votes in Congress, and for opening up avenues of participation in exist-ing structures of foreign policymaking. But critics point to the "Washingtonitis" that often plagues these strategies. They con-tend that focusing on policymakers asks that solutions come from the same people who are causing the problems. Moreover, it allows the government to define the agenda, forcing opposi-tion groups to be reactive rather than proactive.

Many supporters of the group, Pledge of Resistance, for ex-ample, grew weary of being called out week after week for ral-lies and demonstrations. While the Pledge was initially set up as an "emergency response" system, Pledge organizers soon found themselves constantly preoccupied with responding solely to government initiatives. Thus engaged, they found it dif-ficult to build a strong organizational base or do the long-term planning that would allow them to address the full breadth of government policies. As a result, some Pledge groups aban-doned the emergency response focus, and took on issues like protesting the deployment of their states' National Guard

troops in Central America or targeting local military installa-
tions. Others looked for ways to form more positive ties with
Central Americans, through sister cities and other direct links.

An attendant dilemma facing policy-focused groups is the difficulty in keeping people involved once U.S. connections become less obvious. The defeat of contra aid in Congress in 1988
and the Arias peace plan made it seem then as if the crisis in Nicaragua had eased. Activist groups around the country had a
hard time convincing people that Nicaragua remained in deep
trouble and needed continued support. "Some think the answer
is to find other creative Nicaragua-related campaigns, like lifting
the embargo," says Bill Nygren of the Pledge. "Others say we
should go where the 'shooting wars' are, shifting our focus to El
Salvador. And still others are trying to find ways we can address
an even broader range of issues, such as the U.S. military presence in the Philippines, without losing our constituency or becoming too dispersed."

Policy-focused campaigns must be specific in order to be engaging. But building a successful protest or lobby may engender a
trade-off between short-term victories and long-term goals. The
narrow focus of government-focused campaigns often inhibits
people from seeing U.S. foreign policy as a whole and from working to change it more broadly. Anti-intervention groups have divided up the foreign policy pie country by country—hence the
Committee in Solidarity with the People of El Salvador, the Network in Solidarity with the People of Guatemala, the Free South
Africa Movement, the Washington Office on Haiti. "These groups
are really strong on the needs of one country, or even a region,"
comments Dorie Wilsnack, formerly with Mobilization for Survival. "Without them, we wouldn't see the debate on the U.S. role
in these countries to the extent we see it today.

"But there is a problem with these relatively narrow focuses, a
problem which becomes increasingly evident in these times of
heavy U.S. involvement in the Middle East. On the one hand,
you have a network of activists poised to respond to the needs
of individual countries. On the other hand, you have the U.S.
government, which is essentially carrying out similar policies all
over the world. We need to see more linking of Central American issues with South African issues, with Asian causes, and con-
solidate these efforts to support anti-intervention in the Middle

East, a region that is terribly underrepresented in our activist community. Only then can we move beyond reacting to U.S. initiatives, and reform foreign policy as a whole."

Finally, policy-focused activists grapple with the constant tension between the policies they'd *like* to see, and what is realistic to expect from Congress. The winter 1988 contra aid vote on $46 million for "humanitarian" purposes provides an example of how this tension can divide even the strong anti-contra aid community.

Some of the organizations in the movement, like the Pledge, remained adamantly opposed to any aid going to the contras, and urged their networks to pressure representatives into voting against the aid. But others saw the $46 million as the lesser of two evils, and supported the vote. They reasoned that if the Democrats' $46 million aid package failed, an even stronger Republican aid package would follow.

The $46 million package never did pass in Congress, and in fact was followed by another defeat by Republican aid advocates. But the process is indicative of how exasperating it is to play by Washington's rules. "This vote brought up the tensions that exist between groups that are driven by the grassroots and groups that take their cues from their allies in Congress," reflects Father Bill Callahan of the Quixote Center, one of the groups that opposed the vote. "The groups with a Washington focus accuse the others of being unrealistic. Their concern is to come up with legislation that has a good chance of passing. The grassroots groups are not as concerned with what is possible but with what ought to be. I think the lesson of this vote was to trust the grassroots. For, as we saw in this case, what ought to be is sometimes also politically possible."

Environmentalists Lobby Multilateral Institutions

Another group that relies heavily on lobbying as a strategy for change is the environmental community. Environmentalists have become involved in lobbying efforts to stop U.S. tax dollars from destroying the environment and the livelihood of indigenous people. These groups not only look at U.S. bilateral programs, i.e. government-to-government aid, but they also scrutinize multilateral institutions such as the World Bank and the International Monetary Fund (IMF). Since the United States is the largest donor to these institutions, it also dominates the decision-making process.

Both the World Bank and the IMF have come under heavy attack from development and environmental groups for fostering policies that exacerbate hunger and environmental degradation. In 1983, environmentalists launched a campaign to stop World Bank funding of the Polonoreste project in Brazil. This multimillion-dollar project, aimed at "developing" the agricultural and industrial capacity of the Amazon jungle, caused irreparable human and ecological damage. The area suffered from deforestation, invasion of Indian lands, and destruction of a biologically significant rain forest.

Through a persistent campaign of letter-writing, lobbying, and citizen education, an international coalition headed by the Environmental Defense Fund succeeded in stopping World Bank funding of the project in 1984. The group went on to stop the Inter-American Development Bank from funding a similar scheme in the state of Acre, in northern Brazil. The coalition also succeeded in getting legislation passed that requires the U.S. executive director of the World Bank to increase environmental staff, involve nongovernmental and independent analysts, and orient development projects towards respecting and serving local populations.

"These reforms are just the beginning," comments Environmental Defense Fund attorney and campaign leader, Bruce Rich. "Our long-term objective is to change the whole approach to development taken by the multilateral institutions, from capital-intensive, large-scale projects to small-scale, labor-intensive projects using appropriate technologies.

"The fact that financing of the Polonoreste and Acre projects was stopped shows that the banks are sensitive to public opinion. Citizen involvement in these campaigns, through letters to the banks and to U.S. government officials, is key to our success, and to the survival of indigenous rain forests and populations."[3]

Some activists remain doubtful about the effectiveness of such efforts to reform multilateral development institutions. They argue that the World Bank's environmental department is understaffed and underfunded with little decision-making power. They point to the Inter-American Development Bank, which has done virtually nothing to set up any environmental department.

Randy Hayes, Director of the Rainforest Action Network, is one such skeptic. "While some of our actions are targeted at reaching Congress and staff at multilateral institutions, we see citizen education as more important for achieving the kinds of long-term changes necessary for reversing the damaging effects of multilateral development projects.

"For us, the challenge is no less than constructing new institutions to replace the World Bank. It is no small task, but we hope that a new institution can be born which will really respond to the needs of the poor."

No small task, indeed. But Randy Hayes and fellow environmentalists are already laying the groundwork for a better bank. Working first through European Green parties and eventually with other governments, Randy is proposing the formation of the first Conservation Bank. "It actually wouldn't be a bank at all, since it would not be realizing any short-term profits. It would be a granting institution.

"We are asking that European governments pull their money out of the World Bank, and reinvest it in this new bank. Then, we'd like to establish guidelines for the use of the money. Fifty percent of the money would go strictly to conservation projects, or repairing ecological damage. The other 50 percent would go to support sustainable local development in 'buffer' zones around the pristine rain forests, to further thwart steamroller-type development. We'd also like to see that no more than 50 percent of the money goes to governments. The more that goes to citizen-led groups, the better. We may even want to work with groups like Oxfam, granting large portions of money to them to distribute to the Third World groups, since they're already involved and know more than we could about who's doing good work.

"There is no way the World Bank could ever be in charge of conservation," Randy concludes. "It would be like asking the fox to guard the hen house. We need independent institutions that can promote sustainable development and begin to reverse the damage that's been done already."

Unloading the Debt Burden

One issue that has been particularly difficult to organize around in the United States is the debt crisis. The world of banking and finance appears too abstract for ordinary people to grasp.

Yet the debt is arguably the most crucial issue confronting the Third World today. The $1 trillion in debt saddling Third World governments is reputed to be responsible for the death of thousands of babies every day, as governments are forced to cut back on vital services like health care in order to pay back the Western banks.

One of the factors that stymies potential activism around the debt is that there is no consensus within the progressive community on solutions to the crisis. Some adhere to the position espoused by Third World leaders such as Cuba's Fidel Castro that the debt should be totally repudiated. Others take a more moderate stand, saying that the debt should be reduced, perhaps pegged to a certain percentage of a nation's export earnings (the position taken by Peru's President Alan Garcia). Still others maintain that simply canceling or reducing the debt only takes Third World elites off the hook and is no guarantee that the poor will benefit. These activists call for a "3-D" approach (debt relief, development, and democracy)—reduce the debt, put the money saved into a development fund, and allow the fund to be administered by democratically-elected commissions made up of representatives of different sectors of the population, including workers, peasants, and women. This, they contend, is the only way to ensure that the money saved from the clutches of the banks will not end up in the pockets of the local elites.[4]

Despite the controversy, all debt activists agree that the debt must gain more awareness in the public eye before any solution will be achievable. One man who has made a personal commitment to this is John Ross, a journalist and self-described investigative poet. John used a three-week hunger strike and U.S. educational campaign to raise people's awareness of the impact of the debt on the Third World poor. From September 21 to October 16, 1987, John traveled from Mexico City to San Francisco, to

Los Angeles, to New York, to Washington D.C., and back to Mexico City. In each city he spent a day in front of the largest Latin American creditors—Citicorp, Bank of America, Chase Manhattan—distributing leaflets and making a public statement.

"There comes a bump in every journalist's life," John wrote, "when the words begin to turn in on the reporter. For me, the last straw fell at midnight, July 2, 1987. I heard on my radio that 18 braceros (Mexicans who cross the border to find work) had been found asphyxiated in a locked boxcar on a railroad siding in Sierra Blanca, Texas. I subsequently banged on my typewriter and wrote what became the call to action for Words into Deeds, a grassroots group taking action against the debt:

> Eighteen youths, in the first flower of life, 18 young men dead in a Texas boxcar. A boxcar full of the millions more who defy jail and the Migra's stern new laws to go north, because south of the border, the cost of tortillas has risen 400 percent and the peso has lost 600 percent against the dollar in the past 1000 days and half the work force has no work . . .

"When I'd make my statement in front of one of the U.S. banks, people would stop to talk and offer their solutions to the debt problem. It showed me that people really are thinking of this as a major issue; they realize that it affects the health of our own economy."

John got some good radio and newspaper coverage, but he thinks the next step has to be more dramatic. "I'm inspired by the environmentalists, the civil rights and anti-war movements that have made such great strides in getting their cause noticed. I need to build an organization from the names of supporters I collected, but I need help and time to do so. I think the next step should be an occupation of the International Monetary Fund, by at least fifty people. The debt isn't solely a result of IMF policies, but redressing such policies is a good place to start. It's the only way to get some ink."

John Ross's is the most dynamic U.S. approach to the debt crisis according to Bill Hall, environmental activist and author of numerous articles on the debt. "In the United States, and to a lesser extent in Canada and Europe, the debt hasn't reached a popular consciousness. To people in the Third World, on the other hand, debt is not merely an issue left to banks and economic elites—it is an issue of survival day in and day out. When food and transportation subsidies are cut, when employment is cut back and social services curtailed, all in the name of the debt, the debt is no longer a crisis of bank profitability but of food and work and shelter for the poor. John Ross is trying to bring this message to Americans in a way no debt conference or scholar has been able to do."

European experience can provide inspiration to North Americans on how to make the debt crisis a public issue. The campaign undertaken by Oxfam in England during the height of the African famine in 1984-85 is a good example. Oxfam recognized the hypocrisy of sending emergency relief while at the same time forcing Africa to repay its onerous debts to Western banks. "We tried to figure out how to make this a public issue—since no one in Britain cared a hoot about the debt in countries five thousand miles away," recalls John Clarke, then campaign director for Oxfam-UK. "But we knew that people were concerned about the money they gave for famine relief through groups like Live Aid. So we decided to compare the aid to debt service, and show that for every one pound we gave, we took two away."

Oxfam's campaign slogan was "Don't Stop the Giving, Stop the Taking," and it focused on the scandal of the obscene transfer of wealth from Africa to the West. "We talked about how the economic drought was every bit as harmful as the climatic drought," says John Clarke. "And we tried to be as provocative as we could, telling people that we are pissing into the wind by giving with one hand what we are taking away with the other."

Oxfam plastered the country with posters, took out ads in local newspapers, did street theater to catch media attention, and went on radio and TV talk shows. The campaign generated such a groundswell of public support that the African debt suddenly became an issue in the British Parliament, and the Lawson plan (named for Nigel Lawson, Chancellor of the Exchequer) was proposed as an initiative to forgive Africa's public debt and reduce the interest rate on the private debt.

As the debt crisis continues to increase the suffering of the Third World poor, both North Americans and Europeans must search for ever more creative ways of making the issues visible and demanding solutions from their governments and banks.

Campaigning Against Nuclear Weapons

The peace movement is another front that uses actions such as demonstrations, lobbying, and educational campaigns to try to change government policy. But it has often been difficult to fuse the concerns of the peace movement with the concerns of Third World activists. "For a long time, the U.S. peace movement has been primarily a white, middle-class movement divorced from struggles of the Third World," claims Puerto Rican peace activist, Ana Cuilan. "It has largely ignored the effects of nuclear testing on the Third World people who are the guinea pigs in these experiments. And it has ignored the non-nuclear wars that are killing people every day throughout the Third World. The inability to merge the U.S. anti-nuclear sentiment with the concerns of Third World people has been one of this movement's great weaknesses."

Recently, there has been a merging of these concerns with respect to the Pacific Rim. The countries and islands of the Pacific Rim have witnessed a tremendous upsurge in the number of nuclear weapons based and tested in their region. The United States has set off sixty-six atmospheric atomic blasts in the Marshall Islands. The French have tested one hundred nuclear bombs in the atmosphere and underground near Tahiti. The presence of nuclear weapons creates environmental and health hazards for Pacific islanders, leads to increases in prostitution around military bases, and distorts national priorities away from addressing the needs of the poor. Realizing that they cannot reverse these trends without the help of U.S. citizens, activists in the Pacific have called upon North Americans to join their battle against the bases.

North American groups like Mobilization for Survival, the Campaign Against U.S. Military Bases in the Philippines (CAB), the Pacific Campaign to Disarm the Seas, the Greater Victoria Disarmament Group, and the Friends of the Filipino People have joined with their overseas counterparts in Australia, Belau (Palau), the Philippines, Aotearoa (New Zealand), Fiji, Japan,

Korea, and Samoa to protest nuclear testing and weaponry in the Pacific.

One specific campaign these groups are taking on is pressing U.S. and Filipino policymakers to oppose stationing U.S. troops and weapons at Subic Naval Base and Clark Air Force Base in the Philippines. The bases are on land which is leased to the U.S. military, but the lease expires in 1991. In the short term, the bases bring in money for the government of the Philippines. In the long term, they create dependency on the United States, which undermines Filipinos' national sovereignty and their ability to present viable alternatives for improving the local economy.

Through lobbying, exchanging speakers, and organizing educational events for U.S. and Filipino audiences, the transnational alliance works from all sides to build more peaceful ties between the Philippines and the United States.

"We need to lessen the influence of the military on all of our lives, starting with our foreign policy," says Boone Schirmer, an active member of the Friends of the Filipino People. "Keeping the bases in the Philippines undermines the Filipino people's right to self-determination, since such a tremendous show of foreign power exercises undue influence.

"The current Filipino constitution calls for a nuclear-free Philippines. Filipino organizations frequently hold demonstrations to protest against the bases. My responsibility is to alter my own country's role in this. But my work is only a piece of an international program, and it will take all sides working effectively to succeed."

Changing the Face of U.S. Foreign Aid

A handful of other government-focused activist groups have taken up a different piece of the puzzle—changing the thrust of official U.S. development assistance.

A breakdown of U.S. foreign aid reveals that a full two-thirds of U.S. assistance to the Third World is not development aid but security assistance, delivered either in the form of direct military aid or cash payments to "friendly" Third World governments. The militarization of U.S. foreign policy was ominously boosted during the Reagan administrations, when the number of countries receiving U.S. military aid jumped from 57 to 89. Most recipients of U.S. military largesse did not face external threats, but used the security assistance to quell an increasingly impoverished citizenry organizing for change.

Even the small portion of money earmarked for "nonmilitary" development aid rarely reaches the poor. Channeled as it is through governments primarily interested in maintaining their privileges at the expense of the poor, it is no wonder that such aid often ends up in the pockets of corrupt politicians and military leaders, or finances large-scale, top-down projects that provide no benefits to the poor. Decades of failed development have proven that aid delivered through the powerful rarely reaches the powerless.[5]

Many anti-hunger activists focus their attention on U.S. development assistance. Some, like Results, lobby for *more* development assistance, particularly for programs like child immunization or women's development activities. Since 1986, Results has been working in concert with UNICEF and the World Health Organization to raise the amount of government money granted for overseas health programs. In 1987 it launched a campaign to get over six hundred legislators in the United States, Great Britain, Canada, and Australia to urge the president of the World Bank to increase its lending to developing countries, to convert some of the loans to grants, and to increase lending to women.

Complex in structure, Results requires a heavy commitment from its members—three meetings, several conference calls, and the background reading contained in three or four newsletters every month. "Most grassroots groups don't ask much of their members, and therefore don't get very far. One of our major discoveries is that people will do what you ask of them. We ask that our partners be able to speak on the issues, not just write about them. It takes extra work to be able to speak out," says Sam Harris of Results.

The largest anti-hunger lobbying group is Bread for the World, or "Bread." Bread coordinates lobbying for over forty thousand members through a grassroots, ecumenical network. Among its major campaigns are lobbying for increased resources to women in development programs, and seeking legislative responses to alleviate the debt burden on the Third World poor.

"Over the years, Bread has consistently worked to redirect foreign aid resources to more beneficial purposes," says Larry Hollar, Director of Issues for Bread for the World. "We believe that existing U.S.AID resources can be much more effective in helping the poorest of the poor. But we've also seen that it takes a lot more than lobbying to redirect AID money for these policies to be highly successful. We need greater commitment to these policies by high-ranking AID officials, more effective oversight by Congress and advocacy groups, and of course, a major reduction in the military and security aid that undermines far too much of the good that development aid can accomplish."

Bread is not only concerned about the amount of development aid the U.S. government commits to Third World countries, but also the manner in which this aid is administered. It realizes that no matter how much aid is allocated to Third World countries, the institutional structures channeling the aid must be accountable to the needs of the Third World poor and to the public—not to U.S. government strategic interests. Simply asking for more money, or asking that the money be reshuffled through the same institutions but into different programs, is not going to solve this problem of accountability.

"The current subordination of U.S.AID to the political and strategic criteria of national foreign policy colors the programs that the agency can and does pursue," says Bread's President, Arthur Simon. "For example, in Central America, where humanitarian assistance is completely overshadowed by military and security considerations, the opportunities are severely diminished for flexible, sensitive aid that will be supported by local communities to meet their own needs."

Among the groups with which Bread is working on aid issues is The Development Group for Alternative Policies (Development GAP), a Washington-based education and advocacy group on Third World development. The Development GAP is calling for the creation of an independent development assistance agency that would be autonomous from the State Department and U.S. strategic interests.

"At The Development GAP, we would like to see development aid structurally removed from the State Department," says co-founder, Steve Hellinger. "In discussions with members of the House Foreign Affairs Committee, we are asking that all government development aid be funneled through independent organizations directly accountable to Congress.

"We already have successful examples of how this can work. The Inter-American Foundation (IAF) and the African Development Foundation are congressionally-funded programs, with a mandate to promote grassroots development in Africa, Latin America, and the Caribbean. Although, for example, the IAF board shifted to the right under the Reagan administrations, the quality of the IAF's project funding has remained high. Part of this is due to an experienced field staff with a lot of local knowledge, responsiveness, autonomy, a modest budget, and a desire to consult with the poor themselves about the types of programs that need funding—all fundamentally important principles that we recommend following. But these organizations' ability to deliver aid to the people who need it most also lies in their distinct mandate to help the poor—not to serve the strategic interests of our government."

Based on this type of a model, The Development GAP and Bread recommend that development aid be channeled through a new and independent bilateral aid institution, the Inter-American Foundation, the African Development Foundation, and an Asian equivalent. Steve Hellinger continues, "The amount of aid is not the issue. To be successful, aid programs must be responsive to the poor, help build their organizations, and promote only those policies formulated on the basis of popular involvement. To me, the only other alternative is to get rid of all foreign aid, and that's simply not realistic.

"Additionally, multilateral and bilateral aid institutions have promoted policies of export-led growth that helped lead the Third World into the current debt crisis. We cannot focus just on aid without looking at trade and debt policies. We do this at The Development GAP, and work closely on these issues with environmental, labor rights, and church organizations."

Larry Hollar of Bread for the World also feels that focusing solely on aid issues can obscure the myriad other ways that U.S. policies have a negative effect on Third World development—issues such as militarism, trade, and debt. He agrees that minor shifts in U.S. aid policy are not enough and thinks that anti-hunger advocates need to address more of the roots of hunger—although such large, controversial issues are not easily handled in a lobbying campaign.

"Some of our work at Bread has been on relatively non-controversial issues such as advocating emergency and relief measures, including increased food aid for famine areas or aid programs for women and children. While we've done well at those things, we also need to tie militarism and war together with hunger more, and we need to focus more on the debt crisis. We need to talk about why there's massive unemployment and racism here at home, and ask other difficult questions that are going to point the way toward dealing with hunger in the long run. We're starting to do that with our work around southern Africa—making the links between hunger, war and apartheid. But we, and others like us, at times have tread too lightly on those big issues."

James Steele, another Bread staffer, adds that success in lobbying on development aid should be measured not only in terms of the bills it helps to pass, but also by the disastrous conservative initiatives it helps to thwart. "Our clear-cut victories may be slim," says James, "but you also have to look at what we've helped to *prevent*. It takes a staff of full-time lobbyists just to counter the attacks of those who oppose a social justice agenda! We have to keep showing legislators that there are people who care about hunger issues, and that they're not just refugees from the 60's, because that's sometimes the mentality on Capitol Hill."

Seeking Policy Alternatives From the Ballot to City Hall

Another strategy for influencing U.S. foreign policy is through the electoral process itself. Jesse Jackson's 1988 Presidential campaign galvanized a broad cross-section of the U.S. public, with a profound message of social change and government responsibility not only in domestic policies but also in our dealings with the Third World. Speaking with unprecedented strength for the disenfranchised both at home and abroad, the Jackson campaign brought issues like U.S. policy toward southern Africa,

Central America, and the Middle East to the forefront of the campaign platform.

"There was a time when community organizers didn't think it was correct to be involved in electoral campaigns, that our whole goal was to build power on the outside of the electoral process and to put pressure on our elected officials," explains Dwight Pelz of Citizen Action, a federation of groups with over two million members involved in campaigns, lobbies, and grassroots organizing. "I think over time we realized that we could get involved in elections, retain our integrity, and actually use electoral politics to help build the organizations we were working for. And we realized that we needed to do that. It is what you call an inside/outside strategy."[6]

Elections also open up avenues for lobbying groups to play more of a formative role in policymaking. The election year 1988 was a turning point for Neighbor to Neighbor, whose staff decided to use what they had learned from lobbying to work on electoral campaigns for Congressional representatives with progressive policies toward Central America. "It's one way to stop feeling like we can only at best react to U.S. policy in Central America, and instead feel like we are part of the process of building better relations with the region," explains Robyn Macswain of Neighbor to Neighbor.

But election year or no election year, finding new forums for involvement is crucial for grassroots groups wishing to have a voice in policymaking. The Center for Innovative Diplomacy (CID) is developing an exciting if somewhat unorthodox alternative to Washington's exclusive domain over foreign affairs—building a national program to involve municipal governments in the foreign policy arena.

"Municipal foreign policies offer many benefits," explains CID's Director, Michael Shuman. "They help democratize foreign policy, giving expression to otherwise excluded voices. They render U.S. officials more accountable to American citizens. And finally, they are more creative because local officials are forced to develop nonviolent approaches to global problems to which national officials might too eagerly apply military solutions."

Michael contends that involvement in foreign policy benefits the cities as well. It can bring them more trade, more cultural exchange, and less border chaos. But perhaps most important is the role that city-based foreign policies could play in revitalizing the democratic process here at home.

CID holds leadership training and educational seminars for city officials, to strengthen their involvement in foreign policies. CID already counts almost two thousand mayors and city councilmembers as supporters—officials who participate in foreign policymaking at the municipal level. "What we offer are the tools for working with city governments, for those people who want to get involved at this level," adds Michael. "We can help people identify key elected officials in their cities. We also offer a 'menu' of possible city-based initiatives in our quarterly *Bulletin*. Through this newsletter, people can see what has worked and what hasn't worked in other cities. My hope is that eventually, every city government that wants one will have a foreign policy bureau of some kind, and that international relations will be pursued more aggressively from the perspective of local ties."

The idea of municipal foreign policies is not as radical as it may sound, when we consider how active city governments already are in some of the most heated foreign policy issues of our time. Stopping the military influence on community economic development comes home in local efforts to stop the "homeporting" (basing in U.S. ports) of battleships. Since 1984, one such battle has raged in San Francisco, where the Navy, and then-mayor Dianne Feinstein wanted to homeport the battleship U.S.S. Missouri. Economic and environmental studies and the city's policies of non-discrimination in hiring (policies that run counter to the Navy's) indicated that the problems of homeporting might be greater than the benefits its proponents projected.

"The Navy has responded to our efforts by proposing to base other ships here, hoping to catch us when our backs are turned," says Eric Ferry of the Coalition for a Safe Bay. "We've succeeded in stalling their efforts, but we haven't won yet. We do constant outreach to keep local people informed of what's happening, and supply the Mayor's office with position papers on the issue. We're also on the offense, working with community groups to propose economic development alternatives for the areas the Navy was going to take over."

Asked how he sees his work connected to similar efforts

abroad, Eric adds, "Our connections to the Third World are integral. The economic and political impact of U.S. bases is strong
anywhere you look. We see areas become dependent on the
military for their very livelihood, which doesn't do much for the
cause of peace."

Homeporting is one issue that reflects the role of local governments in foreign policymaking. Another example is official
U.S. relations with the apartheid government of South Africa.
While U.S. diplomats were talking "constructive engagement,"
cities divested billions of dollars from South Africa. More than
seventy cities, thirteen counties, and nineteen states helped
move the Reagan administration to replace constructive engagement with limited economic sanctions.[7]

Twenty-seven U.S. cities and one state offer sanctuary for refugees from El Salvador and Guatemala, placing local governments at odds with official U.S. policy as carried out by the
Immigration and Naturalization Service. Eleven states—
Colorado, Hawaii, Maine, Massachusetts, Vermont, Minnesota,
Arkansas, Iowa, Kansas, Ohio, and Rhode Island—participated
in a lawsuit to restore states' authority over their National Guard
units, in protest against the thousands of Guardsmen deployed
in Central America. Add these to the hundreds of sister city
projects already in existence in the United States and Canada,
and you have a base of thousands of localized foreign policy
efforts.

Critics from the left and the right are concerned that municipal foreign policies can divert already scarce resources from
local programs into more "glamorous" international projects.
Another common criticism is that foreign affairs are simply not
part of the domain of local governments. But CID points to all
the ways cities are already linked to global issues. Perhaps the
biggest reminder for U.S. cities of their connection to foreign
policy is the $300 billion U.S. military budget. Dollar for dollar,
money cut from such programs as General Revenue Sharing and
Community Development Block Grants is being siphoned off
into MX missiles and Star Wars research. Even those communities that benefit in the short term from military projects are
beginning to worry about the long-term boom and bust consequences of dependence on military spending.

Michael Shuman adds, "The purpose of establishing a foreign

policy arm of local government is not to sap scarce funds. Rather it is to increase funds through trade and demilitarization, and to see that the use of funds allocated to international programs is accountable to the community. We also don't want to see one mayor put together one kind of foreign policy program, and then another mayor take over the office and do something completely different. Foreign policy is not for the P.R. purposes of the mayor's office. What we're pushing for is a full examination of the possible links between U.S. and Third World communities—in trade, peacemaking, travel, diplomacy, education, aid, and cultural and technical exchange. And the pursuit of these links would be in the hands of local citizens."

Education for Action

While activists are busy trying to change U.S. bilateral and multilateral policies through immediate actions like demonstrations, lobbying, and electoral campaigns, most agree that the hope for meaningful, long-term change in U.S. policy lies in our ability to create a concerned, well-informed public. For that, education and developing a sense of critical thinking are key.

"I talk to groups around the country about the role our government plays in places like El Salvador and the Philippines," says Sara Miles, an expert on U.S. military strategies in the Third World. "The facts are so depressing that people ask me how I can possibly continue to do the work I'm doing without feeling defeated. Ultimately, I believe our only hope for countering immoral government policies is to educate, educate, educate. That hope keeps me going."

Organizations such as the Institute for Policy Studies, the Resource Center, and Bread for the World provide alternative sources of information on the impact of U.S. foreign policy. But their audience is multiplied many times over by groups using their materials in creative educational projects, helping to get the information out to the grassroots in this country. Such educational work is not necessarily attached to a specific piece of legislation or a candidate, but based on the necessity for continued examination of our role in the Third World.

The Freedom Fund in Seattle has been organizing caravans

which travel from state to state, bringing speakers and educational displays on U.S foreign policy to churches, schools, and community centers along the way. Among the displays is a sampling of alternative media sources, such as *Utne Reader*, *The Nation*, and *The Progressive*. Vivian Sharples is an organizer with the Freedom Fund. "It's exhausting work, being on the road for weeks at a time, setting up event after event, putting up and taking down the displays, coordinating the press and the speakers. But it's also exhilarating, because we are convinced that education is empowerment and we can see how people are moved and inspired by our message. They're not going to get this message in their local papers or on the evening news, so we've got to bring it directly to them in their communities."

Wendy Marks was a speaker for the Christic Institute on one of the Freedom Fund's caravans. "The underlying message we are conveying is that we can't believe everything we read or hear from Washington. Our government, and particularly our foreign policy, has gotten out of control and is being made by characters like Ollie North who are totally unaccountable to the American public. We need to take back control of our government, and we can only do that through a grassroots educational campaign that convinces people of the need to create a new foreign policy based on respect for the law and moral principles."

The Interreligious Foundation for Community Organization (IFCO) does similar grassroots education on U.S. policy in Central America. IFCO targets a particular state for a week-long campaign, then coordinates with local peace and justice groups to set up events in hundreds of schools, Rotary and Lions' Clubs, church and community gatherings. The speakers come from all over the country and from Central America as well, bringing a message that U.S. policy must be changed from the bottom up. "The week's campaign is just the beginning," says IFCO's Sharon Haas. "Then we follow up with the local groups, helping to strengthen their activities, hooking them up with new audiences, discussing future strategies with them. It becomes a shot in the arm for the local organizers."

Groups like the Women's International League for Peace and Freedom work through local chapters to educate citizens on important policy issues such as disarmament, racism, and anti-intervention. Other groups try to fill in where the U.S.

government cuts off the flow of information. The Seattle Center for Palestinian Information is a coalition of three peace groups that came together when the U.S. State Department closed the Palestine Information Office in Washington D.C. The Seattle Center now distributes information on the Middle East formerly provided by the Palestine Information Office, and has created an organizing center for Middle East work.

Artists and entertainers contribute to the educational process by tying their work to U.S. foreign policy concerns. Winning Democracy in El Salvador is a campaign to raise awareness of the connection between U.S. tax dollars and the repression and death squad activity in El Salvador. Artist John Baldessari designed a billboard for the campaign, depicting a killing by anonymous assassins, to be displayed in San Francisco and New York subway stations. The signs were initially rejected by the New York Transit Authority, but the controversy itself helped increase public awareness about El Salvador.

Stories of the impact of U.S. policy are even more powerful when they come firsthand. Some groups are educating the public by bringing people from the Third World here to talk with U.S. audiences. Women for Racial and Economic Equality brings women from southern Africa to raise awareness of the conditions under which families there live. The Third World Women's Project at the Institute for Policy Studies likewise sponsors Third World activists on educational speaking tours throughout the United States.

A unique example of grassroots education is the Africa Peace Tour, organized by a coalition of eight religious groups, including the Unitarian Universalist Service Committee, the American Friends Service Committee, and Maryknoll Fathers and Brothers. In 1986, the first year of the annual tour, churchworkers, academics, and representatives from Africa targeted the southern United States and visited fifty cities. Speakers tried to help southerners understand the links between their region's poverty and the poverty of the Third World. Peace Tour delegates explained to audiences how U.S. Steel, for example, closed its Birmingham, Alabama plant in 1982, displacing ten thousand workers, only to invest in a new facility in South Africa that employed six thousand workers at one-quarter to one-tenth of U.S. wages. Tour delegates also drew connections between U.S.

foreign policy and starvation in Africa, showing how U.S.-backed military groups divert African governments' resources from effectively dealing with famine.

The Labor Network on Central America has brought Salvadoran workers to the United States to mobilize labor solidarity. "After American workers get that firsthand information, they can really relate to the problems of Salvadoran workers, and are moved to participate in some way," according to Fred Schwartz, a volunteer with the Labor Network on Central America. Labor activities since the Salvadorans visited have ranged from organizing a human rights rapid response network to forming sister unions.

New groups have also cropped up to take the mainstream media to task for its biased reporting on foreign policy issues. Fairness and Accuracy in Reporting (FAIR) publishes a newsletter with articles examining major media coverage of controversial issues like Central America and the Middle East. Project Censored sponsors annual awards for the year's best stories ignored by the mainstream press.

In all these educational efforts, the bottom line is not merely to provide information about hunger and poverty in the world, or about U.S. foreign policy. The role of education is to counter the fact that we are largely denied the truth about our government's role in the Third World. Education helps us understand how our legitimate national interests—which are first and foremost to build a more stable and peaceful world—are undermined by our present militaristic policies. Armed with a new vision of our national interest, North Americans can then embrace the structural changes necessary to end injustice, and contest U.S. policies that block such changes from taking place.

No Easy Battles: Hope and Success Keep You Going

Pitting ourselves against U.S. policies in the Third World is a painstaking, often frustrating task. It means confronting some of the most entrenched business and military interests in the country. It means competing with conservative lobbies with highly paid and professionally trained staffs who have ready access to policymakers.

But citizen involvement is the best way to ground foreign policy in democratic principles. It is the only way we can hope to give a voice to the voiceless—the majority of people in the Third World who directly suffer under U.S. military and economic policies.

Vietnam veteran, Brian Willson, reminds us that change begins with individual commitment. "The decisions that are being made by policymakers should reveal to the people of the United States that our solution is not just in Washington. This realization represents a paradigm shift that's happening in this country. It's empowering, and it's liberating.

"There is hope, tremendous hope. It's in the consciousness of human beings. I'm very hopeful that people are beginning to see that the solution is within each of us, as we work with one another. There is no security without justice, and that's what I'm promoting, the security of the world which comes from everybody working for justice."

Changes at the national level signal this shifting political tide. Howard Wolpe, Chairman, of the U.S. House of Representatives Subcommittee on Africa throughout the Reagan years, reminds us of the power of grassroots organizing to affect the national agenda.

"In this day and age, it is often said that average citizens don't have much impact on national decisions, domestic or foreign policy questions. What has happened with respect to southern African policy and specifically South African policy is testimony to the enormous power that individual citizens can exercise, even on foreign policy issues. It was in fact the grassroots campaign nationally—ranging from everything from divestment efforts on campuses and within local governments to the non-violent civil disobedience campaigns to the more general broadening of the debate within the church community as well as within the campuses across this country—that really transformed the political environment and made it possible for the Congress to set a new course with respect to our approach to South Africa. It was a classic instance of where grassroots mobilization made the difference in American foreign policy."[8]

The government cannot be used to further our goals until it shares our goals. We must continue to speak out against a definition of national security that undermines the security of hungry people at home and abroad. And we must continue to forge solid people-to-people ties with our Third World counterparts.

Throughout the country, students help raise much-needed funds for organizations such as Oxfam that strive to "bridge the gap" between the First and Third Worlds.

8

Money Matters

We have already delved into an array of possibilities for financial activism: purchasing alternative trade goods rather than conventional imports, boycotting products and corporations which violate ethical principles, and investing in socially responsible funds. These examples illustrate how using our consumer power is in itself a form of activism. Every dollar spent responsibly casts a vote for economic justice, for better labor policies, for human rights and peace, or for sustainable environmental policies.

But money counts on another level as well. Whether we are talking about the small, low-budget groups described throughout this book, or the larger development organizations working overseas, a stable funding base is a basic ingredient for success. For the smaller groups, individual donations are key to securing that base. Directly aiding these organizations is yet another way to invest in your principles and help build an internationalist movement with a strong, secure future.

Where Does the Money Come From?

Nonprofit organizations have four sources of funding: the U.S. government, corporations, foundations, and individuals. Most of the multimillion-dollar development organizations get the bulk of their funds from the U.S. government. CARE, for example, obtains three-fourths of its $450 million budget from the government, mostly in the form of food donations. Only a handful of the larger development groups—groups like Oxfam America, the Mennonite Central Committee, the Unitarian Universalist Service Committee, and the American Friends Service Committee (AFSC)—do not use U.S. government money for their overseas work. And virtually none of the small grass-roots efforts mentioned in this book get government support.

Corporations have in recent years made substantial contributions to mega-events like We Are the World, the effort by performing artists to raise money for emergency relief to Africa in the wake of the 1984 famine. "We could not have done these major events—We Are the World or Hands Across America—without corporations," says Marty Rogol, director of USA for Africa, the group that administers the funds.

USA for Africa never felt co-opted by corporate sponsorship—but then again, the message it was conveying was not a threatening one. USA for Africa was trying to help people in an emergency, not challenge the system that allows such emergencies to happen. "Corporations aren't going to support nonprofits that are working against them," Marty Rogol points out, "just as nonprofits shouldn't accept money from corporations if they have conflicting values."

Perhaps the most exciting aspect of corporate sponsorship of USA for Africa was employee involvement. "Citibank's participation was completely initiated by employees," Marty explains. "Monsanto was amazed at the surge in morale after they sponsored Hands Across America. So I would suggest that individuals who want to support nonprofits look to their workplaces and try to generate employee support for the project."

But others argue that corporations are only interested in giving to high-profile groups that will bring them sufficient publicity for their donations. The student-run Overseas Development Network, for example, spent a good deal of energy soliciting corporate support to no avail. "Corporations just weren't interested in giving money to a small group like ours," says staffer, Mary Kroetch. "We finally rethought our strategy and realized that our time would be better spent building up a base of support among concerned individuals."

Corporate gifts to all nonprofits account for only 5.2 percent of private donations. And in the 1980s, with a sluggish economy and tighter budgets, there has actually been a retrenchment in corporate philanthropy. The 1986 tax reforms also hurt nonprofits by reducing the financial incentives for giving.

Foundations are another key source of income. The Foundation Center, a national organization providing the public with information on philanthropic giving, lists over twenty-five thousand foundations that contribute to nonprofit work. Most focus on domestic activities and are wary of funding more risky, creative projects such as people-to-people ties. There are, however, some smaller, more progressive foundations that are more likely to fund innovative work with the Third World. The Funding Exchange in New York is an umbrella organization for fifteen progressive foundations that have provided seed money to scores of new organizations. In 1987 they provided some $3 million to nonprofits seldom funded by the more conventional institutions.

But Jerry Kohn of TECNICA, a group providing technical assistance overseas, warns against counting on any foundations for ongoing support. "While you can often get some support for the first few years, it's certainly not a stable source of income. We send out lots of proposals, but it's a real hit-and-miss proposition. We cross our fingers and hope one of them will come through, but we can't depend on it."

Some groups do get substantial funding from foundations, but heavy reliance on foundation support—particularly if only from one or two sources—can jeopardize an organization's long-term viability. Foundations fold, divide up, change their funding priorities—and organizations that are overly dependent on them can be left high and dry.

Individual Donors: The Financial Backbone

To establish a long-term, stable funding base, nonprofits must rely almost exclusively on one source: individual donors like ourselves. But bombarded by requests for money, how can we distinguish between one group and another? How can we make educated decisions about which groups to support?

The first step is to set some priorities. Which type of work do you find most compelling—direct material aid, human rights work, educational campaigns in the United States, lobbying efforts to change U.S. policy? Is there a particular region or country that most concerns you?

Another important distinction hinges on whether you wish your contribution to be strictly humanitarian or whether you want it to also make a political statement. For example, some donors want their money to serve as an antidote to the money our government spends on foreign military assistance, so they channel their donations to groups opposing foreign policies gone awry. "I know I can't cover the globe," says Alice Hamburg, a donor to numerous progressive causes. "So when I give to international causes, I try to focus on areas where the United States bears heavy responsibility for what's going on—like in Central America. I also support organizations on the cutting edge of social change, organizations like Committee in Solidarity with the People of El Salvador (CISPES) or Witness for Peace—which are often under attack by our own government."

Once we have made our own personal choices, then comes the task of determining which are the best groups to support within the categories we have chosen. Some donors actively search for the right organization to fund. Doug Johnson, for example, became interested in international hunger during the height of the African famine in 1984 and decided he wanted to support development work overseas.

"I was forty years old at the time, and had a little extra money," he says, "but I didn't know much about development issues or the different organizations that existed. I went to the libraries, and I talked to friends who had been involved in development work. I told them what my criteria were: I wanted an organization with effective field operations, where the money really got to the people. I wanted an independent organization, which for me means it has no religious affiliation and doesn't take money from the U.S. or any government. I wanted an organization that has a vision of a new world order, and addresses that vision in their work. Based on these criteria, Oxfam and World Neighbors were the two organizations that stood out."

Most of us, however, don't search out groups to support. Instead we find ourselves responding to appeals we receive. Here are some questions you might consider when sorting through the choices:

• *What does the organization's annual report say?*

Do you agree with its stated goals and the activities it carried out in the past year? Look at the board of directors and advisory board. Does it represent a cross-section of people from different backgrounds? Is there anyone whose name you recognize and respect? "If a group has someone on the board of directors that I respect," an anonymous donor told us, "then I feel more assured that the organization is well run. I noticed that I was getting several letters signed by Robert White, and since he used to be an ambassador, I was interested. Then I heard him speak, and I was really impressed."

Look at the organization's budget and see where the bulk of the funds come from. Groups that receive substantial government or foundation support, for example, are less dependent on your gift. How large is the group's budget? "It's hard to choose which groups to support," says donor, Ethel Sands. "One of the criteria I consider is how much of a difference my contribution will make. I often give to groups with very small budgets or groups that are in the process of expanding."

Other donors prefer to fund larger organizations that have greater visibility. If we only support small, low-budget groups, they argue, than none can grow big enough to make much of a difference.

• *What percentage of the organization's money goes for fundraising and administrative costs?*

If the annual report doesn't provide that information, you can ask the organization for a more detailed financial statement. Katherine Milroux is very concerned about the overhead costs of organizations she funds. "I get a printed list of the administrative costs of all the nonprofits I'm interested in," she says. "Anyone with their head on straight doesn't want to give to a group with high administrative costs."

The National Charities Information Bureau says that a group should spend no more than forty cents on each dollar for fundraising and administration. The Better Business Bureau's Philanthropic Advisory Service allows fifty cents. But such figures can

198 BRIDGING THE GLOBAL GAP

be misleading because groups use different accounting procedures—what one group describes as a funding appeal, a more
sophisticated group may call an educational campaign. Younger
organizations are also forced to spend more money on fundraising than older, more established groups.

Oxfam's Moli Steinert warns against judging an organization
solely by its overhead costs. "It's important to look further than
the percentage, to see how the money is spent and who it
serves," Moli insists. "For example, we at Oxfam have to spend
more on fundraising than a group that gets most of its funds from
the U.S. government. We also spend more on administration
than some groups because it's much more expensive to admin-
ister many small-scale projects than a few large ones. So the
very factors which make us appealing to some donors also push
our costs up."

Bob Bothwell, Director of the National Committee for Responsive Philanthropy, agrees with Moli. "You can't evaluate an organization by relying on a simple percentage. The best policy is
to give to an organization whose goals you believe in and one
which is on the road to accomplishing those goals. For example,
last year we spent 27 percent of our budget on fundraising and
administration. All that tells you is that we spent 73 percent of
our budget on something else. We could have all been sitting in
the park all year thinking about how the world could be a better
place. You have to read an organization's materials and see
what it's done. And if you're not sure you believe what you read,
call and ask someone to discuss the programs with you."

• *What is the salary of the highest paid staff?*

Some donors feel that by looking at the salaries of the staff—
particularly the top executives—you can get an idea of the organization's priorities. Some of the larger organizations give
hefty salaries to the top executives—CARE pays $90,000 a year,
Save the Children $98,000. "I think there's something wrong
when an organization working around hunger issues pays any of
its staff over $50,000," one donor told us. "If someone has such
an extravagant lifestyle that $50,000 isn't enough, then he or she
chose the wrong career."

At the other extreme are small organizations with low-paid or
volunteer staff. "As soon as a volunteer group starts paying
someone a salary, they become tied into the federal system and

it gets very costly since they have to pay unemployment taxes, medical benefits, and so forth," says Paul Haible of Vanguard Foundation. "On the other hand, organizations with no paid staff are very unstable. Some groups try to compromise by giving stipends of $400-500 a month, but they have a very high staff turnover. If a group wants to keep a stable staff, they must think about what constitutes a living wage."

Some groups, like New El Salvador Today (NEST), have made a conscious decision to keep salaries low and to pay all staff members the same. "We are all paid $9,600 a year, with an additional $2,400 for those with children," says NEST fundraiser, Lisa Lloyd. "We get the same pay because we feel we are part of a cooperative effort and that each of us contributes equally to that effort. And the reason we keep our salaries low is that our job is to get as much money as possible down to people in El Salvador who really need it. The only way we can do that is if we take less for ourselves."

How Much Can I Afford to Give?

Most of us give in a haphazard fashion to causes that reach us at a given moment. "I get inundated by requests for money," sighs Carol Jansen, "and it's always so difficult for me to decide who to give to and how much to give. So I end up acting according to the mood I'm in—if I'm feeling compassionate or hardnosed, generous or miserly."

Is there a more systematic approach to giving? How many of us have made a commitment to give away a certain percentage of our income each year? How much *should* we be giving?

There are, of course, no set answers. The Biblical starting point is the tithe—one-tenth of one's income. Many secular leaders, like Gloria Steinem of the Ms. Foundation, also advocate giving away 10 percent.

Ten percent may sound like a tall order, especially since most people presently give away less than 2 percent of their income. But anti-hunger activists like Tom Peterson of *Seeds* magazine think that for some, 10 percent is far too low. "Ten percent of $10,000 is a substantial contribution, 10 percent of a million dollars barely cuts into discretionary income," argues Tom. "Some people set a basic level of income they need to live reasonably, then give away the bulk of their income beyond that."

Mary Thompson is one such person. With her sizable inheritance, she could afford to live high on the hog. Instead, Mary lives as frugally as possible so she can give more away, and ends up donating 50 percent of her income every year. "I might even give away more, except the tax laws penalize you for giving more than 50 percent," Mary explains. "Some of my friends think I'm crazy, but I feel really privileged to be able to do it."

It is certainly easier to give away a hefty portion of your income if your income is large to begin with. But some of the largest donors to progressive causes are by no means wealthy. In fact, 85 percent of donations to nonprofits come from families earning $50,000 or less.

An extreme example of a low-income person who donates a major portion of his earnings is Bob Heald, a baker who earns $12,000 a year. A few years ago, Bob started to think creatively about his own income, and found that his desire to support change in the Third World and his desire to have a simpler lifestyle could reinforce each other. He decided to live an ecological, minimally consumer-oriented lifestyle, leaving him money to give to a variety of anti-hunger organizations, including Food First and Oxfam America.

"Now I find I can live on $2-3,000 a year and I make $10-12,000, so I give away about 75 percent of my income. I'm a tax resister, and it's very important for me to channel my money away from the government and toward social change."

Bob has a group of friends who share his lifestyle, and they draw strength from each other. "What I've given up is minor compared to what the poor in the Third World do without," says Bob. "Anyway, I don't consider it a sacrifice; I've found a lot of happiness in a simple lifestyle."

Other Ways to Contribute

Even people with limited discretionary income can still support their favorite groups. It just means having to be more creative.

Beverly Francis of Mount Sterling, Iowa, is a mother of four scraping to get by on her musician husband's low salary. "Even though we are poor by U.S. standards," says Beverly, "we are wealthy by world standards and feel a need to do something about our brothers and sisters throughout the world who are going hungry." While reading *Walking* magazine, Beverly and her husband got an idea. They would, as a family, do a two-week walk to raise money for combatting hunger. They'd get friends and neighbors to sponsor them, and give talks at church and community groups along the way.

"Since then we've been training every weekend, walking eight miles. Our two youngest, who are two and five, get some help along the way but they're doing pretty good on their own. We figure the two-week walk is a test run. If we make it, then we'd like to walk two thousand miles from Iowa to Oregon, where our parents live. We'll have to take the kids out of school for a few months, but what better education could they get? It's our chance to do something as a family to help other families."

Jennifer Hofer is a senior high school student in Oakland, California. What she lacks in monetary wealth she makes up for in enthusiasm. In 1987 Jennifer helped organize students, faculty, and parents to raise money for Oxfam projects in Mozambique. They ended up raising $2,500 from 330 students.

"I've become progressively more active every year," Jennifer remarks, "and I plan to keep volunteering during college. I don't have a lot of money, but I'm young and I have a lot of time and energy. So I figure I can make my own little dent by helping to raise money for causes I believe in."

Aside from fundraising, a good way to support an organization is to volunteer some of your time working there. Global Exchange, for example, functions almost exclusively on volunteer labor. The volunteers range from university teachers on sabbatical who share their research skills, to high school students who pack books, to technicians who help streamline the computer system. Kim Harris and Liana Shamlian, college students at the University of California at Davis, commute from Davis to San Francisco on Saturdays and holidays to volunteer at Global Exchange. "We do a bit of everything," says Kim. "We help set up the computer database, design flyers, organize on campus for visiting speakers, raise material aid for Third World groups. For us it's a great relief after spending the week with our heads buried in books to get out and do something about the things we believe in."

Rosario Morales is a Salvadoran single mother who makes her living cleaning houses. "I can barely support myself and my daughter, and I work so hard everyday that when I come home I don't have energy for anything else. But I do want to help Central Americans who are in worse shape than I am—people who are being persecuted by death squads, people who are literally starving. So whenever the local Central American groups have events, I help out doing childcare, making tamales to sell, whatever. It's just important for me to be doing something for people who are suffering."

Other ways to support organizing work is through in-kind donations. "Any professionals—printers, lawyers, performing artists, caterers, publicists, construction workers, computer experts, writers, translators, teachers—can offer their skills," says peace activist Claire Greensfelder. "And office supplies—your old typewriter or desk or computer software—are usually a great boon to nonprofits, especially the smaller ones." When Richard and Julia Quint remodeled their house, they not only donated their old furniture to a nonprofit group, but they also decided to use their home to host a benefit for a different group every year. A San Francisco philanthropist went even further: he remodeled an auto body shop into a beautiful office space and meeting room/gallery/video screening room that he makes available to nonprofits for special events.

Another way to boost an organization is to help publicize its work—inviting a speaker to your church or school, prodding the local media to write a story on the group, getting the organization's written material into community libraries and bookstores. "Whether it's donating your money, time, or skills," Claire Greensfelder insists, "there's a way for everyone—regardless of their income level—to make a contribution to a cause they believe in."

Investing in the Future

Robert Harkins, a door-to-door canvasser for Seattle's Central America Peace Campaign, has seen how giving can act as a tremendous boost to the donor's own spirit. "One time when I was canvassing, an elderly man answered the door," Robert recalls. "He was barely able to walk. I gave him my introduction about what was happening in Central America and he said, 'There ain't nothin' you can do anyway.'

"But he invited me in, and by the end of our discussion he hobbled over to his desk and wrote me out a check for $25. 'You know, young man,' he told me,' many years ago I used to be a Wobbly (a member of a progressive union, the Industrial Workers of the World, active in the early 1900s). But they beat us for what we were saying, kicked us, knocked us around so that I lost hope. From talking tonight, you've made me realize that there is hope that things can be straightened out.'"

Alice Hamburg, a longtime contributor to causes she cares deeply about, feels a great sense of purpose in strengthening organizations that share her vision through financial contributions. "I believe that anyone who is knowledgeable about the world has to care, and anyone who has more than enough has to share. I give as much time, energy, and money as I can. I try to live economically so I can contribute as much as possible. It's my responsibility as a citizen. I do have my family to think about. But aside from that, my primary effort is social justice."

Through financial activism, we are building a vision of how we would like to reshape our society. By investing our dollars and energy in these unique institutions, we are investing in the most precious resource we have—the future. For the more we strengthen and unify this movement for change, the closer we will be towards achieving our vision. That foresight was crystal clear to the eighty-year-old Hawaiian woman who sent in a sizable check to Neighbor to Neighbor, a grassroots lobbying group aimed at changing U.S. policy toward Central America. The note she included with her check read, "This is the best inheritance I could leave my grandchildren."

Benjamin Linder, engineer and clown, was killed by contra gunfire in Nicaragua in 1987. Today, thousands of U.S. internationalists carry his spirit and commitment to all corners of the world.

Photo by Oscar Cantarero

9

Internationalism
Today and Tomorrow

The internationalist movement identified throughout this book is not just a phenomenon of the 1980s. Its roots reach as far back as our own struggle for independence, which was aided to a large extent by the solidarity of Europeans. North Americans have, in turn, come to the aid of foreign struggles. The members of the Abraham Lincoln Brigade, who in the 1930s joined the Spanish Republic in its fight against Franco's fascism, are a prime example.

While earlier internationalists took up arms to fight for what they felt were just causes, most of today's progressive U.S. internationalists seek nonviolent forms of support. Some who do so are morally committed to the principle of nonviolence; others recognize that they have other skills that could make a greater contribution. But for many, a shift in the perception of what constitutes international support has come through recognition of the role the U.S. government often plays in *blocking* change abroad. For them, the real challenge lies in changing policies here at home.

The protest movement against the Vietnam War marked a turning point in U.S. history. It provoked millions of U.S. citizens to question the government's right to interfere in the internal affairs of other countries. While some vehemently supported the U.S. intervention in Vietnam, others took an isolationist position, arguing that the United States should keep out of that country's affairs. Still others felt that U.S. engagement in foreign issues was crucial, but they sought a type of involvement that would put us on the side of those fighting for justice. This search for an ethical and moral U.S. foreign policy forms the basis of today's internationalist movement.

During the Vietnam protests, students stood at the forefront of groups challenging U.S. foreign policy. After all, it was the youth who were being called upon to fight and die in the name of a highly suspect U.S. "national interest." Today, students still play a critical role, though not a dominant one. The strength of the present internationalist movement comes from the fact that it is dominated by no one group—not students, not political parties, not trade unions. This movement is impossible to categorize by class, ideology, or trade.

Many of today's activists are motivated by religious convictions, however. They are Catholics, Protestants, Jews, and Muslims, working both in church-based groups and in community groups composed of believers and non-believers alike. This diverse religious community has provided the spark for many of today's burning peace and justice issues in Central America, southern Africa, and the Middle East.

Many religious activists trace their commitment to social change to the profound transformation in the Catholic Church in Latin America. The introduction of liberation theology in the late 1960s led church workers throughout Latin America to examine the roots of oppression in their societies, and to work side by side with the poor toward changing the structures that perpetuate poverty and injustice. This commitment, known as the "preferential option for the poor," led to the formation of thousands of Christian communities, in which small groups gathered to discuss the Bible in light of their own situation. Together they sought common solutions to overcome their plight. The flowering of these Christian communities has provided the fuel for many of the social movements that have been changing the face of Latin America over the past decade.

So great was the impact of liberation theology in Latin American countries that it forced the religious community in the United States to re-examine its teachings and practices. Influenced by their Latin counterparts, thousands of Catholics and non-Catholics alike underwent a fundamental shift of emphasis away from charity and toward active involvement in movements for social change.

One of the great strengths of today's activists—whether religious or not—is that they are deeply rooted in their communities. Students, war veterans, civil rights advocates, and other activists of the 1960s have since grown up and spread out into the small towns and cities across the United States. Central American activists are heads of their PTAs, anti-apartheid activists are town council members, material aid coordinators are church leaders, corporate gadflies are college professors. This rootedness has two implications: activists are more likely to have influence in their communities and therefore an ability to reach out to more people, and they are more likely to shoulder issues in a serious fashion, digging in for the long haul as opposed to flitting from one issue to the next.

Thanks to travel and communication opportunities, today's activists are building ongoing, personal ties with the Third World. While it is true that several million U.S. citizens went to Vietnam, most did not go of their own volition. They were sent by their government to fight a war they knew little about, in a country they knew nothing about. As of 1988, over one hundred thousand North Americans had visited Nicaragua—not as fighters but as peacemakers. The proximity of Central America to the United States facilitates these people-to-people contacts. As the dynamism of these contacts has caught on, thousands more have visited communities in Africa, Asia, the Caribbean, and the rest of Latin America.

The ties formed through these exchanges run so deep that they are bound to last for many years. As Gary Gunderson said of his African sister city counterparts, "It used to be possible to walk away from the issue of hunger, to find some other diversion. But now, I can't walk away from my friends."

Today's internationalist movement is all the stronger for being forged in the midst of the Reagan era. The Reagan administration's relentless attacks on progressive movements throughout the world were a key mobilizing force in the United States. But U.S. activists soon discovered that they, too, had become subject to government repression. FBI agents infiltrated organizations like the Committee in Solidarity with the People of El Salvador (CISPES); scores of people returning from visits to

Nicaragua faced government harassment upon their return; and sanctuary workers have been indicted. Rather than squelch the spirit of internationalism, this persistent offensive has rallied the will and determination of many activists.

Given this movement's breadth and depth, it is no wonder that it can boast major accomplishments to date. It has been a critical factor in deterring the United States from a military invasion of Nicaragua, and has succeeded in matching contra aid from the government with humanitarian aid from citizens. It was instrumental in forcing the Reagan administration to impose sanctions against South Africa. It has helped free hundreds of political prisoners from Third World jails. It has provided much-needed technical and material aid to strengthen poor people's organizations. And it has created ties of goodwill and mutual respect with hundreds of Third World communities.

Avoiding the Pitfalls: Learning From the Past

The evolution of internationalism has not been one of steady growth and maturation. Since internationalism is largely a *response* to international affairs, the momentum ebbs and flows depending on the administration in power, the visibility of the problem (i.e., a "shooting war" versus the debt crisis), and the degree to which our government is involved.

With the end of the Reagan era in the United States, the movement must consider its own fragility. Recognizing their strengths and weaknesses, internationalists will be in a better position to forge a broader coalition capable of a good deal more than mere reaction to periodic crises. For this, a look at the past can be instructive.

Both the civil rights movement and the anti-war movement of the 1960s changed the fabric of U.S. society in fundamental ways. Not only did they affect the issues at hand—racism in the United States and the U.S. war against Vietnam—but they unleashed a broad progressive movement for change. The pervasive rejection of "business as usual" and the profound search for alternatives led to an explosion of powerful social movements—the black consciousness movement, the women's movement, the environmental movement, the gay rights movement, the anti-nuclear movement.

But by the end of the 1970s, this dynamic force for change was on the defensive. A new wave of conservatism—in part a reaction to the successes of the 1960s and 1970s— was sweeping the nation, bringing Ronald Reagan into the White House and dismantling hard-won gains in everything from social services to university reforms. With the New Right came the ascendancy of a different breed of reactionary social movements such as church fundamentalism, anti-abortion campaigns, and anti-busing zealotry. Representing itself as the standard-bearer of traditional U.S. values—family, patriotism, a strong America—the New Right was able to mobilize a populist base and take control of the nation's political and social agendas.

Why were the progressive movements so easily overshadowed? First and foremost, they were "movements" and not "a movement." Their predominant focus on single issues, while initially vital for mobilizing distinct constituencies, became devastating in the long run. Largely ignoring their common interests, these movements insisted that their issue was *the* issue and would only become muddled and weakened by being mixed with other issues. The forces of the right did not have to "divide and conquer"; the progressives were so divided that conquering was easy.

Today the tables have once again turned. At the end of the Reagan era, the right wing was in disarray. Its foreign policy has been a total disaster: billions of dollars in military aid to Central America have not achieved the goal of unseating the Sandinistas or defeating the Salvadoran guerrillas. The policy of constructive engagement in southern Africa has neither weakened apartheid nor stopped South Africa's aggression against its neighbors. The Middle East is wracked by war and civil conflict. And the Iran-contra scandal shook public confidence in the government's ability to conduct foreign affairs.

As in the 1960s, there is again a deep-seated, fundamental discontent with "business as usual." The millions who supported Jesse Jackson's 1988 presidential campaign suggest that we are poised at the beginning of a new era, when people from all walks of life are demanding sweeping changes in both domestic and foreign policies. The new internationalist movement has a unique opportunity to be a key player in building and shaping this momentum for change.

Building Internal Strength

The first order of business is to fortify the individual organizations that comprise the movement. There are literally thousands of groups dealing with some piece of the international puzzle. A look at the groups working on Central America alone shows the remarkable growth of this movement. When the Texas-based Central American Resource Center began compiling a nationwide list of Central American organizations in 1985, it found a few hundred groups. By 1987 the number had jumped to over one thousand. And these are only the groups that the Center has been able to document!

The internationalist movement is a loose, fragile federation of thousands of groups—some affiliated with national organizations, others completely autonomous. And while it is true that scores of new organizations crop up each year, many fall apart due to lack of direction, lack of resources, mismanagement, or infighting.

To ensure their survival and growth, individual groups must recognize the importance of having clear goals, a plan to achieve those goals, and a funding base which makes that plan viable. But perhaps even more important, they must create internally democratic and participatory structures that will prevent them from turning into "one-person shows," thus crippling both their reach and longevity. They must ask themselves: do all participants have input in the decision-making process? Are leadership skills transferred to younger and newer members? Are all participants empowered to speak for the organization, to represent its work to the outside world?

Groups cannot expect to change the "outside world" if they cannot learn to work together in a supportive and democratic fashion.

Building a Multi-Racial, Multi-Ethnic Movement

Another key to organizational strength is the drive toward ethnic, racial, economic, and sexual diversity. The present internationalist movement is predominantly white and middle class. While the white, middle class is certainly a crucial sector, the success of these organizations will ultimately depend on their ability to reflect our broader society.

Sister city programs have been criticized for not engaging the minority community. At the 1987 U.S-Nicaragua sister city conference, a representative from Detroit—the only black delegate out of some 350—challenged the sister cities to deepen their commitment to a struggling society like Nicaragua by deepening their commitment to the sectors of their own cities struggling for similar survival, and creatively involving them in all activities.

Alternative tourism is inherently biased towards people with money and time to travel. Some travel groups have responded to this bias by making low-income or affirmative action scholarships available for every trip they offer.

It is critical that the movement be inclusive from the start. Our understanding of poverty and racism in the Third World can only be enriched by seeing the issues through the eyes of fellow citizens who struggle with them in their everyday lives. The divestment campaigns that have sprung up on campuses and in communities across the country are teaching us all lessons about this.

The divestment drive is unique in that black, white, and Third World students have worked together in multiracial coalitions. But it also brings to light some of the problems we must overcome to build such alliances. For instance, some students have pointed out that while white activists have no trouble protesting U.S. foreign policy and injustice abroad, they seem much less ready to understand and address the "less glamorous" issues of poverty and racism at home. In some cases, black students are invited to join white-led campaigns.

Black students have criticized this approach for failing to seek alliances across racial lines from the start. They have also charged that the priorities of most white student activists—

direct action, protest politics, global critiques of U.S. policy—
implicitly discredit the choices some black students have made
in their struggle against racism, such as working against financial
aid cuts on campus or working in Jesse Jackson's campaign.

Pushing each other to confront the troubling social problems
is the promise of multi-racial campaigns. The 1987 National Student Convention at the Massachusetts Institute of Technology
began with long, painstaking workshops on racism and sexism.
The roots of anti-racism campaigns at the University of
California-Berkeley, the University of Michigan, and Columbia
University can be traced to the debate started in the divestment movement over how a multi-racial student movement
should respond to racism in our own backyard. One student
commented, "As black students, we found it impossible to work
with those who were willing to challenge racism only from five
thousand miles away."[1]

The debates on racism raging within activist organizations
today are not only healthy, but absolutely necessary if this internationalist movement is to survive and flourish.

Collaborating With Similar Groups

Establishing closer ties among groups doing similar work is
also vital to this movement's success. How might human rights
groups work together for a stronger voice, for instance? How
might the boycott and the socially responsible investment
groups join forces? Shouldn't there be closer collaboration
among the technical assistance, material aid, and trade groups?
How can educational work in the United States become better
integrated into direct aid activities?

Some facets of the internationalist movement have already
attained a significant level of coordination. The alternative
trade groups meet twice annually—once in the United States,
once in Europe—and producer groups in the Third World have
begun to organize their own international conferences.

These gatherings offer the trade groups a time for reflection
and for sharing technical information. On the agenda at the 1988
U.S. trade conference was an initiative from Paul Freundlich of
Co-op America. Paul is proposing that all U.S. groups form a co-

operative marketing campaign—the FAIRTRADE Foundation—
and a national network of Third World shops, modeled after
their namesakes in Europe. "We need to increase our efforts to
compete with importers like Pier 1 and Cost Plus," Paul told us.
"If we really want to help Third World producers gain access to
new markets, we need to think bigger and work together. It
might mean that some groups give up a particular piece of the
pie, but it also means that the pie itself gets a whole lot bigger."

U.S.-Nicaragua sister cities are making concerted efforts to
coordinate as well. The first national gathering of representatives from U.S.-Nicaragua friendship projects was held in 1986.
At each annual meeting since, knowledge about travel and
transport has been shared with newer participants. Speakers
offer the latest ideas for galvanizing new sectors of their
community.

The 1988 U.S.-Nicaragua Sister City Conference held in
Managua addressed the question of where to go from here.
What are the larger roles sister cities can play to be more effective in supporting Nicaraguan development initiatives? How can
they work toward reshaping official U.S-Nicaraguan relations?
How can they address issues of poverty and homelessness in
the United States?

The anti-apartheid movement would greatly benefit from
closer internal coordination. One member of the divestment
community confessed to us his worst fears about the future of a
movement he worked so hard to build: "Some of our organizers
have focused so narrowly on the issue of divestment that once
they got their universities to divest, they were barely able to
sustain student involvement in anti-apartheid or other educational activities."

Other divestment campaigns, however, have been successful
in sustaining student interest. A number of campaigns moved
from university victories to become part of city and state divestment campaigns. At Johns Hopkins University, students pressured Maryland National Bank not only to stop financing U.S.
trade with South Africa, but to increase its lending to low-
income Baltimore communities. Other student groups that
lost divestment battles turned to education and cultural exchanges, pursuing a long-term strategy of forming more positive
direct ties between North Americans and black South Africans.

A wider sharing of the successes and failures within the anti-apartheid movement would help breathe new life into these very trying—and sometimes losing—battles.

A recent, positive trend in the internationalist movement shows some groups starting to move from a single-issue or single-country focus to a broader compass. TECNICA, which has been sending technicians to Nicaragua to support development work since 1984, has recently begun working in southern Africa—Zimbabwe, Mozambique, and Tanzania. MADRE, a group that originally focused solely on women in Nicaragua, has begun to support other Central American and Caribbean women. The American Committee on Africa is pursuing three-way sister city ties, linking U.S. and Nicaraguan cities with cities in southern Africa. The Seattle Nonviolent Action Group commits acts of civil resistance on issues ranging from Central America to South Africa to the Middle East. The Unitarian Universalist Service Committee, which has a strong human rights program in Central America, is starting a similar program in the Philippines. Broadening the scope is essential to both understanding and creating the common ground between different struggles.

But no group can work on every issue in every region of the world. The establishment of some type of annual forum or other form of communication—a sort of United Nations for internationalists—would allow internationalists to exchange ideas and better coordinate *all* sectors of this movement.

Reaching Out to the Broader Community

As the internationalist movement broadens its scope, it must simultaneously broaden its audience. Some groups are addressing this need by deliberately targeting the "unconvinced." Their educational forums are not aimed at the progressive community, but at conservative churches, local PTAs, and men's and women's clubs like the Rotary, Lions, and Soroptimist Clubs. They are putting greater emphasis on high schools—teaching classes, showing films, introducing new curricula, forming debate clubs—to broaden the students' horizons during their crucial formative years.

Others are creating new formats for delivering the same

message. Our society is, unfortunately, not a very literate one, so books and other written material will necessarily only reach a limited audience. The anti-apartheid movement has recognized this and has searched for innovative ways to broadcast its cause. The Sun City video and record attract young people through music and dance. The Stetsasonic rap group and the band Special A.K.A. package the anti-apartheid message in a language and beat that appeal to wide audiences. Artists Against Apartheid has spread the word through murals and other public art forms.

Another form of outreach has involved more sophisticated uses of the mass media. Demonstrations and acts of civil resistance are often planned with an eye toward what will make a splash on the six o'clock news. Groups like the Seattle Media Project coach activist groups on everything from how to write press releases and get stories in the local press to what to wear when interviewed on television. Some groups hire professional media consultants like Washington D.C.-based Fenton Communications or New York-based Pro-Media to get publicity for a critical demonstration or a newly released report.

Broadening the audience also means strengthening our connections to more mainstream political institutions. In Chapter 7, Michael Shuman suggested strengthening local governments' ability to bring people together from all sectors of the community to participate in some aspect of foreign policy-making, and building institutions capable of employing thousands of citizens dedicated to international peace. "An emerging challenge for the peace movement may no longer be how to stop the next weapons system in Congress, but rather how to launch the next visionary, well-funded foreign policy out of City Hall," Shuman speculates.

The anti-nuclear movement also offers useful insights into successful outreach strategies, since it has moved from working on the fringes to affecting major policy changes. "The first time nuclear power and its opponents became a major public issue was in 1977, when two thousand protesters occupied the construction site of the Seabrook, New Hampshire nuclear power plant," recalls peace activist, Bill Moyer. "National and international news coverage put the public spotlight on this challenge to nuclear energy for two solid weeks, as fourteen hundred demonstrators were arrested and remained in armories that served as jails. Only months later came the occupation of the Diablo Canyon, California nuclear construction site.

"There has been no new order for a nuclear power plant in the United States since 1978; every order made during the past eleven years has been canceled. Moreover, there is no indication that there will be any new orders in the foreseeable future, despite the fact that the government and the electrical industry still want a nuclear America.

"Before the 'take-off' of the movement at Seabrook, however, there was a solid decade of ripening social conditions and quiet organizing. It is the care taken in these preliminary stages, invisible to major media coverage, that makes a social movement seem to appear from nowhere. . . .

"The history of the anti-nuclear power movement exemplifies the prerequisites for establishing a large social movement: an issue that can be seen as a 'backyard' or personal one for many people; a stage of going through normal channels to prove why it won't work; the creation of experts within the movement; a network of active people around the country; and adequate training for nonviolent action."[2]

But crucial to reaching a wider audience is making these international issues more relevant to people's everyday lives. To achieve this, the movement must learn to address the domestic ramifications of our government's foreign policy.

Making the U.S. Connections

Very tangible links exist between domestic and foreign issues, but the internationalist movement is only beginning to make them common knowledge. Internationalists must refine their analysis to make it clear that eliminating poverty in the Third World is not only morally correct but in our self-interest as well.

- The jobs of U.S. workers are intimately tied to living conditions in the Third World. As long as millions of Third World workers are denied the right to organize and forced to accept subsistence wages, U.S. companies will continue to move overseas in search of a cheaper, more docile labor force.

- We cannot have healthy, vibrant trade relations with the Third World while the majority of its people remain too impoverished to participate in the market.
- The bloated costs of our militarized foreign policy robs us of much-needed resources for domestic use. During the first three years of the Reagan administration, the cost of U.S. intervention in Central America alone was estimated at $9.5 billion a year, roughly equivalent to the cuts in Aid to Families with Dependent Children, Food Stamps, Medicaid, Child Nutrition Programs, and Social Security Block Grants during the same period.[3]
- The U.S. government, in its eagerness to underwrite covert wars, has either turned a blind eye to or actively participated in the drug trade—from heroin in Southeast Asia in the 1960s and 1970s to cocaine in Latin America in the 1980s.[4] Our foreign policy of collaborating with drug dealers is directly connected to the drug epidemic that is devastating U.S. communities.
- As long as there is hunger, there will be instability in the world. People who are forced to watch their children die of malnutrition are, sooner or later, likely to rebel. Eliminating hunger is therefore a prerequisite for building a world of peace and stability.
- Our present foreign policy is undermining our own democracy. A policy of supporting unpopular regimes in the Third World requires a policy of deceiving the U.S. people. The Iran-contra hearings brought this to the fore: activities carried out without the knowledge and approval of our elected congressional officials bypass the checks and balances so fundamental to the functioning of our democracy. We are left with a foreign policy unaccountable to the public, a policy which is—by definition—undemocratic.

Redefining Democracy

Internationalists have returned from the Third World with a better understanding of the connections between foreign and domestic policies. Their experiences abroad have also made them re-examine some of their notions about basic issues like freedom and democracy. Many have learned from their Third World neighbors that a narrow focus on political rights—such as the right to cast a ballot every few years—is meaningless for people who have no jobs, no health care, no education, no decent housing, no food for their children. This is why so many Third World struggles have defined democracy as a merging of both political *and economic* rights, such as the right to a piece of land to farm or the right to accessible health care.

Many U.S. internationalists have internalized this expanded concept of democracy, and have decided to work for economic rights here in the United States. We've seen a priest who returned from Central America challenged to organize his community to demand jobs and better government services. We've seen U.S. women returning from China intent on improving the quality of daycare in their states. We've seen U.S. construction brigades in Nicaragua coming back to work on housing issues in our own inner cities.

The internationalist movement is also having a healthy effect on revitalizing our political structures. Sister city ties have inspired many more North Americans to participate in local government. Internationalists are demanding more accountability from government officials, and they are getting more involved in the political process—keeping abreast of government activities, meeting regularly with elected representatives, and encouraging the media to do accurate, in-depth reporting on international issues.

Internationalists increasingly recognize that the dichotomy between domestic and foreign issues is false. "When you look at the Americans who joined the Abraham Lincoln Brigade to help the Spanish resistance to fascism," says Johns Hopkins professor, Vicente Navarro, "they were the same people committed to change on the domestic front. And when you look at the internationalists of today, they are the same people who are fighting for rent control in the cities or for a national health care system or for decent housing. The very concept of internationalism is based on the understanding that there is no such thing as 'their' problems and 'our' problems."

Philip Kane, one of the "tourists" from Chapter 1, came to the same conclusion after his trip to South Africa. "What became very clear on our trip is that we are all affected by the same forces. The forces that keep people impoverished in South Africa are the same ones that keep them impoverished in the South Bronx. No matter where we are, we must fight against injustice. No matter where we are, we must reach out to each other. As Martin Luther King said, 'The world in which we live has become a single neighborhood. It is a world in which we live in geographical oneness, and we are all challenged to make it spiritually one...I can never be what I ought to be until you are what you ought to be. You can never be what you ought to be until I am what I ought to be. This is the way the world is made.'"

We hope this book provides you with some of the inspiration and tools to take up this challenge.

Global Exchange Resource Guide to Internationalist Organizations

T his guide includes the organizations mentioned in *Bridging the Global Gap*, as well as many other important internationalist organizations. The guide is divided into chapters, listing groups that do the kind of work described in each chapter of the book. Organizations that carry out various types of activities—material aid, human rights, and tours, for example—may be listed in several sections. Checking the index will help you find in which sections a particular group is listed.

This is by no means a complete list, and we apologize to the many wonderful groups—both local and national—that we have inevitably left out. This is no reflection on their activities, rather a reflection on the shortcomings of our research and space limitations. We plan to expand this guide with each new edition, and ask that you please write to us with the names and addresses of groups—particularly those working on the national level—you think should be added to the list.

We are also aware that a list of this nature is quickly outdated. Sometimes groups are formed to respond to an immediate need, and then disappear when their task is completed. Others lose their funding and are forced to close their doors. Please help us keep this guide current by letting us know if a group has changed its address, changed the focus of its work, or ceased to exist.

CHAPTER 1
Travel with a Purpose

The following is a very selective listing from hundreds of alternative tour options. For a more complete list, send $7 to Alternative Tours, Global Exchange, 2940 16th Street, Room 307, San Francisco, CA 94103.

CEDAM International
Fox Road
Croton-on-Hudson, NY 10520
(914) 271-5365

CEDAM (Conservation, Education, Diving, Archeology, Museums) coordinates one and two week expeditions for novice and experienced divers, explorers, photographers, videographers, archeologists, and marine biologists. Membership is open to anyone with enthusiasm for the conservation and preservation of the planet. Led by professionals, CEDAM tours include the Galapagos Islands, Mexico, Belize, Venezuela, Honduras, and the Red Sea. Costs range from $700 to $1,300 per person.

Center for Cuban Studies
124 W. 23rd Street
New York, NY 10011
(212) 242-0559

The Center organizes numerous trips to Cuba. Each tour has a specific focus, such as health care, film, religion, architecture and urban planning, or the economic system. Trips, according to U.S. Treasury Department restrictions, are limited to professionals in the field, and journalists. Prices vary between $700 and $1,050 for the one-week and ten-day trips.

Center for Global Education
c/o Augsburg College
731 21st Avenue South
Minneapolis, MN 55454
(612) 330-1159

Travel seminars coordinated by the Center are designed to introduce participants to the reality of poverty and injustice in the Third World. Over twenty trips a year go to Central America,

Mexico, the Caribbean, and the Philippines. Additionally, the Center plans travel seminars for other church, community, and professional organizations. The trips often have themes, such as health care, Christian base communities, human rights, or the church in social transformation. Costs range between $875 and $1,895, including airfare. Some scholarships are available.

Church Coalition for Human Rights in the Philippines
P.O. Box 70
110 Maryland Avenue N.E.
Washington, DC 20002
(202) 543-1094

The Coalition educates the public on the human rights situation in the Philippines through two-week learning tours. The itinerary includes discussions with church leaders, grassroots organizers, Philippine and U.S. Embassy officials, sugar workers on the island of Negros, and others. Cost is about $1,750.

Earthwatch
P.O. Box 403
Watertown, MA 02272
(617) 926-8200

Earthwatch volunteers work with scientists and scholars on academic research expeditions in thirty-seven countries and seventeen states. Expeditions vary from studying rock art in Italy to making documentaries on Brazilian festivals. Volunteers participate for two weeks or more. The Earthwatch catalog lists research projects with costs ranging from $600 to $2,500.

EPOCA
Earth Island Institute
300 Broadway, Suite 28
San Francisco, CA 94133-3312
(415) 788-3666

EPOCA (Environmental Project on Central America) sponsors reforestation brigades to Nicaragua. The brigades complement the long-range environmental plans developed by the Nicaraguan Institute for Natural Resources and the Environment

(IRENA), which include planting tens of thousands of trees to provide windbreaks and protect Nicaragua's farmland against flooding and erosion. Environmentalists and non-environmentalists are welcome to join the fifty-member brigades.

Gemquest
Global Education Motivators, Inc.
Montgomery County Intermediate Unit Building
Montgomery Avenue & Paper Mill Road
Erdenheim, PA 19118
(215) 233-9558

Gemquest organizes study and travel programs that promote cultural understanding through extensive people-to-people interaction, homestays, and university study abroad. Educators and students of all ages are invited to participate in numerous trips to all areas of the world, including Kenya, China, Costa Rica, Southeast Asia, Japan, India, Australia, and New Zealand.

Global Exchange
2940 16th Street, Room 307
San Francisco, CA 94103
(415) 255-7296

Global Exchange has a tour program designed to help people get more involved in supporting Third World development efforts. Its tours go to Central and Latin America, the Caribbean (particularly Haiti), and southern Africa. Some limited scholarships are available for low-income people who pledge to increase their activism upon their return.

Habitat for Humanity
419 West Church Street
Americus, GA 31709
(912) 924-6935

Habitat for Humanity is a nonprofit Christian housing ministry that works to build or renovate homes for the inadequately sheltered in the United States and in twenty countries around the world. Volunteers donate labor and money for materials. Homes are sold at no profit, with a no-interest mortgage repaid over a fifteen to twenty-five year period. Volunteer commitments range between one week and three years.

International Bicycle Fund (IBF)
4247 135th Place S.E.
Bellevue, WA 98006-1319
(206) 746-1028

IBF sponsors educational tours of Africa to encourage people-to-people contacts, along with studies of local culture, economics, and history. Three or four bicycle tours are offered each year to West Africa (Togo, Ghana, Ivory Coast), East Africa (Kenya), Cameroon, and other countries. Costs are approximately $1,000, not including airfare.

Inter-religious Foundation for Community Organization (IFCO)
402 West 145th Street
New York, NY 10031
(212) 926-5757, (212) 229-1657

IFCO sponsors study tours to Nicaragua, featuring visits with farmers, women's organizations, church groups, opposition figures, and government leaders. Participation is open to anyone, especially those willing to talk to groups in the United States about their experiences in Nicaragua. Cost is approximately $1,150 including airfare. Limited scholarships are available.

Into Africa Tours
RR 1 Box 2880
Plainfield, VT 05667
(802) 454-8630

Into Africa Tours seeks to facilitate cross-cultural understanding and cooperation by linking North American travelers with Kenyan communities. Along with safaris into Kenya's national parks and cultural tours of Nairobi, travelers visit the countryside to speak with village people and observe development projects. Also included is a homestay on a family farm. Three tours are offered each year. Cost is approximately $1,500 (sliding scale), not including airfare.

MADRE
121 W. 27th Street, Room 301
New York, NY 10001
(212) 627-0444

MADRE is a women's friendship committee working to build links between women in Central America, the Caribbean, and the United States. The U.S. women who visit El Salvador with MADRE talk to people in refugee camps, meet with women who are political prisoners, question U.S. Embassy representatives, and often help deliver donated supplies. In Nicaragua, they speak with women in hospitals, schools, and community settings. One or two ten-day delegations are organized a year.

Marazul Tours, Inc.
250 West 57th Street, Suite 1311
New York, NY 10107
(212) 582-9570, (800) 223-5334

Marazul Tours is a well-known coordinator of alternative tours. Many of the organizations in this guide enlist Marazul's expertise in planning trips to Nicaragua and Cuba. While most of its tours focus on Nicaragua and Cuba, future alternative travel experiences will be offered in Vietnam, Argentina, Brazil, Colombia, Mexico, and Uruguay.

Mekong Travel
c/o Merle Ratner
P.O. Box 302
Prince Station
New York, NY 10012
(212) 420-1586

Mekong Travel leads two sixteen-day tours each year to Vietnam. In an effort to understand the past and current conditions of the country, group members visit schools, hospitals, and tunnels of the wartime underground. Also included are discussions with Vietnamese government representatives, unions, and women's groups. Mekong can tailor the experience to meet specific interests. Approximate cost is $2,375, including airfare from New York.

National Council of Churches
Travel Seminar Office
475 Riverside Drive, Room 851
New York, NY 10115
(212) 870-2044

National Council of Churches Travel Seminars strengthen ties between the ecumenical movement within the United States and abroad. A four-week trip to the Philippines and Korea includes visits to churches and church projects; a two-week itinerary in the Soviet Union includes worship and dialogue with Soviet Christians, visits to peace and friendship societies, and trips to historic and cultural sites. A network of participants is forming to encourage and support follow-up activities.

Network in Solidarity with the People of Guatemala (NISGUA)
1314 14th Street N.W.
Washington, DC 20005
(202) 483-0050

NISGUA sponsors delegations of activists to Guatemala. The itinerary includes meetings with trade unionists, peasant groups, and church and government representatives, as well as visits to "model villages" controlled by the military. Tours are open primarily to individuals active with Central American solidarity movements. Costs are approximately $350, not including airfare.

Our Developing World
13004 Paseo Presada
Saratoga, CA 95070
(408) 379-4431

Our Developing World leads study tours to Africa and Central America to help travelers become better aware of development issues in the Third World. It is one of the few organizations leading tours to southern Africa (Mozambique and Zimbabwe), and plans to initiate tours to the Philippines as well. It also maintains an ongoing link with tour participants, encouraging them to become involved in activist work.

Palestine Human Rights Campaign (PHRC)
220 South State Street, Room 1308
Chicago, IL 60604
(312) 987-1985

PHRC has conducted tours of Israel, the occupied West Bank, Jerusalem, and Gaza since 1982. The trip is an intensive experience that puts participants in contact with decision-makers and residents to discuss the vital issues facing Israelis and Palestinians. Included are tours of Palestinian villages and overnight stays in Arab homes and Jewish kibbutzim. Trips last for seventeen days and cost $1,600, including airfare from Chicago.

Plowshares Institute
P.O. Box 243
Simsbury, CT 06070
(203) 651-9675, (203) 658-6645

Plowshares seminars are designed to be immersion experiences. Participants are asked to do serious advance reading and preparation, participate in discussions of their experiences, explore alternative approaches to global issues, and make a covenant to share their experiences with others for at least one year after the trip. The Institute plans programs to East Africa, South and Southeast Asia, and Australia. Costs vary with location. Limited scholarships are available.

Servas International
11 John Street, Suite 706
New York, NY 10038
(212) 267-0252

Servas does not offers tours, but provides a unique service to individual travelers: it links travelers with host families, facilitating deeper, more personal contacts among people of diverse cultures and backgrounds. Members offer housing (usually for short stays), meals or company to international travelers and are extended similar courtesies when travelling abroad. In addition to hosts throughout the United States and Europe, Servas also has members in dozens of Third World countries, from Antigua to Zimbabwe.

Tour de Caña
c/o Bikes Not Bombs
P.O. Box 7293
Philadelphia, PA 19101
(215) 222-1253

Tour de Caña is a bicycling tour of Nicaragua that includes visits to the Bikes Not Bombs Managua workshop and other bicycle assembly shops, and daily swims in Lake Nicaragua, volcanic lagoons, and the Pacific Ocean. Tours, led by seasoned bilingual cyclists, begin in Managua and proceed southwest. Buses, meals, and accommodations are provided by TurNica, the Nicaraguan tourist agency. The ten-day tours are offered annually and cost approximately $850, including airfare from Mexico City.

The Travelers Society
P.O. Box 2846
Loop Station
Minneapolis, MN 55402
(800) 342-2788

The Travelers Society gives priority to making alternative tours accessible to families and grandparent/grandchildren groups. Trips arranged to the Soviet Union and to the Middle East. Programs are tailored to meet the needs of special interest groups. The nonprofit Society also helps raise funds to subsidize the cost of the trips for particular groups, such as teachers.

U.S.-Indochina Reconciliation Project (USIRP)
5808 Greene Street
Philadelphia, PA 19144
(215) 848-4100

USIRP sponsors tours of Vietnam, encouraging U.S. citizens, particularly educators, to find common ground with their Vietnamese counterparts. Itineraries include visits to areas of natural beauty and historical significance, as well as meetings with government representatives and aid officials. Three-week trips cost approximately $2,600, including airfare.

Venceremos Brigade
64 Fulton Street, Room 1101
New York, NY 10038
(212) 349-6292

Venceremos Brigade, a project of the Cuban Friendship Institute, organizes trips to Cuba that combine work with travel and educational opportunities. Itineraries include visits to hospitals, factories, and cooperative farms, as well as meetings with representatives of youth groups, neighborhood committees, and members of the National Assembly. Several trips are offered each year, including special interest tours for health professionals, women, children, and individuals interested in music or film.

Volunteers for Peace International Workcamps (VFP)
Tiffany Road
Belmont, VT 05730
(802) 259-2759

VFP work camps provide an opportunity for young people of all nationalities to work together on two- and three-week projects. VFP coordinates placement in over eight hundred camps in thirty-six countries listed in an annual International Workcamp Directory. VFP aims to promote international peace and understanding through hands-on construction, agricultural, and other cooperative work. Costs range between $75 and $90, plus travel expenses.

Wilderness Expeditions
310 Washington Avenue S.W.
Roanoke, VA 24016
(703) 342-5630, (800) 323-3241

Wilderness Expeditions provides opportunities for travelers to explore the jungles of Peru, and emphasizes jungle conservation in areas where ecosystems are rapidly being destroyed. The trips support a program affiliated with the International Society for the Preservation of the Tropical Rainforest, as well as a

Peruvian Children's Fund orphanage. Expeditions range from two days to two weeks.

Witness for Peace (WFP)
P.O. Box 567
Durham, NC 27702-0567
(919) 688-5049

WFP is a grassroots, faith-based movement committed to changing U.S. policy toward Central America through nonviolent action. Working with Nicaraguan churches, WFP maintains a permanent presence of U.S. citizens who want to gain an understanding of the effects of U.S. involvement in Central America by sharing in the daily lives of Nicaraguans. Delegations also have discussions with church, government, and opposition leaders, and they participate in work projects and worship services. WFP sponsors both long-term teams and short-term delegations. While most trips are to Nicaragua, some visit other Central American countries on their way to Nicaragua. A two-week trip costs $900 to $1,000, including airfare.

Resources

Center for Responsible Tourism
2 Kensington Road
San Anselmo, CA 94960
(415) 453-2280

The Center does research and education on the impact of tourism on Third World peoples. While the Center does not organize tours, it does offer resources and information for individuals and groups interested in responsible tourism. The Center publishes an occasional newsletter, *Responsible Travelling*, and distributes *Contours*, the quarterly newsletter of the Ecumenical Coalition on Third World Tourism.

CHAPTER 2
Partners with People

This section lists national partnership organizations, as well as a few local groups with specific strengths that may be useful to groups develop-ing new partnership activities.

Africa Exchange
2940 16th Street, Room 307
San Francisco, CA 94103
(415) 648-7015

Africa Exchange, a project of Global Exchange, publishes re-sources for activists and provides information on linking U.S. communities with southern African organizations working against apartheid and for democratic development.

American Committee on Africa (ACOA)
198 Broadway
New York, NY 10038
(212) 962-1210

Building on the ties that already exist between U.S. and Cen-tral American cities, ACOA is working to create three-way rela-tionships by connecting existing partners with African cities, hospitals, schools, and other community institutions.

Berkeley City Council
Peace and Justice Commission
City Center Building, 2nd Floor
2180 Milvia Street
Berkeley, CA 94704
(415) 644-6317

Berkeley has six sister cities, including the first U.S.-Black South African township partnership. Berkeley places political and foreign policy issues high on the list of criteria when choos-ing a partner and a program of activities.

Canadian Organization for Development through Education (CODE)
321 Chaptel Street
Ottawa, Ontario K1N 7Z2
Canada
(613) 232-3569

CODE supports sister school programs throughout Canada, and already coordinates partnerships with schools in Uganda, Kenya, the Caribbean, and the Philippines.

Committee in Solidarity with ANDES (COSANDES)
2940 16th Street, Room 305
San Francisco, CA 94103
(415) 861-2121

COSANDES partnerships support the work of ANDES, the national teachers' association in El Salvador. Funds raised through educational, social, and athletic events benefit the Salvadoran literacy campaign, families of disappeared teachers, and schools. COSANDES also arranges tours of El Salvador for North American teachers.

Faith Without Borders
c/o Network in Solidarity with Guatemala (NISGUA)
1314 14th Street N.W., Room 16
Washington, DC 20005
(202) 483-0050

Founded in 1985, Faith Without Borders links Christian-based communities in the United States with Guatemalan counterparts for the purpose of communication, education, and Christian commitment. Faith Without Borders expects that U.S. partners will do much more than send money, and considers community education about Guatemala its key focus.

Friendship City Projects
38899 Boulder Canyon Drive
Boulder, CO 80302
(303) 442-0460

Friendship City Projects is one of several active U.S.-Nicaragua partnerships. This group is famous for accomplishing a lot with few resources—for example getting a truck and driving to Nicaragua to visit its sister city.

Girl Guides of Canada
50 Merton Street
Toronto, Ontario M4S 1A3
Canada

Canada's version of the Girl Scouts has included an extensive partnership program since 1984, linking young people in
Canada and Third World communities. Funds raised to support
the partnerships go to youth and development programs in the
Third World.

International Development Education Association (IDEA)
120 Woodland, Suite 2
San Anselmo, CA 94960
(415) 456-9196

IDEA supports partnerships between San Francisco Bay Area
schools and community groups and Third World communities,
organizing material aid campaigns, tours, and work brigades.

International Sister Restaurant Project
c/o The White Dog Café
3420 Sansome Street
Philadelphia, PA 19104
(215) 386-9224

Café owner, Judy Wicks, was inspired to start a sister restaurant project after a visit to Nicaragua, and is now working to add
Soviet and Tanzanian restaurants to her "family." She appeals to
her clientele to travel with her, learn about the country's political, economic, and cultural situation, and help establish sister
ties. She also plans to put together cook exchanges.

Labor Network on Central America
P.O. Box 28014, Department F
Oakland, CA 94604
(415) 272-9951

Since 1983, the Labor Network has been bringing together
labor activists focused on Central American issues that concern
working people. It espouses an anti-interventionist and pro-
labor policy. The Labor Network itself does not sponsor or

oversee sister union programs, but can provide information on partnership activities carried out by affiliated trade unions.

MADRE
121 W. 27th Street, Room 301
New York, NY 10001
(212) 627-0444

MADRE is helping to support the Nicaraguan government's efforts to provide childcare to all who need it through its Day-care Center Twinning Program. Once twin centers are assigned, children, teachers, and parents exchange photographs, draw-ings, messages, and school supplies as a means to learn about each other.

Mexico-U.S. Diálogos
51 Eighth Avenue
Brooklyn, NY 11217
(718) 230-3628

Mexico-U.S. Diálogos links different social sectors—farmers, unions, academics—in the United States and Mexico to create a deeper understanding between the two nations and to develop a new vision for mutual development.

Network of Educators Committees on Central America (NECCA)
P.O. Box 43509
Washington, DC 20010
(202) 667-2618

A number of NECCA members have active partnership pro-grams involving schools and teachers' unions. NECCA also works on curriculum projects to teach about Central America in U.S. schools.

New El Salvador Today Foundation (NEST)
P.O. Box 411436
San Francisco, CA 94141
(415) 864-7755

Since 1983, NEST's sister city program has supported the efforts of displaced people in El Salvador to repopulate their villages and restore community construction and development. As of 1988 NEST had seven U.S.-Salvadoran partnerships.

New Haven/Leon Sister City Project
965 Quinnipiac Avenue
New Haven, CT 06513
(203) 467-9182

The New Haven partners have been especially successful at linking a wide variety of community groups—sanitation workers, schoolchildren, daycare centers, universities, artists, and poets—with their counterparts in Leon, Nicaragua.

Partners of the Americas
1424 K Street N.W., Suite 700
Washington, DC 20005
(202) 628-3300

Partners, which was founded by the U.S. State Department during the Alliance for Progress years of the 1960s, is the largest private voluntary organization promoting ties between the United States, Latin America, and the Caribbean. The partnerships carry out economic development projects and all kinds of social and business exchanges. The organization maintains a pro-business, pro-U.S. foreign policy stance, and funding for the partnerships comes from a hundred major corporations, foundations, and government agencies such as AID and USIA.

Peace Corps Partnership Program
M-1210
806 Connecticut Avenue N.W.
Washington, DC 20526
(800) 424-8580, ext. 227

Peace Corps Partnerships was established to provide financial assistance to Peace Corps projects in the Third World. Many are not long-term partnerships, but are a means to transfer material aid and allow former Peace Corps volunteers to maintain their ties with the Third World communities they worked in.

Philippine Workers Support Committee (PWSC)
P.O. Box 11208
Moiliili Station
Honolulu, HI 96828
(808) 595-7362

The Philippine Workers Support Committee is a network of independent chapters and committees in the United States carrying out activities to support Philippine workers. PWSC publishes the Philippine Labor Alert, which reports on Philippine labor news as well as on critical labor issues arising in other countries. PWSC encourages members to support workers' struggles through various actions, including sister workplace projects between North American and Philippine employees of the same companies.

Project Self-Help and Awareness (PSA)
975 Prairie Queen Road
Cambridge, WI 53523
(608) 986-3815

PSA links Wisconsin with Mississippi in a sister state program. While not a transnational partnership, PSA is a good example of a way to strengthen regional ties within the United States and may be useful for groups wanting to form three-way partnerships. PSA participants travel between the two states and live with each others' families and friends. The Wisconsin partners try to help the Mississippi partners carry out their housing and agricultural development projects, providing technical assistance, marketing schemes, and material assistance.

Project Tanzania
P.O. Box 12000
Raleigh, NC 27605
(919) 890-6007

Project Tanzania is unique in that it is sponsored in part by Raleigh's local TV station (WRAL). While the community sends assistance from North Carolina to Shinyanga, Tanzania, viewers learn about the ecology, customs, and daily life in their

Tanzanian sister city. A study guide and video for fourth graders have also been developed, including lessons in Swahili.

Seattle/Managua Sister City Association
P.O. Box 24883
Seattle, WA 98214
(206) 329-2974

The Seattle/Managua Association has weathered some difficult political battles to keep its partnership going, and now has one of the largest organizations in the country, with a full-time staff and many volunteers.

Seeds Sister Cities Project
222 E. Lake Drive
Decatur, GA 30030
(404) 378-3566

Decatur is officially linked with a city and a village in Burkina Faso, West Africa. The Decatur group sends representatives to Africa about once a year, and hosts visitors from Burkina. The group involves a number of different community sectors in the partnership program, from city officials to health professionals to university researchers.

Sister Cities International (SCI)
1625 Eye Street N.W., Suite 424-26
Washington, DC 20006
(703) 836-3535

SCI was founded in the late 1950s and is now the largest coordinating body for sister city programs. SCI advocates official bonds between cities, and does not advocate issue- or politically-oriented relationships. Funds for activities are raised by nonprofit organizations formed in each city. Approximately 15 percent of the national budget comes from memberships; the rest comes from endowments, corporations, and government agencies such as USIA and AID.

Sister Parish
c/o Clergy and Laity Concerned
10 East Mt. Vernon Place, Suite 1
Baltimore, MD 21202
(301) 962-8333

Sister Parish links U.S. congregations with base Christian communities in Central America for education, exchange, and technical assistance. Sister Parish hopes to create similar links throughout Latin America and in other parts of the world.

Towns and Development Movement
c/o ICDA
Rue des Bollandistes 22
1040 Brussels, Belgium
Tel: 0032.2.734.23.32

ICDA is one of many European organizations participating in the Towns and Development Movement, which links European cities and villages with Third World communities. ICDA is a coordinator of the movement, and can provide information on other groups throughout Europe.

United Towns Organization (UTO)
2 Rue de Logelbach
F-75017 Paris, France
Tel: 47.66.65.10

UTO has been coordinating partnerships for European towns since 1957. Recent partnerships include East and West Germany, Poland and Morocco, Togo and France, and Great Britain and France.

U.S. South Africa Sister Community Project
2601 Mission Street, Room 400
San Francisco, CA 94110
(415) 824-2938

U.S. South Africa Sister Community Project, founded in 1987, links U.S. cities with black communities in South Africa. Because of the government's policy of racial classification, certain areas are designated for whites only. The purpose of the partnerships is to recognize the black communities, and in doing so, pressure the government not to carry out its policy of forced removal. By 1988 the Sister Community Project linked four U.S. communities (Louisville, St. Paul, Milwaukee and Berkeley) with black communities, with the goal of establishing twelve partnerships by the end of 1989.

Wisconsin Coordinating Council on Nicaragua (WCCN)
P.O. Box 1534
Madison, WI 53701
(608) 257-7230

WCCN is an umbrella organization for Wisconsin's many Nicaragua groups (Wisconsin and Nicaragua have been sister states since 1964). One of the country's most active partnerships, WCCN has also coordinated national conferences for some sixty Nicaraguan sister city programs, and can refer people to the local organizations in their areas.

Resources

Center for Innovative Diplomacy (CID)
17931 Sky Park Circle, Suite F
Irvine, CA 92714
(714) 250-1296

CID publishes materials on citizen diplomacy. The quarterly *Bulletin of Municipal Foreign Policy* provides commentary on city-based foreign policies, and highlights city policymaking in the areas of arms control, Central America, South Africa, economic conversion, homeporting, human rights, and U.S.-U.S.S.R. relations. *Building Municipal Foreign Policies*, by co-founder Michael Shuman, provides a resource guide and historical overview for the citizen foreign policy movement. The book has good examples of successes and of obstacles faced by municipal foreign policymakers; it makes a strong argument in favor of citizen initiatives as a means to democratize U.S. policymaking. Available for $6 from CID.

Friends in Deed: The Story of U.S.-*Nicaragua Sister Cities*
By Sheldon Rampton, photographs by Liz Chilsen
Wisconsin Coordinating Council on Nicaragua (WCCN)
P.O. Box 1534
Madison, WI 53701
(608) 257-7230

Friends in Deed is the history of the U.S.-Nicaragua sister city movement, as told by activists who have been involved since 1964. It also provides detailed advice for people considering a Nicaraguan or other sister city project.

Sister City Training
c/o Jobs With Peace
76 Summer Street
Boston, MA 02110
(617) 338-5783

The Sister City Training Program is a project of Jobs with Peace, and brings together local organizers to share information and technical assistance.

Villagers Magazine
P.O. Box 1
55 McCaul Street
Toronto, Ontario M5T 2W7
Canada
(416) 863-9734

Villagers is a high-quality, colorful, quarterly publication put out by Village-to-Village Applied Integrated Development, a Canadian nonprofit education foundation. Each issue features art, articles, poetry, commentary, and stories from Canadian partners and local groups.

CHAPTER 3
Aid: From Charity to Solidarity

The following is a partial listing of organizations providing material and technical assistance to Third World grassroots groups. Some offer opportunities for voluntary service, at home or abroad. The first section lists professional and solidarity groups that provide general development assistance. The rest of the list is divided by type of assistance—architecture and construction, arts and popular culture, organized labor, public health and medicine, teaching and research, transportation, student programs, and family, women's and children's programs.

For an extensive list of professional U.S. development groups working overseas, contact InterAction, 200 Park Avenue South, New York, NY 10003. For additional listings of opportunities for volunteer work abroad, send $7 to Global Exchange, 2940 16th Street, Room 307, San Francisco, CA 94103.

General Development Assistance Organizations

American Friends Service Committee (AFSC)
1501 Cherry Street
Philadelphia, PA 19102
(215) 421-7000

AFSC is the Quaker world service organization, providing direct material assistance to grassroots groups in Asia, Africa, Latin America, the Caribbean, the Middle East, and poor U.S. communities. AFSC also supports an extensive U.S. educational program through its regional offices that coordinate human rights campaigns, cross-cultural school programs, foreign policy programs, and local material aid projects.

American Jewish World Service (AJWS)
729 Boylston Street
Boston, MA 02116
(617) 267-6656

AJWS was founded in 1982 and has since grown to support grassroots development projects in Asia, Africa, and Latin America. AJWS also carries out development education efforts in U.S. Jewish communities. Regional associates groups represent the organization locally and participate in their own educational and aid campaigns.

Bishop Tutu Refugee Fund
P.O. Box 18207
Washington, D.C. 20036

The Bishop Tutu Refugee Fund raises money to support South African refugees—both internal and external—created by the apartheid government. It funds agricultural training for refugees, provides education and scholarships, and supplies refugee centers with needed goods.

Central America Exchange
2940 16th Street, Room 307
San Francisco, CA 94103
(415) 255-7296

Central America Exchange, a project of Global Exchange, was founded in 1988 to provide material assistance and human rights advocacy to grassroots organizations in Central America, and to educate North Americans about U.S. foreign policy. Much of its emphasis has been on building people-to-people ties with Honduras, a country that has become the center of U.S. military policy in the region.

Chile Humanitarian Aid
347 Dolores Street, Suite 109
San Francisco, CA 94110
(415) 863-0681

Chile Humanitarian Aid raises money to fund grassroots projects in Chile, supporting indigenous peoples and helping political prisoners and their families. It also does educational work in the United States on Chilean issues.

Church World Service (CWS)
475 Riverside Drive
New York, NY 10115-0050
(212) 870-2257

A member of the National Council of Churches, CWS supports overseas development projects to benefit the Third World poor. Additionally, CWS carries out development education, refugee resettlement, and policy research and advocacy on Third World issues in the United States.

Eritrean Relief Committee (ERC)
475 Riverside Drive, Room 251
New York, NY 10115
(212) 870-2727

The Eritrean Relief Committee is the U.S. arm of the Eritrean Relief Association, an indigenous African relief and development organization founded on the principles of self-help and the support of basic human rights to food, shelter, and peace. The ERC funds projects supporting Eritrean refugees who are under attack by the Ethiopian military and suffering from the effects of drought.

Florida Association of Voluntary Agencies for Caribbean Action (FAVA/CA)
1311 Executive Center Drive, Suite 118
Tallahassee, FL 32301
(904) 877-4705

FAVA/CA runs a people-to-people technical assistance program, providing volunteers in the fields of health, social services, education, agriculture, and business. Volunteers typically spend one to two weeks on assignment in a Latin American or Caribbean country, responding to needs identified by the host country. FAVA/CA also offers professional exchange programs for mid-level managers and technicians.

Foundation for International Training
200-1262 Don Mills Road
Don Mills, Ontario M3B 2W7
Canada
(416) 449-8838

The Foundation sponsors projects in Africa, the Middle East, and the Caribbean in community and cooperative development, industry administration, and management. Volunteers should have some overseas experience as well as experience teaching a technical skill. Assignments are for six to eight weeks. All overseas expenses are paid, and a small honorarium is offered.

Grassroots International (GI)
Box 312
Cambridge, MA 02139
(617) 497-9180

GI supports grassroots development projects in the horn of Africa, Lebanon, the Philippines, and South Africa. It also concentrates on educational activities in the United States.

International Development and Education Association (IDEA)
120 Woodland Ave, Suite 2
San Anselmo, CA 94960
(415) 456-9196

IDEA was founded in 1986 to build a bridge between people in the San Francisco Bay Area and people in the developing world. IDEA conducts community education programs and sets up partnerships between U.S. and Third World groups. In 1989, for example, IDEA took California high school students to rural Kenya to work with local high school students building a school library.

International Development Exchange (IDEX)
777 Valencia Street
San Francisco, CA 94110
(415) 621-1494

IDEX links U.S. community groups (schools, churches, rotary clubs) with grassroots development projects in the Third World for the joint purposes of mobilizing material aid and using the projects to educate U.S. groups about the Third World.

International Voluntary Services (IVS)
1424 16th Street N.W., Suite 504
Washington, DC 20016
(202) 387-5533

IVS provides technical assistance volunteers to small-scale rural development projects in the Third World. Volunteers serve a minimum of two years, usually in agriculture, small business and cooperative development, public health, or technology. Volunteers have been sent into Central and South America,

Asia, Africa, and the Caribbean. Participants must have a degree in a relevant field, and at least two years practical experience. Room, board, and travel expenses are provided.

Lasting Links
6231 Leesburg Pike, Suite 612
Falls Church, VA 22044
(703) 241-3700

Lasting Links maintains a database of Third World development projects, and makes the list available to U.S. groups that wish to develop partnerships to help fund the projects.

Mennonite Central Committee
21 South 12th Street
Akron, PA 17501
(717) 859-1151

Mennonite Central Committee works in fifty countries throughout the world, providing material and technical assistance in the areas of health, agriculture, education, social services, and community development. U.S. volunteers are recruited to work on these projects, and MCC pays for their transportation, living expenses, and a small stipend. MCC asks that volunteers be Christian, actively involved in a church group, and willing to adhere to its nonviolent principles.

Middle East Children's Alliance
2140 Shattuck Avenue, Room 207
Berkeley, CA 94704
(415) 548-0542

Middle East Children's Alliance provides medical aid, and educational and recreational materials to children in the Israeli-occupied territories. It also takes groups of U.S. citizens to the Middle East to witness the conditions of the occupation, and tries to raise awareness among the U.S. public about Middle East issues.

New El Salvador Today Foundation (NEST)
P.O. Box 411436
San Francisco, CA 94141
(415) 864-7755

NEST provides emergency relief and community development assistance to repopulated zones in rural El Salvador. NEST also helps educate North Americans about conditions in El Salvador and U.S. policy there.

Nicaragua Network
2025 I St. N.W., Suite 212
Washington, D.C. 20006
(202) 223-2328

The Nicaragua Network is an umbrella organization for many U.S groups providing material aid to Nicaragua. It also works to stop U.S. funding of the contras, and to educate U.S. citizens about Nicaraguan reality.

Nicaragua Appropriate Technology Project (NICAT)
P.O. Box 158
Bellingham, WA 98227
(206) 647-1752, (206) 321-1367

NICAT volunteers work with governmental and private agencies in Nicaragua in alternative energy and agriculture. NICAT also does education in the United States to raise funds for its projects and to counter U.S. military intervention. Projects include setting up an appropriate technology library and a mobile water-testing and purification lab, donating surveying equipment, constructing a small-scale hydro-electric plant, and training local machinists and operators.

Oliver Law Fund
5465 S. Ridgewood
Chicago, IL 60615
(312) 702-8570

The Oliver Law Fund was established in 1987 in order to send technical trainers and medical graduates to work in the Front Line States in southern Africa—particularly Mozambique,

Angola, and Namibia. Room and board is covered by the sponsoring government; the fund covers transportation costs. The purpose of the Oliver Law Fund is to link the black community of Chicago with people struggling for freedom in southern Africa.

Overseas Development Network (ODN)
P.O. Box 1430
Cambridge, MA 02238
(617) 868-3002

ODN is a network of college activists across the United States who organize educational and fundraising events on third world development issues. ODN chapters are essentially autonomous, but relate to each other for national campaigns.

Oxfam America
115 Broadway
Boston, MA 02116
(617) 482-1211

Oxfam Canada
251 Laurier Avenue West Suite 301
Ottawa, Ontario K1P 5S6
Canada
(613) 237-5236

Oxfam-UK
274 Banbury Road
Oxford OXF2DZ
England
(44) 8-655-6777

Oxfam (first established in the U.K.) is now one of the oldest and largest private development assistance organizations in the world. Oxfam supports material and technical aid projects in Asia, Africa, Latin America, the Caribbean, and the Middle East. Each national organization is autonomous, but they share the goals of supporting grassroots efforts of the poorest members of society, building institutions to sustain these efforts, and educating citizens of industrialized countries about the political and economic realities of the third world.

Partners for Global Justice
4920 Piney Branch Road N.W.
Washington, D.C. 20011
(202) 723-8273

Partners for Global Justice has a long history of providing volunteer opportunities in Third World countries and of empowering U.S. citizens to influence public policy effectively. Volunteers spend one year in a third world country working with cooperatives and community organizations. A second year is devoted to work on human rights or direct service with groups in the United States.

Plenty USA
P.O. Box 90
Summertown, TN 38483
(615) 964-3992

PLENTY sponsors a limited number of volunteers who work on community-based development projects in food production, health care, construction, and integrated village technology in Central America and Africa.

Quest for Peace
Quixote Center
P.O. Box 5206
Hyattsville, MD 20782
(301) 699-0042

Quest for Peace is the material aid campaign that has matched, dollar for dollar, the money Congress allocated to the contras with real humanitarian aid to the Nicaraguan people. It is now focusing on removing the U.S. economic embargo against Nicaragua.

SHARE Foundation
Box 16, Cardinal Station
Washington, DC 20064
(202) 635-5540

SHARE (Salvadoran Humanitarian Aid, Research, and Education) raises money for programs benefiting the poor of El Salvador, including refugee groups seeking to repopulate their villages. It funds dental and health clinics, leads delegations of

U.S. religious leaders to El Salvador, and places U.S. volunteers in rural villages as protection against official harassment.

TECNICA
3254 Adeline Street
Berkeley, CA 94703
(415) 655-3838

TECNICA has sent hundreds of volunteers from the United States, Canada, and Europe to work in Nicaragua since 1985, and has since expanded to include programs in southern Africa. TECNICA volunteers train technicians and professionals, solve technical problems, and recommend and install appropriate technology. TECNICA places long- and short-term volunteers, who pay their way and a fee for administrative costs. TECNICA volunteers include specialists in computers, engineering, agriculture, health care, and manufacturing.

Unitarian Universalist Service Committee (UUSC)
78 Beacon Street
Boston, MA 02108
(617) 742-2120

The UUSC has focuses on human rights and grassroots development in its overseas work. Its development program provides material and technical assistance to grassroots groups in Africa (mainly West Africa and the Horn of Africa), Central America and the Caribbean, and India.

Venceremos Brigade
64 Fulton Street, Room 1101
New York, NY 10038
(212) 349-6292

A project of the Cuban Friendship Institute, Venceremos Brigades offer one of the few ways U.S. citizens can bypass U.S. laws barring travel to Cuba. Annual trips bring groups of twenty to thirty people to work and live with a community in Cuba. Members of the Brigade are expected to do educational work later in the United States to help improve U.S.-Cuba relations.

Volunteers in Asia
P.O. Box 4543
Stanford, CA 94305
(415) 497-3228

At the request of Asian institutions, Volunteers in Asia places volunteers in teaching, village technology, and community development positions in East Asia and the Pacific. The *Appropriate Technology Sourcebook* and an easily portable microfiche library of a thousand technical books are examples of the group's creative projects for technical aid.

Volunteers for Peace, Inc. (VFP)
Tiffany Road
Belmont, VT 05730
(802) 259-2759

VFP coordinates work brigades throughout the world. Ten to twenty people from several countries join a community project in construction, environmental, social, agricultural, or maintenance work. VFP serves as an information and referral center for these international opportunities. Volunteers pay all travel expenses, although some brigades cover room and board.

War on Want
Three Castles House
1 London Bridge Street
London SE1 9SG
England
(44) 1-403-2266

War on Want is an organization providing funding for innovative projects in the Third World designed to improve material conditions and raise people's consciousness. It is involved in educating the British public about development and foreign policy issues.

YWCA/USA
726 Broadway
New York, NY 10003
(212) 614-2700

YWCA/USA links YWCAs in the United States with YWCAs in Third World countries through the World YWCAs Cooperation for Development Program. Program grants provide funding for projects initiated and led by the local YWCA. Such programs include vocational crafts for women in refugee camps in Jordan, tree planting campaigns in Botswana, and economic empowerment for women in Zambia. Within the United States, YWCAs organize study groups to consider the issues faced by different areas of the world.

Issue-Specific Material and Technical Aid Organizations

AGRICULTURE

Farm Youth Exchange
c/o National Farm Union
250-C Second Avenue South
Saskatoon, Saskatchewan S7K 2M1 Canada
(306) 652-9465

The Farm Youth Exchange is a joint effort between Canadian farm organizations and several Caribbean farmers' groups to exchange experiences and technical information, and to develop young leaders with a broad understanding of domestic and international farm issues. Approximately twenty-eight young people participate in each exchange, spending six weeks in Canada and six weeks in the Caribbean.

Humanitarian Assistance Project for Independent Agricultural Development in Nicaragua (Hap-Nica)
802 Monroe
Ann Arbor, MI 48104
(313) 761-7960, (313) 764-1446

Hap-Nica is a project of the New World Agricultural Group (NWAG) and the Guild House Campus Ministry in Ann Arbor. UNAG (Farmers and Ranchers Union), ATC (Farmworkers Union), and ISCA (Higher Institute of Agricultural Science) in Nicaragua propose agricultural development projects, and Hap-Nica responds with research and volunteers. Examples of Hap-Nica projects include introducing new plant species for cultivation, soil testing and development, setting up cooperative enterprises, and ecological research.

Innovations et Reseaux pour le Development (IRED)
Case 116, 3 rue de Varembe
CH-1211, Geneva 20
Switzerland

IRED coordinates exchanges between Third World peasant groups in many countries, including Mali, Sri Lanka, China, Rwanda, and India. Exchanges of people are often followed by exchanges of tools, seeds, and techniques.

International Alliance for Sustainable Agriculture (IASA)
Newman Center, University of Minnesota
1701 University Ave. SE, Room 202
Minneapolis, MN 55414
(612) 331-1099

IASA works to provide alternatives to capital-intensive, chemically-dependent agriculture and to facilitate the exchange of information and ideas among sustainable agriculture groups throughout the world. Their *Resource Guide to Sustainable Agriculture in the Third World* is a compilation of resource-efficient, ecologically sound agricultural practices used by farmers and development groups in the Third World.

New World Agriculture Group (NWAG)
802 Monroe
Ann Arbor, MI 48104
(313) 761-7960

NWAG is an affiliation of agriculturalists, researchers, and teachers concerned with ecological agriculture. Research and work opportunities, including projects in Cuba, Nicaragua, and the United States, are highlighted in its quarterly newsletter. NWAG also advocates international cooperation through conferences and symposia, sister-laboratories, and literature exchanges.

North American Farm Alliance (NAFA)
NAFA/UNAG Joint Dairy Project
P.O. Box 8445
Minneapolis, MN 55408

NAFA is a progressive coalition of North American farm groups working on social justice issues. UNAG is the 120,000-strong Farmers and Ranchers Union in Nicaragua. Together, these two groups run a dairy in Boaco, Nicaragua. The dairy will produce milk and direct a regional dairy extension program with a team of veterinarians from MIDINRA (Nicaraguan Ministry of Agriculture) and the University of California at Davis. The dairy also plans to produce a special brand of "solidarity cheese" to be marketed worldwide as a product of Nicaragua-North American cooperation.

Rodale Research Center
33 E. Minor Street
Emmaus, PA 18098
(215) 967-5171

Rodale Research Center is a leading advocate of farming techniques, called regenerative agriculture, that are neither chemically dependent nor environmentally damaging. Rodale shares its findings and successes through publications such as *Organic Gardening Magazine*, and through its international outreach programs.

Third World Aprovecho Institute
80574 Hazelton Road
Cottage Grove, OR 97424
(503) 942-9434

The Institute, in cooperation with the Permaculture Institute of North America, sponsors intensive workshops for North, South, and Central American farmers, policymakers, foresters on "permaculture"—small-scale and ecologically sound agricultural and energy systems.

World Neighbors
5116 North Portland Avenue
Oklahoma City, OK 73112-2098
(405) 946-3333

World Neighbors is a development organization based on the belief that small-scale, locally controlled, and technologically appropriate agricultural systems are the keys to food self-sufficiency, and that such projects do not require tremendous infusions of capital to be successful. World Neighbors supports food production projects in Third World countries through research, material aid, and technical support.

ARCHITECTURE/CONSTRUCTION/DESIGN/ENGINEERING

Architects and Planners in Support of Nicaragua (APSNICA)
P.O. Box 1151
Topanga, CA 90290
(213) 455-1340

APSNICA projects include construction brigades, research delegations, material aid campaigns, and technical assistance programs. APSNICA also publishes a monthly newsletter, *Framework*. The construction brigades are made up of both skilled and unskilled volunteers who pay their way to Nicaragua and live and work with Nicaraguans on rural cooperatives. Part of APSNICA's emphasis is on training local men and women in all aspects of building houses. APSNICA also sends professionals in architecture, soil science, planning, engineering, and hydrology.

Brigada Compañeras
264 Willow Avenue
Somerville, MA 02144
(617) 628-3754

Brigada Compañeras supports AMNLAE (The Nicaraguan Women's Association) by building vocational schools where women can learn carpentry and other trade skills. After the schools are constructed, tools are donated to the Nicaraguan women.

Earth Shelter
63 Burbank Street, Room 15
Boston, MA 02115
(617) 424-8423

Earth Shelter is a nonprofit architectural group organized in 1986 to develop politically and environmentally responsive design projects while educating the public for social change. Its projects stress sensitivity to culture, use of indigenous materials, and each project's potential for widespread application. Earth Shelter is part of Project Breaking Ground, which has been active in Nicaragua since 1983. Its book, *Machine Guns and Musicians: Architectural Design in Revolutionary Nicaragua*, is available for $20.

Groundwork Institute
1126 Delaware Street
Berkeley, CA 94702
(415) 527-6266

Groundwork is an affiliation of architecture, construction, and planning professionals wishing to demonstrate that affordable, environmentally sound, and attractive housing can be accessible to all. Using local materials and traditional designs, Groundwork trains rural people in construction techniques. In turn, locals agree to train others and pass on their knowledge. Since 1978 Groundwork has consulted on projects in Nicaragua, Cuba, and Grenada.

Habitat for Humanity
419 West Church Street
Americus, GA 31709
(912) 924-6935

Habitat for Humanity is a nonprofit Christian housing ministry that works to build or renovate homes for the inadequately sheltered in the United States and in twenty countries around the world. Volunteers donate labor and money for materials.

Homes are sold at no profit, with a no-interest mortgage repaid over a fifteen to twenty-five year period. Habitat volunteers make one week to three year commitments to projects.

International Design Assistance Commission (IDAC)
c/o Segal and Gale
1185 Avenue of the Americas
New York, NY 10036
(212) 730-0101

In 1985, a number of design associates concluded that their profession largely ignored the needs of the vast majority of the world's population, and formed IDAC. IDAC is a loose federation of volunteer designers, who take on design projects at the request of international agencies. To date, IDAC designers have worked on water pumps, communications systems, and solar energy cookers in the Third World.

Veterans-Vietnam Restoration Project
716 Locust Street
P.O. Box 69
Garberville, CA 95440
(707) 923-3357

This veterans-initiated project sends twelve-person teams to Vietnam to work on construction projects, build medical clinics, rebuild orphanages and, in general, restore relations with the people of Vietnam.

ARTS AND POPULAR CULTURE

Artists Against Apartheid
180 Prospect Park West
Brooklyn, NY 11215
(718) 768-1731

Art Against Apartheid began in 1982 with the formation of coalitions of U.S. artists and art organizations. Campaigns solicit artists' support for the anti-apartheid movement, using all possible platforms and art forums to educate people about South Africa.

Artists and Writers Action Committee (AWAC)
P.O. Box 177
Station G
Toronto, Ontario M4M 3G7
Canada

AWAC works with artists and writers in Nicaragua and Chile, publishing their work and information about the political situation in these countries. AWAC's work also involves raising funds and gathering materials for artists' and writers' projects, and promoting cultural exchange among Canada, Nicaragua, and Chile.

Baseball Diplomacy, Inc.
12335 Santa Monica Blvd.
Santa Monica, CA 90025
(213) 453-8547

Baseball Diplomacy—also known as "Bats Not Bombs"—was founded in January 1986 by volunteers who raised the money to bring the twenty-four member Nicaraguan national baseball team to the United States. The 1987 project sponsored the Mexican national team at California State University at Long Beach. Future plans for other sports events include an Israeli-Jordanian soccer tour.

Caribbean Exchange
2940 16th Street, Room 307
San Francisco, CA 94103
(415) 255-7296

Caribbean Exchange, a project of Global Exchange, uses celebrations of Caribbean culture to raise funds for grassroots development programs and to educate Americans about the politics and culture of that region. Through the sale of Haitian folk art, for example, Caribbean Exchange is able to provide musical equipment to Haitian groups helping to organize and in-spire rural activism.

Jugglers for Peace
c/o Club Volcano
P.O. Box 4524
Pahoa, HI 96778
(808) 965-8756

Jugglers for Peace collects donated juggling equipment from U.S. manufacturers and brings it to Nicaragua. Volunteers also teach Nicaraguans how to juggle and organize community events. Jugglers for Peace is planning to expand into other countries.

Nicaraguan Cultural Alliance
1627 New Hampshire Avenue N.W.
Washington, DC 20009
(202) 387-4371

Nicaraguan Cultural Alliance focuses on exchanges of culture and ideas through sponsorship of Nicaraguan artists and exhib-its in the United States. It sends Chicano and Latino cultural del-egations to Nicaragua, and protests U.S. policies limiting free trade and travel between the United States and Nicaragua.

Potters for Peace (PFP)
c/o Quest for Peace
P.O. Box 5206
Hyattsville, MD 20782
(301) 699-0042

PFP began in 1986 when some Washington D.C. artists sold their work to raise money for a pottery cooperative in Estelí, Nic-aragua. PFP helped twenty Nicaraguan women potters purchase materials for their kiln. PFP has since grown into a national or-ganization, organizing potters to support Nicaraguan artists with research, material aid, and training.

U.S./Nica Printers Project
Box 282, 3309-1/2 Mission Street
San Francisco, CA 94110

The U.S./Nica Printers Project promotes democratic development through education and the written word. This group includes booksellers, publishers, writers, teachers, and librarians. The Project raises money to keep several printing presses rolling in Nicaragua, as well as for supplies, parts, and maintenance training. The Project supports presses that serve the literacy and education campaigns, the mass organizations, and the newspaper, El Nuevo Diario.

ORGANIZED LABOR

Action in Support of the Mexican Garment Workers
c/o Nationwide Women's Program
American Friends Service Committee (AFSC)
1501 Cherry Street
Philadelphia, PA 19102
(215) 421-7000

Out of the devastating earthquakes in Mexico City in 1985 grew the New Independent Union of Seamstresses (the "19th of September" Union), organized after factory owners refused to compensate families of women who perished in factories after the quake. AFSC has mobilized a national network of people supporting the growth of this unique union in Mexico. Activities of the U.S. network include sponsoring exchanges between Mexican and U.S. garment workers, and material aid and letter-writing campaigns.

Backing the Front Line
c/o CUSO
1602 12th Avenue
Regina, Saskatchewan S4P 0L8
Canada
(306) 525-2900

Backing the Front Line focuses on the Front Line States in southern Africa, particularly on Mozambique and Zimbabwe. It ties labor unions and other community groups with their equivalent organizations in southern Africa. One example is the partnership between Canadian Grain Services Union and the Mozambican National Workers Union of Food and Drink Industries. Canadian union representatives have traveled to Mozambique to survey health and safety conditions and to bring medical supplies needed because of the war.

Chile Union Education Project
c/o Oxfam Canada
251 Laurier Avenue West, Suite 301
Ottawa, Ontario K1P 5S6
Canada
(613) 237-5236

Union leaders from Canada organize fundraising and educational campaigns to assist workers in Chile. The funds go to train workers in occupational safety and health, coping with technological change, and collective bargaining, labor legislation, and labor history.

Hometowns Against Shutdowns
68 Kentwood Boulevard
Bricktown, NJ 08723
(201) 840-1723, (201) 462-3271

In 1986, 3M Corporation told 350 of its workers at a plant in Freehold Township, New Jersey, that they would lose their jobs due to a plant shutdown and relocation. In an unprecedented show of international solidarity, an estimated three hundred black South African workers staged a protest strike at the 3M plant in South Africa. The two unions issued a joint statement, which was also endorsed by musicians and others against apartheid in both the United States and South Africa. The partnership continues, as U.S. workers write letters of protest against the imprisonment of Amon Msane, the chief shop steward at the 3M company's plant near Johannesburg.

262   BRIDGING THE GLOBAL GAP

International Commission for the Coordination of Solidarity Among Sugar Workers (ICCSASW)
11 Madison Avenue
Toronto, Ontario M5R 2S2
Canada
(416) 597-8454

ICCSASW sponsors international conferences for sugar workers to discuss common concerns and issues relating to sugar production and development. Topics include debt, diversification of the industry, layoffs and mill closures, international quotas, and working conditions. ICCSASW also publishes *Sugar World*, a newsletter which carries news of sugar workers from around the world.

International Union of Foodworkers (IUF)
Rampe du Pont Rouge 8
CH-1213 Petit-Lancy, Geneva
Switzerland

The IUF is a five-continent federation of food sector trade unions. The groups in North America and Europe help subsidize the operations of the Third World groups. The IUF has been a key player in such critical union solidarity actions as protesting the violent repression of Guatemalan Coca Cola workers.

Trade Union Support for Guatemala (TUSGUA)
29 Islington Park Street
London N1
Great Britain

TUSGUA was set up in June 1987 to coordinate British support for the Guatemalan trade union movement. It publicizes trade union activity and denounces the violation of trade union rights in Guatemala.

W.R. Long International Solidarity Fund
B.C. Teachers Federation
2235 Burrard Street
Vancouver, British Columbia
Canada

The teachers' union sets aside about 2 percent of its revenue for solidarity projects focusing on Central America and southern Africa. Among other projects, the fund provides money for exchanges with teachers' unions in other countries.

PUBLIC HEALTH AND MEDICINE

Christian Committee for the Displaced of El Salvador (CRIPDES)
c/o Salvadoran Refugee Committee/CRECEN
P.O. Box 43603
Washington, DC 20010
(202) 265-6345

CRIPDES organizes groups of North American volunteers to accompany displaced persons returning to their homes in El Salvador's rural areas and to help train health promoters. Volunteers must speak some Spanish and be willing to stay in El Salvador for at least two weeks.

Committee for Health Rights in Central America (CHRICA)
347 Dolores Street
San Francisco, CA 94110
(415) 431-7768

CHRICA places community health volunteers in Central America. CHRICA also recruits paid and unpaid volunteers for its own projects, including a maternal and child health project and a mental health program for refugees in Central America.

Flying Samaritans
P.O. Box 633
Sonora, CA 95370
(707) 526-0874

Founded in 1961, the Flying Samaritans has grown to ten California and southwestern United States chapters that maintain fifteen medical clinics in Baja California. Volunteers pay their own way and provide expertise in flying small planes, dental care, prenatal care and health education, optometry, and other basic health services. The projects are affiliated with the University of Tijuana and are not meant to compete with or substitute for Mexican government health programs.

Guatemalan Health Rights Support Project
1747 Connecticut Ave N.W.
Washington, DC 20009
(202) 332-7678

The Guatemalan Health Rights Support Project was established to send needed funding, trainers, and medical supplies to the Guatemalan Health Rights Network (GHRN). GHRN is an "underground" health care system, devised to protect victims of the civil war as they seek the medical treatment they need.

Hesperian Foundation
P.O. Box 1692
Palo Alto, CA 94302
(415) 325-9017

The Hesperian Foundation develops and distributes educational materials aimed at promoting village-centered health care. Most widely distributed is their book, *Where There is No Doctor*, now available in thirty languages. Their other publications include *Helping Health Workers Learn*, *Disabled Village Children*, and *Where There is No Dentist*. The Foundation also helps place U.S. health professionals in projects in Mexico.

Insulin for Life
1868 Church Street
San Francisco, CA 94131
(415) 552-1870

Nicaragua has about five thousand diabetics needing sixty thousand bottles of insulin each year, yet the stock of insulin reaches only about thirty thousand bottles. Insulin for Life raises money to purchase insulin from Denmark, where it is less expensive, and ship it to Nicaragua. Insulin for Life may soon be expanding services to Guatemala and other Third World countries.

Interplast, Inc.
378-J Cambridge Ave.
Palo Alto, CA 94306
(415) 329-0670

Interplast is an organization of volunteer plastic surgeons, pediatricians, anesthesiologists, and nurses who provide free reconstructive surgery to poor people in the Third World. Interplast patients are those who would ordinarily go without help for burns or cleft lips and palates. Interplast has worked on more than thirteen thousand patients in Jamaica, Mexico, Honduras, Peru, the Philippines, and Samoa.

Jubilee Partners
P.O.Box 68
Comer, GA 30629
(464) 783-5131

Jubilee Partners is a Christian-based organization that launched the Walk in Peace Campaign to support Nicaraguan amputees who are victims of contra attacks. Jubilee Partners sends medical teams as well as prosthetic materials and money to Nicaragua. The Nicaraguan recipients are working to decrease their need for outside donations and technical help, and are setting up training for their own people.

National Central America Health Rights Network (NCAHRN)
P.O. Box 407
Audobon Station
New York, NY 10032
(212) 781-0657

NCAHRN is the national affiliation of individuals and groups who support the movement for health and peace in Central America. NCAHRN publishes *Links*, a newsletter for health professionals interested in keeping up on the news about health issues in the region and in finding out about work and volunteer opportunities there. Links has begun covering health issues in other regions as well, including southeast Asia and southern Africa.

Palo Alto-Stanford Medical Aid Committee for Central America (PASMAC)
P.O. Box 9392
Stanford, CA 94305
(415) 856-7572

PASMAC is a voluntary organization providing medical assistance to community health projects in Central America. PASMAC's principal project is a sister hospital in Grenada, Nicaragua, which it supports by sending supplies, medicines, and equipment. It also supports basic health care in rural El Salvador, and sanitation, immunization and health education projects in other Central American countries.

Philippine Assistance for Technology and Health (PATH)
6844 Mission Street
Daly City, CA 94014
(415) 992-0708

PATH benefits community-based organizations in the Philippines in the areas of health and technology by distributing funds and supplies collected in the United States. It also arranges visitor exchanges and other educational tours, and provides North Americans with information on the current socio-economic situation of the Filipino people.

Physicians for Human Rights
408 Highland Avenue
Sommerville, MA 02158
(617) 623-1930

Physicians for Human Rights enlists health workers to use their medical skills in defense of human rights. Its current projects include sending public health workers to South Korea to research the damage done by exposure to tear gas; sending forensic pathologists to look into the deaths of prisoners in Czechoslovakian jails; observing the medical problems related to the use of chemical weapons in Iran and Iraq; and sending a mission of psychiatrists and mental health workers to the West Bank and Gaza to study the psychological damage caused by beatings, tear gas, and rubber bullets. A project in the near future will focus on the effects of social discrimination on AIDS patients.

SEVA Foundation
108 Spring Lake Drive
Chelsea, MI 48118
(313) 475-1351

SEVA places volunteers in medical, agricultural, and other aid projects in thirty-six countries. It is perhaps best known for its work against blindness in Nepal and India.

Southern Africa Medical Aid Project
4428 Ryan Street
Durham, NC 27704
(919) 477-6076

Initiated in 1986, SAMAP's primary focus is supporting the ANC-Holland Solidarity Hospital in Dakawa, Tanzania, which serves political refugees from South Africa suffering from physical and psychological problems. Funds raised go to buy much-needed supplies, although many supplies and medications are also donated.

U.S./Vietnam Friendship Association
Medical Aid Program
P.O. Box 5043
San Francisco, CA 94101

Participants in the Medical Aid Program serve as consultants for health projects in Vietnam and Kampuchea. Projects include restoring a dental college, and designing and implementing a children's preventative dental health program which now serves half a million children. The program is partly funded by the Mennonite Central Committee.

Veterans of the Abraham Lincoln Brigade (VALB)
799 Broadway, Room 227
New York, NY 10003
(212) 674-5552

This group is composed primarily of veterans of the Abraham

Lincoln Brigade, the contingent of U.S. citizens who went to Spain in the 1930s to fight fascism. Some 350 members of the Brigade are still active, and have been raising medical aid for Nicaragua, including sixteen ambulances, six hospital generators, and thousands of dollars in relief aid after the 1988 hurricane. VALB has also started supporting medical clinics in southern Africa. Non-veterans, called VALB associates, also work with the Brigade.

Vosh International
243 N. Linderbergh Boulevard
St. Louis, MO 63141
(314) 991-4100

Founded in 1972, Vosh is a federation of U.S. optometrists dedicated to the improvement of vision for disadvantaged people around the world. Although vision-oriented, other doctors, surgeons, and dentists have travelled and worked with VOSH. Teams may be as large as sixty people. Each member is responsible for travel expenses but supplies are donated. The period of stay is usually no longer than two weeks, during which time volunteers see about three thousand patients a week. VOSH has served in Costa Rica, the Dominican Republic, Guatemala, Haiti, Honduras, Panama, Mexico, Nicaragua, and Jamaica.

TEACHING AND RESEARCH

Association of Arab-American University Graduates
556 Trapelo Road
Belmont, MA 02178
(617) 484-5483

The Association carries out research, publishing, and education in the United States on issues relating to Arabs and Arab-Americans. It publishes *Arab Studies Quarterly*, as well as general materials on Palestine, Lebanon, and Arab culture and history.

Council for International Exchange of Scholars
11 Dupont Circle N.W., Room 300
Washington, DC 20036
(202) 939-5400

The Council helps arrange speaking tours and exchanges between U.S. and foreign academics to foster stronger cross-cultural ties.

Cultural Survival
11 Divinity Avenue
Cambridge, MA 02138
(617) 495-2562

Cultural Survival was founded in 1972 by social scientists concerned with the fate of tribal peoples and ethnic minorities around the world. Cultural Survival responds to requests from tribal groups and local support committees for help or information. Its associates also help design and implement culturally sensitive and useful research programs.

Faculty for Human Rights in El Salvador and Central America (FACHRES-CA)
P.O. Box 8436
Berkeley, CA 94707
(415) 642-5270

FACHRES is a national network of faculty members engaged in human rights work in Central America, especially as it relates to the academic community. It also does educational work in the United States around U.S.-Central America policy.

Highlander Research and Education Center
Route 3, Box 370
New Market, TN 37820
(615) 933-3443

Highlander helps organize adult education exchanges between community activists in Appalachia and in the Third World. Its exchanges have focused on education, labor rights, health care, land use, toxics, and economic development.

Jerusalem Fund
2435 Virginia Avenue N.W.
Washington, DC 20037
(202) 338-1958

Jerusalem Fund was established to provide small grants to low-income Palestinian Arab students to study in Israel. Since April, 1988, the Fund has also started sending emergency medical aid to the occupied territories.

LASA Task Force on Scholarly Relations with Nicaragua
c/o Latin American Studies Association
Sid Richardson Hall, Unit 1
University of Texas
Austin, TX 78712
(512) 471-5551

The LASA Task Force was created in 1983 to ensure that scholarly ties between the United States and Nicaragua remained intact, even after other ties between the two countries were cut. Activities include a newsletter, the establishment of university-to-university ties and exchanges, and setting up academic panels of leading U.S. and Nicaraguan specialists to improve access to information on Nicaraguan-U.S. relations. Other LASA chapters house task forces on scholarly relations with Cuba, Human Rights, and Academic Freedom.

Maestros Por La Paz
2440 16th Street
San Francisco, CA 94103
(415) 863-3778

Maestros volunteers teach English to urban professionals, technical workers, and students in Nicaragua. It sponsors both summer brigades and long-term classes. Brigade members are housed with Nicaraguan families but must pay airfare, food, costs, and administrative fees. Applicants are expected to have teaching experience, good knowledge of Spanish, and experience in a multi-cultural setting.

Network of Educators Committees on Central America (NECCA)
P.O. Box 43509
Washington, DC 20010
(202) 667-2618

NECCA is an affiliation of U.S. committees involved in various educational projects about Central America, including sister-school relations, teachers' tours, and activism against U.S. intervention. NECCA's newsletter provides ideas for teaching about Central America.

Nicaragua School Supplies Campaign
c/o American Friends Service Committee (AFSC)
1501 Cherry Street
Philadelphia, PA 19102
(215) 241-7000

One of many of AFSC's humanitarian assistance programs in Central America, the School Supplies Campaign is a way to involve school children directly in learning about Nicaragua and building ties with Nicaraguan students. AFSC supplies organizational packets to teachers who wish to participate. Each classroom fills a box with the supplies listed, and returns it to AFSC for shipment to Nicaragua.

Science for the People (SftP)
897 Main Street
Cambridge, MA 02139
(617) 547-0370

SftP, in cooperation with the Nicaraguan Council for Higher Education, sends U.S. professors to Nicaragua to teach agriculture, animal husbandry, computer science, ecology, engineering, forestry, medicine, physics, statistics, and mathematics at the college level. Participants make a commitment for a semester or one year, and receive a small stipend.

World University Service
5 Chemin des Iris
1216 Geneva
Switzerland

World University Service is a network of representatives and committees from sixty countries. Its goal is to see that universities have the educational and technical resources to meet community development needs. Major activities include providing college scholarships for political refugees and victims of discrimination, and supporting literacy campaigns and technical training.

TRANSPORTATION

Bikes for Africa
5143 39th Avenue South
Minneapolis, MN 55417
(612) 724-7943

Bikes for Africa is a project of the Minneapolis chapter of Bikes Not Bombs (see below). Following up on the successful delivery of twenty-five bicycles to Mozambique in 1985, the Minneapolis group has developed a project to manufacture all-terrain bikes and carts and to establish an assembly and repair network in Mozambique.

Bikes Not Bombs
Institute for Transportation and Development Policy
P.O. Box 56538
Washington, D.C. 20011
(301) 589-1810

Bikes Not Bombs collects and refurbishes bicycles for Nicaragua, and trains Nicaraguans in bicycle mechanics. So far, it has sent over a thousand bicycles. The campaign publishes a quarterly newsletter, Bikes Not Bombs Update, and organizes bicycle tours to Nicaragua. Tour participants are encouraged to bring a three-speed bike to be donated at the end of the trip.

Haitian Development Fund
P.O. Box 56538
Washington, DC 20011
(301) 589-1810

The Institute for Transportation and Development Policy in Washington D.C., sponsor of Bikes Not Bombs, also sponsors the Haitian Development Fund. The Fund has delivered bicycles to teachers and organizers working with Haiti's national literacy campaign.

International Bicycle Fund (IBF)
4247 135th Place Southeast
Bellevue, WA 98006-1319

The IBF promotes bicycle transportation, economic development, international understanding, and safety education. The organization sponsors lectures and slide shows on topics ranging from transportation planning to African studies. IBF also sponsors bicycle trips to developing countries.

STUDENT-DIRECTED CAMPAIGNS

Fast for Life
c/o Oxfam America
115 Broadway
Boston, MA 02116
(617) 482-1211

Fast for Life is an annual Oxfam campaign, carried out by students in high schools and colleges across the country. Fast for Life raises awareness of hunger and development issues, and raises money for Oxfam programs in the Third World.

National Student Campaign Against Hunger
29 Temple Place
Boston, MA 02111
(617) 292-4823

The National Student Campaign Against Hunger works nationally in forty-five states, on over five hundred campuses. The organization publishes a newsletter, *Students Making a Difference*, providing ideas for student activism against hunger and homelessness. Money raised from the campaign goes to support projects combating hunger at home and abroad.

Overseas Development Network (ODN)
P.O. Box 1430   -and-   P.O. Box 2306
Cambridge, MA 02238   Stanford, CA 94309
(617) 868-3002   (415) 725-2869

ODN is a national student organization with chapters across the United States. Each chapter sets its own agenda, but generally promotes discussion of Third World issues on campus and involves students in building constructive responses to hunger, poverty, and injustice. ODN projects include fundraising for overseas activities, education, and overseas volunteer placements.

FAMILY, WOMEN'S, AND CHILDREN'S PROGRAMS

Children of War
Religious Task Force
366 Marsh Street
Belmont, MA 02178
(617) 484-7528

Children of War sponsors activities to unite young people all over the world. The Children of War Tour brings young people from war-torn countries to the United States to meet with their counterparts in schools, religious groups, and community organizations.

Gabriela
National Women's Coalition
2017 Francisco Street
Berkeley, CA 94709
(415) 841-1439

Gabriela is a national women's network in the Philippines. It has recently established a U.S. International Relations Commission to facilitate educational and solidarity campaigns between U.S. and Filipina women.

MADRE
121 W. 27th Street, Room 301
New, York, NY 10001
(212) 627-0444

MADRE works in conjunction with AMNLAE, the Nicaraguan Women's Association, on a whole range of material and technical aid efforts. MADRE raises money for school supplies and medicines, pairs U.S. daycare centers with Central American daycare centers, sends medical and other professional work brigades to Central America, and produces educational materials for use in the United States.

MATCH
1102-200 Elgin
Ottawa, Ontario K2P 1L5
Canada
(613) 238-1312

MATCH is the only development agency in Canada devoted exclusively to promoting women's equal participation in development. Since 1978, MATCH has funded more than two hundred women's projects in Africa, Asia, Latin America and the Caribbean. MATCH also participates in conferences, tours, media activities, and other educational programs that bring a feminist perspective to development issues.

Mujer a Mujer/Woman to Woman
A.P. 12-709
Col. Narvarte 03020
Mexico, D.F.
Mexico
(905) 564-7566

Mujer a Mujer is a group of U.S. women supporting organizations of poor Mexican women. Among the groups Mujer a Mujer supports are the independent September 19th National Garment Workers Union and the women's section of the Urban Poor People's Movement (CONAMUP). Mujer a Mujer brings U.S. women to meet with their Mexican counterparts, sponsors speaking tours of Mexican women, and provides ongoing financial and technical assistance to the Mexican groups.

Najda
Women Concerned about the Middle East
P.O. Box 7152
Berkeley, CA 94707
(415) 549-3512

Najda publishes a monthly newsletter to keep U.S. women informed about material aid campaigns, human rights work, and other issues confronting Middle Eastern women of all backgrounds.

SISA
Sisterhood in Support of Sisters in South Africa
719 Washington Street, Suite 383
Newtonville, MA 02160

SISA was founded in 1984 as an organization of black women to direct aid to South African women and their families. SISA is committed to increasing the awareness of the need for majority rule and social justice in South Africa.

Somos Hermanas
3543 18th Street
San Francisco, CA 94110

Somos Hermanas concentrates on organizing U.S. working-class women and women of color to get involved in solidarity work with Central American women.

U.S.-Cuban Women's Exchange
c/o Venceremos Brigade
64 Fulton Street, Room 1101
New York, NY 10038
(212) 349-6292

The Women's Exchange works to promote dialogue and understanding between U.S. and Cuban women. U.S. women go on delegations to meet with Cuban women, and then return to do educational work in the United States.

Woman to Woman
5825 Telegraph, Box A
Oakland, CA 94609
(415) 652-4400, ext.415

Woman to Woman supports women's groups in Nicaragua and El Salvador, and sponsors events in the United States to raise money and awareness of women's issues. The money goes to women's unions, child care, legal aid, health, and education.

Women's International Resource Exchange (WIRE)
2700 Broadway, Room 7
New York, NY 10025
(212) 870-2783

WIRE distributes publications written by and for women activists all over the world. The materials deal with issues such as development, education, politics, and culture from a women's perspective.

Women for Racial and Economic Equality (WREE)
130 E. 16th Street
New York, NY 10003
(212) 473-6111

WREE is the U.S. sister organization to the Women's Section of the ANC and the Women's Council of SWAPO. WREE sponsors tours to southern Africa, organizes educational campaigns in the United States, and raises funds to support women's and children's projects in southern Africa.

Women's Skills and Resources Exchange
PO Box 20806
Seattle, WA 98102
(206) 322-1975

Women's Skills and Resources Exchange was founded with the goal of empowering women to work toward world peace. Its focus has been on exchanging skills and resources between North American and Third World women, particularly in Central America.

CHAPTER 4
Championing Human Rights

American Civil Liberties Union (ACLU)
22 Maryland Avenue N.E.
Washington, DC 20002
(202) 543-4651

The ACLU is one of the oldest organizations protecting civil liberties in the United States through court cases, research, media campaigns, and community education. The ACLU also works on international issues such as human rights, refugee legal aid, and immigration.

American Committee on Africa (ACOA)
198 Broadway, Room 401
New York, NY 10038
(212) 962-1210

ACOA speaks out against human rights abuses in Africa. One of its major campaigns is against the repression of the thirty thousand political prisoners in South African jails, 40 percent of whom are children. ACOA also makes a variety of educational materials on Africa available to the public.

American Friends Service Committee (AFSC)
1501 Cherry Street
Philadelphia, PA 19102
(215) 241-7165

AFSC runs human rights education and action programs focused on many different regions and countries. The Philadelphia headquarters can refer people to appropriate local offices.

American-Arab Anti-Discrimination Committee (ADC)
4201 Connecticut Ave. N.W., Suite 500
Washington, DC 20008
(202) 244-2990

ADC defends the rights and promotes the heritage of Arab Americans. It also sponsors "Eyewitness Israel," a project to monitor human rights in the West Bank and Gaza strip. Delegations of ten to fifteen North Americans participate in village life and report on human rights abuses by the Israeli government.

Americas Watch
The Watch Committees
36 West 44th Street, Suite 911
New York, NY 10036
(212) 840-9460

The Watch Committees include Americas Watch, Asia Watch,

Helsinki Watch, the Fund for Free Expression, and the Lawyers Committee for Human Rights. These organizations monitor human rights in their respective regions, work against censorship, and promote the rights of refugees. The Watch Committees also maintain a professional lobbyist to testify before Congress and push for human rights considerations in U.S. foreign policy decisions. The Watch Committees publish *Human Rights Watch*, available for a $20 a year, and number of human rights studies focusing on particular countries.

Amnesty International
322 8th Avenue
New York, NY 10001
(212) 807-8400

Amnesty International, the largest human rights organization, advocates fair treatment and prompt trials for political prisoners around the world. Its London-based research center documents cases and publishes information, but the heart of the organization is a grassroots base of local membership committees. Committees write letters on behalf of prisoners, but cannot work on cases of prisoners within their own countries.

Casa Chile Human Rights Committee
P.O. Box 3620
Berkeley, CA 94703
(415) 845-9398

Since 1981 Casa Chile has worked to support the rights of the Chilean people in their struggle for democracy. Activities include publishing the *Chile Newsletter*, participating in urgent action and human rights campaigns, promoting the boycott of Chilean goods, and sponsoring educational and cultural events.

Center for Constitutional Rights (CCR)
666 Broadway, 7th floor
New York, NY 10012
(212) 614-6464

CCR is a nonprofit legal and educational organization that takes on court cases and educational campaigns defending civil rights, minority rights, and internationally-recognized human rights. CCR has also been active in defending the rights of sanctuary workers.

Christian Urgent Action Network for Emergency Support in the Philippines (CUANES-Philippines)
1821 W. Cullerton
Chicago, IL 60608
(312) 738-3255

CUANES-Philippines is a network of people who receive calls about human rights emergencies in the Philippines and respond by sending cables to officials in the Philippines and the United States. Through their work with the Philippine-based Task Force Detainees, they have been successful in limiting torture and helping to free some detainees.

Church Committee for Human Rights in Asia
5253 N. Kenmore
Chicago, IL 60640
(312) 561-4953

Asian Rights Advocate is a regular newsletter of the Church Committee, focusing on South Korea, the Philippines, and Indonesia. The newsletter provides background information on human rights issues and suggestions for action to release political prisoners and change U.S. policies that have a negative effect on human rights.

Church Coalition for Human Rights in the Philippines and North American Coalition for Human Rights in Korea
110 Maryland Avenue N.E.
Washington, DC 20002
(202) 546-4304

Like the Church Committee for Human Rights in Asia, these offices provide regular mailings to members on the human rights situations in the Philippines and Korea. They also provide suggestions on how to work for more effective action by the religious community.

Council for Human Rights in Latin America (CHRLA)

1236 Kincaid St.   1331 SW Broadway, Room 300
Eugene, OR 97401 - and -   Portland, OR 97201
(503) 484-5867   (503) 295-7783

The Council aims to promote better understanding between the people of North and South America through cultural events, education, humanitarian aid projects, tours, and sponsoring speakers from Latin America. Many of the Council's educational events and conferences focus on the human rights situations in Latin American countries. Human rights reports, records and tapes of Latin American music, and videos and slide shows on Latin American topics are all available through CHRLA.

Food First Information and Action Network (FIAN)

International Secretariat
Postfach 10 22 43
D-6900 Heidelberg
West Germany
Phone: 06222-5 01 08

FIAN supports organizations of the poor in the Third World struggling for land and agricultural labor rights. It sponsors networks for urgent action appeals, and takes on longer-term casework and educational campaigns. FIAN pressures governments to act on existing laws, or to support their citizens' initiatives for new ones. U.S. organizations can contact FIAN to join the network.

Free Individuals Disappeared in Guatemala (FINDING)

1020 S. Wabash, Room 401
Chicago, IL 60608
(312) 427-4351

FINDING is one of several U.S. human rights organizations working with the Grupo de Apoyo Mutuo (GAM), a Guatemalan group supporting the families of the forty thousand disappeared. FINDING provides its members with a woven Guatemalan bracelet as a reminder of the disappeared, and the name of one person for whom letters are to be written. FINDING also educates U.S. citizens about the connection between the repressive Guatemalan security forces and U.S. economic assistance.

Guatemala Human Rights Commission/USA
P.O. Box 91
Cardinal Station
Washington, DC 20064
(202) 529-6599

Through publications, reports, press releases, and other educational materials, the Guatemala Human Rights Commission supports the work of the Grupo de Apoyo Mutuo (GAM). The Commission does not have its own response network at the grassroots level, but cooperates with other local and national groups working on behalf of the disappeared in Guatemala.

Human Rights Advocates (HRA)
2918 Florence Street
Berkeley, CA 94705
(415) 841-2928

HRA provides publications and resources to lawyers and others who wish to inform themselves of human rights standards, and how these standards can be applied to local, national, and international law. HRA uses human rights standards to argue for the rights of welfare recipients, sanctuary workers, migrant workers, disabled people, and the hungry.

Humanitarian Law Project
6250 Franklin Avenue
Los Angeles, CA 90046
(213) 850-1183

The Humanitarian Law Project promotes respect for international law, especially as it affects refugees and displaced persons. *Protocol* is the organization's quarterly newsletter, providing in-depth explanations of current cases and issues.

Humanitas International

P.O. Box 818
Menlo Park, CA 94026
(415) 324-9077

Humanitas programs denounce repression wherever it is found. Projects include conferences and speaking tours of key peace activists from America, Eastern and Western Europe; advocacy on behalf of victims in the Soviet Union, Eastern Europe, Asia, and South Africa; and publication of organizers' resources and country updates.

Inter-Church Committee on Human Rights in Latin America (ICCHRLA)

40 St. Clair Avenue East, Suite 201
Toronto, Ontario M4T 1M9
Canada
(416) 921-4152

ICCHRLA works with Canadian parishes, congregations, and other community groups to develop support for human rights organizations in Latin America. ICCHRLA also intervenes on behalf of victims of human rights abuses through phone, letter, and telegram campaigns, and with fact-finding missions. A regular newsletter provides information to all member organizations.

International Defense and Aid Fund

P.O. Box 17
Cambridge, MA 02138
(617) 491-8343

The International Defense and Aid Fund raises funds for the families of black South African children imprisoned by the apartheid government. The money is used to help pay legal expenses to get these children out of jail, as well as to help support their families.

Lafontant Joseph Memorial Human Rights Fund
c/o Caribbean Exchange
2940 16th Street, Room 307
San Francisco, CA 94103
(415) 255-7296

Caribbean Exchange initiated the Fund in the name of Lafontant Joseph, a Haitian human rights activist who was slain in July 1988. The money raised goes to human rights organizations carrying out the spirit of his work in Haiti.

Lawyers Committee on Central America
2269 Market Street, Room 189
San Francisco, CA 94114
(415) 661-5559

One of the Watch Committees established to monitor international human rights, the Lawyers Committee specializes in publicizing and fighting human rights violations in Central America, examining U.S. immigration laws and their impact on Central Americans, and educating its members about legal and political issues in Central America.

Lawyers Committee for Civil Rights Under Law
Southern Africa Project
1400 Eye Street N.W.
Washington, DC 20005

The Lawyers Committee for Civil Rights Under Law is an association of eminent members of the U.S. legal profession working to eradicate the vestiges of discrimination and racism in the United States. Recognizing the link between racism and the international struggle for human rights, the Committee established the Southern Africa Project. The Project helps political defendants in South Africa and Namibia get competent legal assistance, seeks to alter laws in this country that are supportive of apartheid and that are contradictory to U.S. civil rights law, and serves as a resource for people concerned with human rights in South Africa.

Marin Interfaith Task Force on Central America (MITF)
25 Buena Vista
Mill Valley, CA 94941
(415) 454-0818

MITF undertakes a wide variety of educational and fund-raising programs on behalf of Central America. Some Task Force members have gone to San Salvador to provide members of the Salvadoran Human Rights Commission with protection by escorting them on their daily business and by keeping the functions of their office going. Members have published a report on the torture of political prisoners upon returning to the United States.

Network in Solidarity with the People of Guatemala (NISGUA)
1314 14th Street N.W., Room 17
Washington, DC 20005
(202) 483-0050

NISGUA carries out a number of programs in support of Guatemala, one of which is a human rights campaign. With more than thirty local committees nationwide, NISGUA operates a rapid response network to write letters and to campaign for arrested and disappeared people. NISGUA has also led delegations of visitors to Guatemala.

Palestine Human Rights Campaign (PHRC)
220 S. State Street, Room 1308
Chicago, IL 60604
(312) 987-1830

The Palestine Human Rights Campaign publishes information and action alerts so that North Americans can write letters on behalf of Palestinian prisoners taken by the Israeli military. The Campaign also publishes information on the conditions of Palestinian refugee camps in Lebanon.

Peace Brigades International (PBI)
4722 Baltimore Avenue
Philadelphia, PA 19143
(215) 727-0989

PBI is an international organization currently involved in nonviolence training and development efforts in Central America, Asia, North America and Europe, and is looking toward involvement in Africa and the Middle East. One of its most active programs is the escort service provided to members of GAM, the Grupo de Apoyo Mutuo in Guatemala. Teams of volunteers spend from two weeks to a year in Guatemala, shielding the relatives of the disappeared from threats and attacks by Guatemalan security forces. Volunteers return home and do follow-up education and speaking about the human rights situation in Guatemala.

Peru Solidarity Committee
Box 3580, Grand Central Station
New York, NY 10017
(212) 964-6730

The Peru Solidarity Committee focuses on human rights education and action in Latin America, with a particular focus on Peru. The Committee publishes a newsletter, *Peru Update*.

Survival International
2121 Decatur Place N.W.
Washington, DC 20008
(202) 265-1077

Survival International (SI) is a nonprofit organization working to advance the human rights of indigenous people. Through urgent action campaigns, SI alerts U.S. citizens to the immediate concerns of indigenous people, from army attacks on tribal Filipinos to the destruction of Brazil's Amazon by internationally-funded developers. Members respond by forming local groups and writing letters on behalf of people facing repression. SI also does educational work and publishes materials on tribal peoples.

Washington Office on Africa
110 Maryland Avenue N.E.
Washington, DC 20002
(202) 546-7961

The Washington Office on Africa (WOA) was established in 1972 by church and trade union groups concerned with political and economic repression in southern Africa. It carries out education and human rights campaigns, and lobbies to improve U.S. foreign policy toward Africa.

Washington Office on Haiti
10 Maryland Avenue N.E.
Washington, D.C. 20002
(202) 543-7095

The Washington Office on Haiti, one of the best sources for news and information about Haiti, initiated the Campaign to Support Democracy and Human Rights in Haiti to provide information to U.S. citizens and engage their support. Letter writing and education are the main tools of the campaign.

Western Sahara Campaign, USA
2556 Massachusetts Avenue N.W.
Washington, D.C. 20008
(202) 387-0412

The Western Sahara Campaign educates the U.S. community about the two thousand disappeared Sahrawis, struggling for Western Saharan independence from Morocco. The Campaign uses speakers bureaus, newsletters, and networking with other human rights organizations. The Campaign also provides humanitarian aid to Sahrawi refugees in Algerian camps.

Witness for Peace (WFP)
Box 29497
Washington, DC 20017
(202) 269-6316

Witness for Peace documents and reports on contra attacks against Nicaraguan civilians. Information is gathered through on the scene witnessing by short- and long-term civilian delegations. A rotating team of thirty U.S. citizens has worked and lived in the war zones since 1983. Witness for Peace also helps raise money for medical and living expenses of victims of contra attacks.

Women for Guatemala
P.O. Box 322
Concordia, KS 66901

Women for Guatemala promotes understanding about women's and children's struggles in Guatemala, and channels aid to refugee women and children living outside Guatemala. Women for Guatemala collaborates with Amnesty International and other human rights organizations to provide names of disappeared women to individuals who wish to write letters on their behalf.

Young Koreans United (YKU)
1314 14th Street N.W., Room 5
Washington DC 20005
(202) 387-2420

YKU, with local chapters across the country, works to mobilize and educate North Americans on militarization, human rights, reunification, and other issues facing Koreans. YKU also works to promote understanding of Korean culture in the United States by sponsoring traditional dance, drama, and other cultural activities.

Resources

Amnesty International Report
Amnesty International Publications
1 Easton Street
London WC1X 8DJ
United Kingdom

These annual reports are among the most up-to-date sources of information on human rights, providing overviews of the political and human rights situation for every country in the world.

Critique: Review of the Department of State's Country Reports on Human Rights Practices
Watch Committees and Lawyers Committee for Human Rights
36 W. 44th Street
New York, NY 10036

Since 1979, the annual *Critique* has been a response to the annual publication of the State Department's *Country Reports*, the official human rights report of the U.S. government. Noting where improvements have been made in the *Country Reports*, *Critique* also shows the uneven quality of official reports, especially about countries under political debate in the United States (Guatemala, Nicaragua, Libya), and about U.S. allies where military forces contribute to human rights abuses.

Human Rights Internet Reporter
c/o Human Rights Internet
Harvard Law School
Pund Hall, Room 401
Cambridge, MA 02138
(617) 495-9924

The *Reporter* is a bi-monthly publication on news and issues in human rights. It includes highlights of fact-finding missions, calendars of events, and reports on the work of other independent human rights organizations. Directories of human rights organizations in different world regions are also available through the Human Rights Internet.

Human Rights Information and Documentation System (HURIDOCS)
c/o HBC
Grensevein 99, N-0663
Oslo 6
Norway

HURIDOCS is a global network of over a hundred human rights organizations. As a service to human rights groups, HURIDOCS provides listings of directories and resource information, advises on information systems and technology for human rights work, and coordinates seminars and consultations among groups working in similar areas to discuss common campaigns and problems.

International Human Rights Internship Program
Institute of International Education
1400 K Street NW, Suite 650
Washington, DC 20005
(202) 842-0062

This internship program offers fifteen to twenty grants each year for individuals to work full-time with human rights organizations. Application deadline is August 31.

The Sanctuary Movement
c/o The Data Center
464 19th Street
Oakland, CA 94612
(415) 835-4692

The Data Center is a nonprofit research center and library offering a clipping service on a wide variety of countries and topics. *The Sanctuary Movement* is a collection of articles and readings that the Data Center has been gathering since 1983.

Seeking Safe Haven - A Congregational Guide to Helping Central American Refugees in the United States
Published cooperatively by American Friends Service Committee (Philadelphia), Church World Service Immigration and Refugee Program (New York), Inter-religious Task Force on El Salvador and Central America (New York), and Lutheran Immigration and Refugee Service (New York).
This booklet is designed for community groups that want to work with refugees. It provides background information on Central American countries, options and guidelines for action, resources, and examples of existing programs. Available through AFSC (see address above).

CHAPTER 5
Fair Trade

This is a short list of U.S. *Alternative Trade Organizations* (ATOs). *For a more complete list of* U.S., *Canadian, European, and other* ATOs, *send* $7 *to Global Exchange, 2940 16th Street, Room 307, San Francisco, CA 94103.*

Co-op America
2100 M Street N.W., Suite 310
Washington, DC 20063
(202) 872-5307, (800) 424-2667

Co-op America is not directly involved in alternative trade, but acts as an umbrella organization for marketing the goods of many trade groups. As a nonprofit, member-controlled, worker-managed association, Co-op America links socially responsible businesses and consumers in a national network. Catalogs promote members' products, and the Organizational Member Directory serves as a networking tool for member organizations and consumers. The quarterly magazine, *Building Economic Alternatives* covers trade and investment issues. In 1989 Co-op America's director launched a bold initiative to create the FAIRTRADE Foundation, whose goal is to create a multimillion-dollar mail order business and a national network of stores selling goods from Third World cooperatives.

Equal Exchange
P.O. Box 2652
Cambridge, MA 02238
(617) 482-4945

Equal Exchange is a food-importing cooperative working with progressive governments and grassroots organizations in the Third World. Its main products are Nicaraguan coffee and tea from the Sarvodaya Movement in Sri Lanka. Equal Exchange is also the U.S. distributor for Stichting Ideele Imports of Holland, one of the largest European alternative trade groups.

Friends of the Third World, Inc.
611 West Wayne Street
Fort Wayne, IN 46802
(219) 422-6821, (219) 422-1650

Friends of the Third World (FTW) is one of the nation's

strongest advocates of alternative trade. In addition to its retail and wholesale operations, FTW initiated the first yearly
conference of U.S. ATOs (a task now fulfilled by a steering committee composed of several ATOs). FTW also helps other
groups start their own stores. FTW puts a heavy emphasis on
education, by running Whole World Books and sending out educational pamphlets with every sale.

Jubilee Crafts
300 West Apsley Street
Philadelphia, PA 19144
(215) 849-2178

Jubilee Crafts is a Christian organization that supports selfhelp development projects. Jubilee Crafts buys from church
groups, cooperatives, and groups with indigenous leadership in
the Third World and impoverished areas of the United States.
Some of their producers include Chilean political prisoners and
Palestinian refugees. Jubilee Crafts educates U.S. consumers
about the economic and political conditions of the artisans. Interested consumers can become Jubilee Partners, helping to
sell crafts at churches, fairs, schools, and other events.

Mayan Crafts
1101 North Highland Room 506
Arlington, VA 22201
(703) 527-5067

Mayan Crafts buys and sells handicrafts of Guatemala's
Mayan Indian refugees, from groups in Mexico and in Guatemala. Its goal is to encourage Mayan cultural traditions and
self-sufficiency, and to educate the U.S. public about the refugees' plight.

MCC SELFHELP Crafts
21 South 12th Street
Akron, PA 17501
(717) 859-4971

The Mennonite Central Committee staffs and runs SELFHELP
Crafts, one of the largest U.S. ATOs. Its warehouse serves more

than seventy shops and retail outlets. SELFHELP Crafts buys from over a hundred groups in thirty-two developing countries; its net sales in 1988 were over $3 million. SELFHELP also provides marketing assistance to poor artisans, including refugees, disadvantaged minorities, and handicapped people. Most of the SELFHELP staff is volunteer, so a high percentage of proceeds from sales is returned to the producers.

One World Trading Company
P.O. Box 310
Summertown, TN 38483
(615) 964-2334

One World Trading is a project of PLENTY USA, a development organization. It markets traditional Guatemalan crafts made by artisans in Guatemala and Guatemalans living as refugees in Mexico.

Pueblo to People
1616 Montrose Boulevard
Houston, TX 77006
(713) 523-1197

Pueblo to People is one of the fastest-growing ATOs involved in mail order retailing. It sells crafts and some foods from cooperatives in Latin America. Pueblo to People tries to support co-ops that not only need income, but are also having a larger social impact. In addition to its catalog, Pueblo to People has two retail stores, in Houston and San Francisco. It supports grassroots change for peasants and artisans by providing a foreign market, technical training, and exposure to democratic methods of organization.

SERRV SELFHELP Handcrafts
500 Main Street
P.O. Box 365
New Windsor, MD 21776
(301) 635-2255

SERRV, one of the largest and oldest U.S. ATOs, buys and markets crafts from over a hundred groups in thirty countries. In 1988, net sales topped $3 million. Most sales are to church groups, which buy its products wholesale or on consignment. SERRV is a project of Church of the Brethren, a small Protestant peace church. It works closely with Church World Service to expand its supply sources and markets. A wholesale catalog and two craft shops, located in Oakdale, California and New Windsor, Maryland, market items for resale or retail.

Thai International Display, Inc.
6030 90th Avenue North
Pinellas Park, FL 33565
(813) 544-2429

The founders of Thai International Display drew on ten years of development work in Thailand to create their alternative marketing business. Products come from Asian producers in fourteen countries and are bought from individuals, cooperatives, or church-affiliated centers. It also rents out audiovisual materials on Asian handicrafts.

CHAPTER 6
The Buck Stops Here: Consumer and Corporate Accountability

The following organizations offer ideas for consumer, trade union, shareholder, and investor activism to build corporate accountability toward the Third World.

Acción International
1385 Cambridge Street
Cambridge, MA 02139
(617) 492-4930

Acción makes small loans to income-generating projects for the poor in Latin America and the Caribbean. While Acción receives U.S. government money, it also encourages private citizens to invest in its loan guarantee fund to further grassroots economic development.

Action for Corporate Accountability (Action)
3255 Hennepin Avenue South, Suite 255
Minneapolis, MN 55408
(612) 823-1571

Action is the central office of the International Baby Food Action Network (IBFAN). IBFAN members include over 150 consumer, social justice, women's, and health workers' organizations around the world concerned about multinationals' compliance with World Health Organization guidelines for marketing infant formula. IBFAN *News*, a bimonthly, and *Action News*, a quarterly, are available from Action.

CANICCOR
P.O. Box 6819
San Francisco, CA 94101
(415) 885-5102

CANICCOR, Interfaith Council on Corporate Accountability, focuses on divestment, the debt crisis, human rights in Central America, pesticides, and economic alternatives. CANICCOR publishes a quarterly newsletter, *Of Prophets and Profits*.

Council on Economic Priorities (CEP)
30 Irving Place
New York, NY 10003
(212) 420-1133

CEP documents and evaluates corporate performance, advocates corporate social responsibility, and educates the public about the consequences of corporate behavior. CEP has a portfolio review service for socially conscious investors. *CEP Newsletter* is published monthly. CEP also puts out reports, studies, and books, including *Rating America's Corporate Conscience*.

Ecumenical Development Cooperative Society (EDCS)
475 Riverside Drive, Room 1003
New York, NY 10115
(212) 870-2665

EDCS is an international organization with headquarters in the Netherlands. Founded in 1974 by the World Council of Churches, it has a predominantly church membership. One of its primary goals is challenging churches in developed and developing nations to provide long-term, low-interest loans to cooperatively-owned businesses started by the poor.

Infant Formula Action Coalition (INFACT)
256 Hanover Street, 3rd Floor
Boston, MA 02113
(617) 742-4583

INFACT began as the Infant Formula Action Coalition, which organized the Nestle boycott. INFACT later turned to organizing around nuclear weapons and has now launched a boycott against General Electric for its role in manufacturing nuclear weapons.

Interfaith Center on Corporate Responsibility (ICCR)
475 Riverside Drive, Room 566
New York, NY 10115
(212) 870-2936

ICCR has been at the forefront of the corporate accountability movement. This project of the National Council of Churches focuses on international issues of human rights, the environment, corporate responsibility, social justice, community reinvestment, nuclear arms and energy, disarmament, and domestic equality. ICCR periodically provides congressional testimony on these issues and helps sponsor shareholder resolutions. Its monthly publication, *The Corporate Examiner*, includes an in-depth report on a different issue each month.

International Organization of Consumers Union (IOCU)
P.O. Box 1045
Penang, Malaysia
Phone: 8850 72

IOCU is an international information network of consumer and citizen groups concerned with hazardous products and substances, especially pharmaceuticals, agricultural chemicals, toys, and household items. IOCU publishes *Consumer Currents*.

Investor Responsibility Research Center (IRRC)
1319 F Street N.W., Suite 900
Washington, DC 20004
(202) 833-3727

IRRC is an information service for institutional investors who wish to assess the social policies of their portfolio companies. The Center conducts research and publishes impartial reports on contemporary business and public policy issues.

Pesticide Education and Action Project/Pesticide Action Network-North America (PAN-NA)
P.O. Box 610
San Francisco, CA 94101
(415) 541-9140

PAN is a worldwide citizens' coalition of groups and individuals opposed to the irrational spread and misuse of poisonous pesticides. Among its activities is the "Dirty Dozen" campaign to expose twelve of the most dangerous pesticides.

Rainforest Action Network (RAN)
300 Broadway
San Francisco, CA 94133
(415) 398-4404

RAN uses letter-writing campaigns, boycotts, and demonstrations to protect the world's rainforests. RAN publishes numerous fact sheets and brochures and two periodicals: the monthly *Action Alert* and the quarterly *World Rainforest Report*. Rainforest Action Groups (RAGS) across the country carry out RAN's work on a local level.

Transnational Institute for Policy Studies (IPS)
1601 Connecticut Avenue N.W.
Washington, DC 20009
(202) 234-9382

IPS's project on transnational corporations launched an international meeting on counterstrategies to transnationals in 1984.

United Nations Centre on Transnational Corporations
Room DC2-1220
2 United Nations Plaza
New York, NY 10017
(212) 754-3176

The objectives of the Centre are to further the understanding of transnational corporations (TNCs), to secure effective international agreements with TNCs, and to strengthen the negotiating capacity of host countries, particularly developing countries.

Women's World Banking (WWB)
104 East 40th Street
New York, NY 10016
(212) 935-2390

WWB, founded in 1977, guarantees loans to women entrepreneurs around the world, particularly in low-income regions, and to women who haven't had access to financial marketplaces. Locally established affiliates review loan applications and select recipients. As of 1987, WWB had made about twelve hundred loans with no defaults.

Resources

Catalyst
64 Main Street, 2d Floor
Montpelier, VT 05602
(802) 223-7943

This bimonthly newsletter focuses on small-scale, decentralized, cooperative enterprises and alternative investment possibilities in the United States. Occasionally featured are businesses and nonprofit organizations working in the third world and with Native Americans. Catalyst recently published a full-length guide to socially conscious investing, *Economics As If the Earth Really Mattered*.

Data Center
464 19th Street
Oakland, Ca 94612
(415) 835-4692

The Data Center's Corporate Profile Service provides information on individual corporations, and the Search Service can prepare customized packets of clippings on topics such as runaway shops and U.S. investments in Latin America.

Insight
Franklin Research and Development Center
711 Atlantic Avenue, 5th Floor
Boston, MA 02111
(617) 423-6655

This monthly covers socially responsible investment, the social performance of different companies, and investment recommendations based on these criteria. The Franklin Research and Development Center is a socially responsible investment advisor.

International Barometer
1025 Connecticut Avenue N.W., Suite 707
Washington, DC 20036
(202) 822-9398

This monthly newsletter is designed to inform business, government, and other opinion leaders of the objectives and activities of issue-oriented organizations in order to facilitate dialogue between business and activists. Subscription rates are designed for the corporate budget ($235 a year); however, publication exchanges with other organizations are possible.

Multinational Monitor
P.O. Box 19405
Washington, DC 20036
(202) 387-8030

This bimonthly magazine includes investigative reports, critiques, and analysis of multinationals.

National Boycott News
Institute for Consumer Responsibility
6506 28th Avenue N.E.
Seattle, WA 98115
(206) 523-0421

This quarterly lists boycotts called by organizations working on human rights, animal rights, peace, labor, and the environment. It explains when and why each boycott is called, allows the corporation being boycotted an opportunity to respond, and gives updates on continuing boycotts.

Social Investment Services Guide
711 Atlantic Avenue
Boston, MA 02111
(617) 423-6655

This guide provides information and resources to advisors on investment funds, and is updated twice a year.

Transnational Information Exchange (TIE)
20 Paulus Potterstrat
Amsterdam 1071 DA
The Netherlands
(020) 766-724

TIE links workers from transnational subsidiaries in different countries to facilitate internationalist strategies in the labor movement. The quarterly TIE *Report* is available in the United States from the Institute for Policy Studies (see above address).

CHAPTER 7
Government By the People

The following groups are involved—through such tactics as lobbying, civil disobedience, and educational activities—in creating U.S. and multinational policies that will be more favorable to the Third World poor.

American Committee on Africa (ACOA)
198 Broadway
New York, NY 10038
(212) 962-1210

ACOA was founded in 1953 to provide political and educational support to African independence struggles. ACOA is involved in human rights work, research, lobbying, and direct aid through the affiliated Africa Fund.

American Friends Service Committee (AFSC)
1501 Cherry Street
Philadelphia, PA 19102
(215) 241-7169

AFSC, supports a wide variety of educational and activist projects throughout the United States to teach people about Third World issues and U.S. foreign policy. Projects include media work, demonstrations, human rights networks, and cross-cultural education through schools. AFSC has a number of regional offices throughout the country to support these grass-roots efforts.

Bread for the World
802 Rhode Island Avenue N.E.
Washington, DC 20018
(202) 269-0200

Bread for the World is a grassroots network of anti-hunger activists who lobby government representatives on foreign and domestic food and hunger policies. Based primarily in Christian churches and community organizations, Bread also has a staff of full-time lobbyists and analysts in Washington D.C. It organizes educational campaigns on issues such as the debt, militarism, and women in development.

Call to Conscience (CTC)
American Friends Service Committee (AFSC)
1501 Cherry Street
Philadelphia, PA 19102
(215) 241-7169

CTC is a network of individuals and groups committed to nonviolent protest of U.S. policy in southern Africa. Activities include organizing demonstrations and vigils, distributing educational materials, making appeals to Congress, and engaging in civil disobedience.

Center for Defense Information
1500 Massachusetts Avenue N.W.
Washington, DC 20005
(202) 862-0700

The Center for Defense Information is a nonprofit, nonpartisan research organization whose staff includes former U.S. military officers as well as civilian experts in military analysis. The Center provides objective appraisals of military forces and defense needs. It supports the reduction of military influence on U.S. domestic and foreign policy, and advocates the prevention of nuclear war. The Center publishes the *Defense Monitor* ten times a year.

Center for Economic Conversion
22C View Street
Mountain View, CA 94041
(415) 968-8798

The Center for Economic Conversion, founded in 1975, is a coalition of individuals interested in disarmament and economic conversion. Its primary aim is to convert the military industry to socially useful production. It serves as a resource center on military, economic, and employment issues for peace, environmental, religious, governmental, and labor groups.

Center for Innovative Diplomacy (CID)
17931 Sky Park Circle, Suite F
Irvine, CA 92714
(714) 250-1296

CID advocates city government involvement in foreign policy issues such as trade, diplomacy, immigration, and aid. It believes that involvement in foreign affairs will not drain city government coffers, but may help recover federal funds for city programs that have been lost to the bloated national military budget. CID publishes the quarterly *Bulletin of Municipal Foreign Policies*.

Center for the Study of the Americas (CENSA)
2288 Fulton Street, Room 103
Berkeley, CA 94704
(415) 540-5006

CENSA undertakes specialized research projects in collaboration with research centers in Central and South America, in order to deepen the understanding of the common interests and struggles of people in these regions.

Central America Resource Center
600 West 28th Street, Room 204
Austin, TX 78705
(512) 476-9841

The Central America Resource Center is a networking organization that supports the work of Central American activists all over the country. It publishes the *Directory of Central America Organizations*, a listing of hundreds of groups around the country working on Central America (also available on mailing labels). It also distributes scholarly books, reports, and articles on the region.

The Christic Institute
1324 North Capitol Street N.W.
Washington, DC 20002
(202) 797-8106

The Christic Institute is an interfaith law and public policy center specializing in investigations, legal work, and public education. Most recently, the Institute has been investigating twenty-five years of secret activity by the military and the CIA (the "Secret Team"), suing those involved in illegal activities, and conducting a massive educational campaign to inform the public about these issues.

Citizen Action
1300 Connecticut Ave. N.W., Suite 401
Washington, DC 20036
(202) 857-5153

Citizen Action is a federation of local canvassing and campaign groups, representing two million individuals in twenty-six states. It organizes actions on a wide range of issues from Central America to toxic waste. Citizen Action puts pressure on government officials by mobilizing an active citizenry.

Citizens for Participation in Political Action (CPPAX)
25 West Street
Boston, MA 02111
(617) 426-3040

CPPAX organizes public rallies and demonstrates against issues such as military intervention and nuclear war. It has had a strong influence in a number of state initiative campaigns such as the Equal Rights Amendment, the Nuclear Freeze, and opposition to the death penalty. CPPAX educates the public through forums, cultural events, fact sheets at polling places, and through a bimonthly newsletter.

Committee in Solidarity with the People of El Salvador (CISPES)
P.O. Box 12056
Washington, DC 20005
(202) 265-0890

Through hundreds of local chapters and affiliates, CISPES works to provide political support to the liberation movement in El Salvador, and to apply human rights and anti-intervention pressure on U.S. policymakers.

Council on Hemispheric Affairs (COHA)
1900 L Street N.W., Suite 201
Washington, DC 20036
(202) 775-0216

COHA publishes research on policy issues affecting Latin America and the Caribbean in *Washington Report on the*

Hemisphere, and organizes public education programs and speaking events.

Data Center
464 19th Street
Oakland, CA 94612
(415) 835-4692

Data Center is a resource library and clipping service on Third World and domestic issues, multinational corporations, individuals, private organizations, and governmental organizations. For a moderate fee, the Center prepares packages of clippings and bibliographies on any of these subjects.

Development Group for Alternative Policies (D'GAP)
1010 Vermont Avenue N.W., Suite 521
Washington, DC 20005
(202) 638-2600

D'GAP was created in 1977 to strengthen the connection between development assistance and social change. D'GAP works to promote effective delivery of aid to the Third World through research and policy efforts.

Ecumenical Program for InterAmerican Communication and Action (EPICA)
1470 Irving Street N.W.
Washington, DC 20020
(202) 332-0292

EPICA was founded in 1968 to provide educational materials for North Americans to help them better understand the political and economic struggles of people in the Caribbean and Latin America.

Environmental Defense Fund
1616 P Street N.W.
Washington, DC 20036
(202) 387-3500

The Environmental Defense Fund has led campaigns to stop the destruction of Amazon rain forests, specifically focusing on the environmental and social impact of the leading multilateral development banks.

Environmental Project on Central America (EPOCA)
300 Broadway, Suite 28
San Francisco, CA 94133
(415) 788-3666

EPOCA is a network of U.S. and Central American activists involved in protecting the environment in Central America. Through research, education, legislative action, and tours, EPOCA shows the links between the U.S. war in the area, poverty, the policies of transnational corporations, and environmental destruction.

Fellowship of Reconciliation
523 N. Broadway, Box 271
Nyack, NY 10960
(914) 358-4601

The Fellowship is a religious, pacifist network of people committed to human rights and nonviolent social change in the Third World. It carries out various education and activist programs.

Friends of the Filipino People
2421 Nation Avenue
Durham, NC 27707
(919) 489-0002

Friends of the Filipino People is working in conjunction with grassroots organizations in the Philippines to educate U.S. policymakers and citizens about U.S. bases in the Philippines.

GATT-Fly
11 Madison Avenue
Toronto, Ontario M5R 2S2
Canada

GATT-Fly is a project of various Canadian churches dedicated to research, education, and action in solidarity with people's organizations that are struggling for economic justice in Canada and in the Third World. They publish a quarterly newsletter, *The Gatt-Fly Report*, as is covers such issues as aid and debt.

Global Exchange
2940 16th Street, Room 307
San Francisco, CA 94103
(415) 648-7015

Global Exchange helps educate North Americans about conditions in the Third World and what they can do to help. It hosts activists from the third world on speaking tours to the United States, and has an ongoing speakers bureau with experts on development, U.S. policy, and activist strategies who are available to talk at schools and community events.

Institute for Food and Development Policy/Food First
145 Ninth Street
San Francisco, CA 94103
(415) 864-8555

Food First publishes books, research reports, and curricula on the true causes of world hunger and the impact of U.S. foreign aid on the Third World. It also has a speakers bureau with experts on world hunger and U.S. policy.

Institute for Policy Studies (IPS)
1601 Connecticut Avenue N.W.
Washington, DC 20009
(202) 234-9382

The Institute for Policy Studies, founded in 1963, is a political research and education center. Areas of focus include Third World debt, domestic policy, national security, foreign policy, international economics, and human rights. The Institute publishes books and policy papers, and conducts seminars and lectures.

Jobs With Peace
76 Summer Street
Boston, MA 02110
(617) 338-5783

Jobs With Peace is a national campaign to divert excessive military spending into the funding of jobs and social programs in such vital areas as education, housing, and health care. The campaign works mainly through creative grassroots organizing and lobbying.

National Council of Returned Peace Corp Volunteers
1319 F Street, NW #900
Washington, DC 20004
(202) 393-5501

The National Council is the only national organization that represents the 120,000 U.S. citizens who have served in the Peace Corp. Its mission is to educate North Americans about global awareness and humane development policies.

National Guard Clearinghouse
438 N. Skinker
St. Louis, MO 63130
(314) 727-4466

The National Guard Clearinghouse does research on National Guard and Regular Reserve deployment to Central America. The Clearinghouse provides reports on the impact of the forces' presence in the region through the bimonthly, *National Guard Update*, and calls for actions in protest of the use of these forces in Central America. A focus of the Clearinghouse is the increasing militarization of Honduras.

National Mobilization for Survival (MfS)
l853 Broadway, Room 418
New York, NY 10003
(212) 995-8787

MfS, founded in 1977, is a grassroots peace and justice organization working for global disarmament, safe energy, peaceful foreign policy, and social and economic justice. It calls for a significant reduction of the military budget and for the diversion of these funds to create jobs and human needs programs. MfS supports and initiates national coalitions for a variety of actions in support of peace and human rights.

National Rainbow Coalition
2100 M Street N.W., Suite 316
Washington, DC 20037
(202) 955-5795

The National Rainbow Coalition was founded in 1984 to end economic, racial, regional, and sexual polarization in the U.S. political process. Its goals include a humane alternative national budget and a fair tax shelter, a toxic-free environment and a non-nuclear world, and a noninterventionist foreign policy based on peace, development, and national self-determination. The Rainbow strives to expand voter participation and ensure enforcement of the Voting Rights Act.

National Wildlife Federation
1412 16th Street N.W.
Washington, DC 20036
(202) 797-6800

National Wildlife Federation is the country's leading conservation group, and is a co-founder of the citizens' movement for environmental policy reform of World Bank projects.

Natural Resources Defense Council (NRDC)
122 East 42nd Street
New York, NY 10168
(212) 949-0049

NRDC, founded in 1970, is a nonprofit membership organization engaged in the protection of natural resources and the environment. NRDC directs an effective environmental protection program that combines legal action, scientific research, and education. Some of its major issues include energy policy and nuclear safety, toxic substance control, clean air and water, preservation of natural resources, and the international environment. NRDC publishes a quarterly magazine, *The Amicus Journal*.

Neighbor to Neighbor (N2N)
2601 Mission Street
San Francisco, CA 94110
(415) 824-3355

Neighbor to Neighbor is a lobbying and public education campaign, organizing constituencies at the grassroots to push their elected representatives to vote for more progressive policies regarding U.S.-Central American relations.

Network in Solidarity with the People of Guatemala (NISGUA)
930 F Street N.W., Suite 720
Washington, DC 20004
(202) 483-0050

NISGUA was organized in 1981 to help coordinate the growing number of U.S.-Guatemala solidarity groups. It now organizes educational, lobbying, and other activist campaigns to end U.S. support for the Guatemalan regime.

New Jewish Agenda
64 Fulton Street, #1100
New York, NY 10038
(212) 227-5885

New Jewish Agenda is a national Jewish progressive organization that works to educate the U.S. public in five main areas: Central America, the Middle East, disarmament, economic and social justice, and feminism.

Nicaragua Network
2025 I Street N.E., Suite 1117
Washington, DC 20006
(202) 223-2328

The Nicaragua Network is engaged in public education, advocacy, lobbying, and direct, people-to-people projects for the purpose of developing friendly relations between the U.S. and Nicaraguan peoples, and ending U.S. intervention in the region.

Non-Governmental Liaison Service (NGLS)
Two UN Plaza, Room 1103
United Nations
New York, NY 10017
(212) 963-3113

NGLS helps link nongovernmental organizations throughout the world, particularly those concerned with grassroots development, and works to ensure that the voices of these organizations are heard within the UN agencies. It is also involved in development education in the United States. Its quarterly publication NGLS News lists development conferences and new resources for development education.

Nuremberg Actions
65 Eckley Lane
Walnut Creek, CA 94596
(415) 933-7850

Since June 10, 1987, Nuremberg Actions has kept a daily vigil at the Concord Naval Weapons Station in California, blocking trains and trucks carrying explosives bound for Central America. Because of its presence, the number of trains leaving the base has dropped from thirty to two a week.

Pacific Campaign to Disarm the Seas
2257 Makanani Drive
Honolulu, HI 96817
(808) 845-6328

The Pacific Campaign is part of a coalition of organizations in nearly a dozen countries working to remove nuclear weapons, military bases, and nuclear test sites from the Pacific Rim, through public education, lobbying, and media campaigns.

Palestine Solidarity Committee (PSC)
P.O. Box 27462
San Francisco, CA 94127
(415) 861-1552

PSC's thirty U.S. chapters work to educate North Americans about the right to Palestinian self-determination and to build a

U.S. policy that promotes peace in the Middle East. Its bi-monthly newspaper, *Palestine Focus*, is a good source of up-to-date information on the Middle East. PSC also collects material aid, such as medical supplies, to send to the West Bank.

Philippine Resource Center
P.O. Box 40090
Berkeley, CA 94704
(415) 548-2546

The Philippine Resource Center is a clearinghouse for information on the Philippines, including materials published in the Philippines, clippings, and materials about grassroots organizations and other actors in U.S.-Filipino relations.

Pledge of Resistance
P.O. Box 53411
Washington, DC 20009
(202) 328-4040

The Pledge of Resistance is a network of organizations across the country involved in a variety of protest actions against U.S. policy in Central America. Among them are civil disobedience, demonstrations, and blocking planes carrying National Guard troops bound for Honduras.

Policy Alternatives for the Caribbean and Central America (PACCA)
1506 19th Street N.W., Suite 2
Washington, DC 20036
(202) 332-6333

PACCA, established in 1982, is an association of scholars and policymakers dedicated to formulating alternative policy recommendations on the U.S. role in Central America and the Caribbean. It has produced a series of books, pamphlets, and other classroom resources that explore policy alternatives.

Project Abraço
Who Owes Whom
515 Broadway
Santa Cruz, CA 95060
(408) 423-1626

Project Abraço (North Americans in Solidarity with the People of Brazil) is a grassroots organization whose main focus is the debt crisis and its devastating impact on the people of the Third World. Through its quarterly newsletter *Who Owes Whom*, Project Abraço advocates long-term restructuring of the international economy, and provides educational tools on the debt crisis.

Rainforest Action Network (RAN)
300 Broadway, Suite 28
San Francisco, CA 94133
(415) 398-4404

Rainforest Action Network is a nonprofit organization working in twelve countries and focusing on the preservation of tropical rain forests. Through newsletters, journals, and information campaigns, the Network keeps the public informed of the critical importance of rain forests, and monitors environmental and cultural damage brought on by their destruction.

The Resource Center
P.O. Box 4506
Albuquerque, NM 87196
(505) 266-5009

The Resource Center conducts research on U.S. government policies, low intensity conflict, multinational corporations, and the workings of private voluntary agencies in the Caribbean and Central America. It distributes books and audio-visual materials on these regions, and also publishes its findings in a quarterly bulletin.

SANE/Freeze
711 G Street S.E.
Washington, DC 20003
(202) 546-7100

Two anti-nuclear organizations, SANE and Freeze, merged forces in 1987 to form SANE/Freeze and work for a bilateral U.S.-U.S.S.R. agreement to stop production, testing, and deployment of nuclear weapons and missiles. SANE/Freeze maintains a national clearinghouse to keep individuals informed on the nuclear priorities of government representatives, and produces educational materials on issues relating to nuclear weaponry.

Ten Days for World Development
85 St. Clair Avenue East
Toronto, Ontario M4T 1M8
Canada
(416) 922-0591

Ten Days for World Development is an annual education campaign conducted by the relief and development agencies of the Anglican, Lutheran, Presbyterian, Roman Catholic and United Churches of Canada, and by CIDA (the Canadian International Development Agency). Topics the campaigns have focused on include the international debt crisis and hunger and poverty in the Third World.

TransAfrica
545 8th Street S.E. Suite 200
Washington, D.C. 20003
(202) 547-2550

TransAfrica is a public information and education center focusing on U.S. foreign policy issues as they affect African and Caribbean countries. Programs include lobbying, publishing and human rights work.

20/20 Vision

29 Taylor Street		1181-C Solano Avenue
Amherst, MA 01002	- and -	Berkeley, CA 94706
(413) 253-2939		(415) 528-8800

20/20 Vision is a lobbying service that provides information on pending legislation about the military to a network of subscribers. Subscribers are asked to spend twenty minutes a month writing or calling their legislators. They are called on for both national and local policies relating to the military, with the goal of reducing the military's dominance over the national budget.

Veterans Peace Action Team (VPAT)

P.O. Box 586
Santa Cruz, CA 95061

VPAT is an outgrowth of the Veterans Fast for Life of 1986, when four veterans fasted on the steps of the U.S. Capitol in protest against U.S policy in Central America. VPAT works with veterans and other peace and solidarity groups to build nonviolent resistance to the militarization of U.S foreign policy.

Washington Office on Africa (WOA)

110 Maryland Avenue N.E.
Washington, D.C. 20002
(202) 546-7961

WOA was founded in 1972 to provide church activists and trade unionists with up-to-date information on southern Africa, and to lobby for a progressive U.S. foreign policy toward the region in general. WOA supports lobbying, media and educational campaigns, and human rights work on African issues.

Washington Office on Haiti

110 Maryland Avenue, N.E.
Washington, D.C.20002
(202) 543-7095

Washington Office on Haiti provides information on the political and economic situation in Haiti, and lobbies for better U.S. policies toward Haiti.

Washington Office on Latin America (WOLA)

110 Maryland Avenue N.E.
Washington, DC 20002
(202) 544-8045

WOLA is a clearinghouse of information on Latin America and

U.S. policy, and publishes its own research and analyses in *Latin America Update*.

Women's International League for Peace and Freedom (WILPF)
1213 Race Street
Philadelphia, PA 19107
(215) 563-7110

Through a national network, WILPF carries out a wide variety of education and legislative action programs on U.S policy, militarism, and development. WILPF focuses on ending the arms race, U.S. intervention abroad, government repression, sexism, and racism.

Words Into Deeds
Grassroots Action Against the Debt
c/o John Ross
Apdo. Postal 198
Delegación Cuauhtemoc,
06002 Mexico DF

Words Into Deeds is the creation of U.S. poet and journalist, John Ross, who in 1987 initiated a coast-to-coast hunger strike to raise awareness about the impact of the debt on the Third World poor. Ross is planning other actions to protest current IMF and U.S. government priorities relating to debtor nations.

World Development Movement
Bedford Chambers
Covent Garden
London WC2E 8HA, England
(01) 836-3672

The World Development Movement represents a coalition of citizens acting on behalf of nongovernmental aid agencies to change government policies. Its actions include lobbying for the redirection of food aid from the United Kingdom, developing guidelines for multinational corporations in the Third World, and seeking solutions to the debt crisis.

SPEAKING TOURS
The following organizations have successfully organized tours of Third World speakers in the United States for the purposes of public education and mobilization. They may be good resources for groups planning tours of their own.

Africa Peace Tour
c/o Maryknoll Fathers
Maryknoll, NY 10545
(914) 941-7590

Freedom Fund
4534-1/2 University Way N.E.
Seattle, WA 98105
(206) 547-7644

Inter-Religious Foundation for Community Organization (IFCO)
402 West 145th Street
New York, NY 10031
(212) 926-5757 or (212) 229-1657

Labor Network on Central America
P.O. Box 28014, Department F
Oakland, CA 94604
(415) 272-9951

Third World Women's Project
Institute for Policy Studies (IPS)
1601 Connecticut Avenue N.W.
Washington, DC 20009
(202) 234-9382

MEDIA RESOURCES

The following are just a few suggestions of publications that provide a critical analysis of U.S. government policies. We also recommend looking at the newsletters of organizations listed in other parts of this resource guide, especially for specific country studies.

EXTRA!
Fairness and Accuracy in Reporting (FAIR)
130 W. 25th Street
New York, NY 10001
(212) 633-6700

FAIR is a progressive media watch group that tries to get more media coverage for peace, public interest, and minority viewpoints. Its newsletter, EXTRA!, is published every six weeks. Subscription rate: $24/year.

Food Monitor
World Hunger Year
261 West 35th Street, Room 1402
New York, NY 10001-1906
(212) 629-8850

Food Monitor is a publication of World Hunger Year, an organization that aims to inform the general public, the media, and policymakers on hunger in the United States and abroad. Subscription rate: $18/year.

In These Times
1300 W. Belmont Avenue
Chicago, IL 60657
(312) 472-5700

In These Times has particularly good analyses of European politics, but also covers many Third World issues. Published forty-one times a year. Subscription rate: $34.95/year.

Mother Jones
1663 Mission Street, 2d Floor
San Francisco, CA 94103
(415) 558-8881

Mother Jones, a monthly, provides occasional investigative reports and analysis of Third World issues and U.S. activist movements. Subscription rate: $24/year.

NACLA *Report on the Americas*
475 Riverside Drive, Suite 454
New York, NY 10115
(212) 870-3146

NACLA *Report* is published by the North American Congress on Latin America, an independent research and information center founded in 1966 to provide in-depth reporting on Latin America and U.S. policy in the region. Subscription rate: $20/year.

New Internationalist
P.O. Box 1143
Lewiston, NY 14092
(416) 591-1381

New Internationalist is a British-based monthly publication that provides insights on a wide variety of Third World issues—militarism, debt, hunger, sexism, and foreign aid. Subscription rate: $25/year.

The Progressive
409 East Main Street
Madison, WI 53703
(608) 257-4626

The Progressive is a monthly magazine of political commentary and investigative reporting. It covers Third World issues primarily as they relate to U.S. policy. Subscription rate: $27.50/year; $19.50 for students.

Seeds
222 East Lake Drive
Decatur, GA 30030
(404) 378-3566

Seeds is a monthly publication on U.S. and world hunger and poses alternatives. Subscription rate: $16/year.

Sojourners
Box 29272
Washington, DC 20017
(202) 636-3637

Sojourners is an independent Christian monthly highlighting popular struggles and the role of the progressive church in the United States and the Third World. Subscription rate: $21/year.

The Nation
72 5th Avenue
New York, NY 10011
(212) 242-8400

The Nation is a weekly that provides a sharp critique of U.S. foreign policy. Subscription rate: $28/year.

Utne Reader
Box 1974
Marion, OH 43305

Utne Reader is a bimonthly that contains excerpts from the best of the U.S. alternative press on issues ranging from peace and the environment to socially responsible investing. Subscription rate: $24/year.

NETWORKING RESOURCES

EcoNet and PeaceNet
The Farallones Institute
15290 Coleman Valley Road
Occidental, CA 95465

EcoNet and PeaceNet are computer-based networks of environmental and peace organizations and individuals. Users can send information to each other, join computer conferences, publicize new materials, and communicate more efficiently than through the telephone or mail.

Third World Resource Directory
Edited by Thomas Fenton and Mary Heffron
Maryknoll: Orbis Books (1984)

This directory lists progressive educational organizations, curricula, films, videos, and other resources on Third World development issues. The authors have since compiled separate directories on Africa, Asia, Latin America and the Caribbean, and women in the Third World. The directories are available through the Data Center (see address above).

Introduction

1. The efforts of the peace movement to use citizen diplomacy as a tool for breaking down superpower rivalry have been in heralded such books as *Citizen Diplomats*, by Gale Warner and Michael Shuman (New York: Continuum, 1987) and films like *People to People* (Educational Film and Video Project: 1983).

Chapter 1

1. Ron O'Grady, *Tourism in the Third World*, pp.75-6.
2. Regional organizations supporting the Coalition include the Center for Responsible Tourism in San Anselmo, California, and the European network called TEN (Third World Tourism Ecumenical European Network).
3. See last page of this chapter for a copy of the Code of Ethics.
4. *Mediterranean Conference*, International Union of Food and Allied Workers' Associations, Estoril, November 5-6, 1985, p.I/4.
5. O'Grady, op. cit., p.70.
6. O'Grady, p.62.
7. Haunany-Kay Trask, "Tourism and the Condition of the Native People," *Third World People and Tourism: Approaches to a Dialogue*, The Ecumenical Coalition on Third World Tourism (F.R. Germany: Horlemann Publizistik, 1986), pp.36-38.
8. O'Grady, p.1.
9. Cathy Cockrell, "I Have Been to the Mountaintop: U.S. Blacks Visit Nicaragua," *Nicaraguan Perspectives*, Summer, 1988.

Chapter 2

1. Gary Gunderson, "Emerging Partners," *Seeds*, February 1986.
2. *Directory and Analysis: Private Organizations with U.S. Connections - Honduras* (Albuquerque: The Inter-Hemispheric Education Resource Center, 1988).
3. For an in-depth examination of how pressure from U.S. government agencies can deeply divide a partnership program, see Terry Allen, *Partners of the Americas: Vermont-Honduras, An Examination of the Role of AID Grants on Vermont Partners and on the People of Honduras*, unpublished manuscript, Dec. 1987.
4. Interviewed on ABC *News Nightline*, May 1, 1987.

Chapter 3

1. "In the Name of God and Charity," *Resource Center Bulletin*, No. 13, Summer 1988.
2. Canadian participants include Canadian Crossroads International, the National Farm Union, and the Quebec Young Farmers. The Caribbean participants are the St. Vincent Farmers Union, the Dominican Farmers Union, and farm representatives from Grenada and St. Lucia.

Chapter 4

1. Sharon Martinas, "You Can Save Lives of Activists in El Salvador," S.F. CISPES *Update*, Vol. 3:4, May/June 1988.
2. Mary Jo McConahay, "The Well-Meaning American," *Image Magazine*, February 7, 1988.
3. Ibid.
4. "Right to Food is Policy for the American Bar Association," *Hunger Report*, U.S. House of Representatives Select Committee on Hunger, VII/87. pp.3-4.
5. According to the 1986 *Amnesty International Report*, the number of political assassinations did drop significantly in this time. Arrest, detentions, and torture, however, remained widespread.
6. In October 1988, the provision of the McCarran-Walter act that denies U.S. visas to "communist" or "subversive" foreigners was overridden for two years, pending review by the U.S. Congress.

Chapter 5

1. Contact Friends of the Third World (see Guide) for information about the date and location of the yearly conferences.

Chapter 6

1. Amy L. Domini, *Ethical Investing* (Reading, MA: Addison-Wesley Publishing Co., 1984), p.203.
2. Ibid, p.9.
3. For more information on the Grameen Bank, see *Development That Works* by Medea Benjamin and Becky Buell (San Francisco: Food First Books, forthcoming 1989).

Chapter 7

1. Some groups are now referring to civil disobedience as "civil resistance" to emphasize that it is the government, not they, who are violating international law and ethical principles.
2. S. Brian Willson quotes excerpted from Vicki Kemper, "The Power Within: A Nonviolent Activist Stands for Truth and Life," *Sojourners*, April 1988.

3. "Citizens Stop the World Bank" in *Seeds*, August 1986, p.18.
4. See Susan George, *A Fate Worse Than Debt* (New York: Grove/Food First, 1988).
5. See Frances Moore Lappe, Rachel Schurmann, and Kevin Danaher, *Betraying the National Interest* (New York: Grove Press/Food First, 1987) and Kevin Danaher, Phillip Berryman and Medea Benjamin, *Help or Hindrance: United States Economic Aid to Central America*, Food First Development Report No.1, September 1987.
6. Quoted in "Promoting Economic Democracy," *International Barometer*, Vol. 3:9, March 1988.
7. Michael Shuman, "Dateline Main Street: Local Foreign Policies," *Foreign Policy*, 65: Winter 1986-87.
8. "Interview with Howard Wolpe," *Africa Report*, March-April 1988, p.39.

Chapter 8

1. Matthew Countryman, *The Nation*, March 26, 1988.
2. Bill Moyer in George Lakey, *Powerful Peacemaking, A Strategy for a Living Revolution* (Philadelphia: New Society Publishers, 1987), pp.210-218.
3. Joshua Cohen and Joel Rogers, *Inequity and Intervention: The Federal Budget and Central America* (Boston: South End Press, 1986).
4. See, for example, Leslie Cockburn, *Out of Control* (New York: Atlantic Monthly Press, 1987) and Alfred W. McCoy, *The Politics of Heroin in Southeast Asia* (New York: Harper & Row, 1973).

About
Global Exchange

T his book is a springboard for a new organization called Global Exchange, based in San Francisco, California. Global Exchange is a nonprofit research, education, and action center, focusing on U.S.-Third World internationalism. It is a clearinghouse for the most up-to-date information on ways you can get involved in this growing movement to end hunger and poverty, and to build peaceful international ties through direct action.

Global Exchange also serves as a sounding board for the internationalist community, generating discussion and dialogue on the future of the movement, and sponsoring conferences and other forums to bring internationalists face to face to discuss common concerns. Finally, Global Exchange sponsors tours all over the third world, allowing more people to see for themselves how North Americans and third world people can work together for change.

Aside from its own mandate, Global Exchange is an umbrella organization for regionally-focused groups: Africa Exchange, Caribbean Exchange, and Central America Exchange. Each Exchange committee carries out its own programs, including tours, material assistance, educational activities, partnership programs, human rights advocacy, and alternative trade.

Global Exchange speakers are available to address students, community groups, internationalists, and other activists on a wide range of topics, including world hunger, grassroots development, sustainable agriculture, militarism, debt, U.S. foreign policy, internationalism, and education and careers in social change. Please write to our Speakers Bureau for information on bringing a Global Exchange speaker to your community.

Global Exchange functions thanks to the hard work of a corps of volunteers. If you are interested in volunteering with us in our San Francisco office, or being a contact person for us in your own community, please let us know.

We also need your ideas for building an even sturdier internationalist movement: new groups to add to the Global Exchange resource guide, other areas of the Third World needing an "Exchange Committee," insights on trade, tourism, human rights work, or other activities from your own experience. We want to hear them! We hope you will use the response form on the opposite page to keep Global Exchange alive. We promise to keep in touch if you do.

Global Exchange
2940 16th Street, Room 307
San Francisco, CA 94103
(415) 255-7296

A

Abraham Lincoln Brigade, 74, 205, 218; See also, Veterans of the Abraham Lincoln Brigade
Accion International, 294
Acosta, Francisco, 50
Action for Corporate Accountability, 143, 294-295
Action in Support of the Mexican Garment Workers, 260
Africa Exchange, 52, 232
Africa Peace Tour, 188, 317
Africa Watch, 98
African Development Foundation, 181
African National Congress (ANC), 66, 97
aid; development, 68, 178, 180, 181-182; economic, 67; to families, 66; financial, 78; humanitarian, 88, 96; material, 68, 84, 87-89; military, 70-71, 178; technical, 68, 78, 80, 82, 84
Allende, Salvador, 141
Allende, Mrs. Salvador, 113
Alliance for Progress, 42, 45
Alternative Trade Organizations (ATOs), 119-139
alternative tourism, 14, 17, 18, 19, 20, 21-37, 211

American-Arab Anti-Discrimination Committee (ADC), 99, 278
American Civil Liberties Union (ACLU), 113, 278
American Clothing and Textile Workers Union (ACTWU), 50
American Committee on Africa (ACOA), 52, 97, 169, 214, 232, 278, 300-301
American Friends Service Committee (AFSC), 64, 188, 194, 242, 278, 301
American Jewish World Service (AJWS), 64, 87, 242
American Institute for Free Labor Development (AIFLD), 51
Americas Watch, 92, 98, 103, 104, 110, 278
Amnesty International, 92, 93-94, 96-98, 106-107, 111, 279
Anaya, Herbert, 101, 112
apartheid, 10, 51-52, 66, 92, 97, 128, 148, 155, 156, 169, 182, 185, 207, 209, 213, 215
Appropriate Technology Project of Volunteers, 69
Appropriate Technology Sourcebook, 69
Architects and Planners in Support of Nicaragua (APSNICA), 80, 255

327

Medea Benjamin is an economist and nutritionist, having worked with the Institute for Food and Development Policy/Food First, the United Nations Food and Agriculture Organization, the Swedish International Development Agency, and government ministries in Nicaragua, Cuba, Guinea Bissau, and Mozambique. Medea is author or coauthor of *Don't Be Afraid, Gringo: A Honduran Woman Speaks From the Heart, No Free Lunch: Food and Revolution in Cuba Today, Help or Hindrance?: Economic Aid to Central America*, and *Development That Works: Grassroots Solutions to Hunger and Poverty*. She is co-founder of Global Exchange and Central America Exchange.

Andrea Freedman works with the San Francisco Center for U.S.-U.S.S.R. Initiatives, promoting citizen diplomacy travel. She has written extensively on grassroots development and citizen activism. She has worked for the Institute for Food and Development Policy/Food First and the World Affairs Council. She is author of *Education for Action: Graduate Studies with a Focus on Social Change* and her articles have appeared in *Building Economic Alternatives, Christian Science Monitor, Seeds*, and *Food Monitor*. She is co-founder of Global Exchange and is an active member of Caribbean Exchange.

Please use this page for suggestions and updates for Global Exchange. You can also use this form to order additional copies of *Bridging the Global Gap* and other resources.

☐ **YES!** I want to support Global Exchange and the internationalist movement. Enclosed is my tax-deductible membership donation of
   ☐ $100   ☐ $50   ☐ $25   ☐ Other: $_____.
(Members will be invited to join upcoming tours and the first Conference on Internationalism, and will stay informed of other Global Exchange activities.)

☐ Please send me more information about Global Exchange.

☐ Suggestions for activist groups not listed in the resource guide. Please include address, phone, and contact person if possible:

_____

_____

_____

_____

_____

☐ Please send me the following:

_____ Copies of *Global Exchange* at $11.95 $_____
_____ Copies of *Alternatives to the Peace Corps* at $5.00   _____
_____ Copies of the *Guide to Alternative Trade Organizations* at $5.00   _____
_____ Copies of the *Directory of Alternative Tours* at $5.00   _____
_____ Copies of *Education for Action: Graduate Studies with a Focus on Social Change* at $3.00 _____

SUBTOTAL $_____
Add 15% shipping (min. $1.00)   _____
CA Residents add 6.5% sales tax   _____
TOTAL ENCLOSED (Payable to Global Exchange) $_____

Name _____

Address _____

City _____ State _____ Zip _____

Phone _____

Mail to:
   Global Exchange, 2940 16th St. #307, San Francisco, CA 94103

Please use this page for suggestions and updates for Global Exchange. You can also use this form to order additional copies of *Bridging the Global Gap* and other resources.

☐ **YES!** I want to support Global Exchange and the internationalist movement. Enclosed is my tax-deductible membership donation of
☐ $100   ☐ $50   ☐ $25   ☐ Other: $_____.
(Members will be invited to join upcoming tours and the first Conference on Internationalism, and will stay informed of other Global Exchange activities.)

☐ Please send me more information about Global Exchange.

☐ Suggestions for activist groups not listed in the resource guide. Please include address, phone, and contact person if possible:

_____

_____

_____

_____

_____

☐ Please send me the following:

_____ Copies of *Global Exchange* at $11.95 $_____
_____ Copies of *Alternatives to the Peace Corps*
at $5.00   _____
_____ Copies of the *Guide to Alternative Trade
Organizations* at $5.00   _____
_____ Copies of the *Directory of Alternative Tours*
at $5.00   _____
_____ Copies of *Education for Action: Graduate
Studies with a Focus on Social Change*
at $3.00   _____

SUBTOTAL $_____
Add 15% shipping (min. $1.00)   _____
CA Residents add 6.5% sales tax   _____
TOTAL ENCLOSED (Payable to Global Exchange) $_____

Name _____

Address _____

City _____ State _____ Zip _____

Phone _____

Mail to:
Global Exchange, 2940 16th St. #307, San Francisco, CA 94103